THE STRATEGIC COMMUNICATION IMPERATIVE

This book proposes a model for directly aligning strategic communication with organisational business planning to enable effective management of mid- to long-term organisational issues.

It argues that current conceptualisations of strategic communication need to be extended to locate it more precisely within definitions of strategy and as an essential element of mid- and long-term business planning. This approach re-positions strategic issues communication in a professional practice dimension that has a specific focus on issues that do not immediately impact on an organisation's ability to achieve its day-to-day business goals.

Full of contemporary examples from business, and including a thorough explanation of how the model can be applied in professional practice, the book will prove illuminating reading for scholars, students, and professionals alike.

James Mahoney is Adjunct Professor in Professional Communication in the News and Media Research Centre at the University of Canberra, Australia. He is a life fellow of the Public Relations Institute of Australia. He is the author of *Strategic Communication: Campaign Planning* and *Public Relations Writing*.

THE STRATEGIC COMMUNICATION IMPERATIVE

For Mid- and Long-Term Issues Management

James Mahoney

Routledge
Taylor & Francis Group

LONDON AND NEW YORK

Cover image: © sesame / Getty Images

First published 2022
by Routledge
2 Park Square, Milton Park, Abingdon, Oxon OX14 4RN

and by Routledge
605 Third Avenue, New York, NY 10158

Routledge is an imprint of the Taylor & Francis Group, an informa business

British Library Cataloguing-in-Publication Data
A catalogue record for this book is available from the British Library

Library of Congress Cataloging-in-Publication Data
Names: Mahoney, James Scott, 1947- author.
Title: The strategic communication imperative: for mid and long-term
issues management / James Mahoney.
Description: Abingdon, Oxon; New York, NY: Routledge, 2022. |
Includes bibliographical references and index.
Identifiers: LCCN 2021036456 (print) | LCCN 2021036457 (ebook) |
ISBN 9781032011417 (hardback) | ISBN 9781032011394 (paperback) |
ISBN 9781003177340 (ebook)
Subjects: LCSH: Business communication. |
Strategic planning. | Organization.
Classification: LCC HF5718 .M344 2022 (print) |
LCC HF5718 (ebook) | DDC 658.4/5–dc23
LC record available at https://lccn.loc.gov/2021036456
LC ebook record available at https://lccn.loc.gov/2021036457

ISBN: 978-1-032-01141-7 (hbk)
ISBN: 978-1-032-01139-4 (pbk)
ISBN: 978-1-003-17734-0 (ebk)

DOI: 10.4324/9781003177340

Typeset in Bembo
by Deanta Global Publishing Services, Chennai, India

For those who think about this; it really matters.

CONTENTS

LIST OF ILLUSTRATIONS

Tables

Figures

Diagrams

PREFACE: A JOURNEY BEGINS

This journey to explore the essential attributes of strategic communication began as a doctoral research project. Along the way it ventured into new territory as its track was influenced by the responses of those who contributed to the research, and the inevitable buffeting that exposure to scholarly works, especially in disciplines other than your own, always gives to ideas and theoretical understandings.

Strategic communication remains at best a translucent concept. The term 'strategic' is often mis-applied to practice which is technical and tactical. Technical in the sense that it relies on outputs involving marketing communication tools, including those used in public relations, to support sales of products and services; tactical in that its focus is almost always in current time frames, which cannot in any way be described as 'strategic.' It is definitely not about dealing with socio-economic and political issues in a dialogic way that resolves them before they impact on market performance. A crucial question for tactical communication, then, is whether, in a given situation concerning a specific issue, its outputs are actually noticed by important stakeholders, read and understood, and generate the desired outcomes: changes in awareness, knowledge, and behaviour.

The significant problem addressed here is that often practitioners are unable to address issues in a strategic way. Even though they acknowledge the ideal approach to professional communication strategic planning and implementation, practitioners can be prevented from acting strategically by senior management or clients who are not convinced of its importance as a high-order, value-added organisational function. While senior managers and clients recognise the need for strategic business planning, they do not equally recognise the strategic communication imperative of dealing with emerging mid- to long-term socio-economic and political issues. To resolve that problem, the book proposes that strategic communication planning be re-imagined and located in a professional practice dimension that would integrate it with organisational business planning.

Associated with this is a proposed new definition of strategic communication to more precisely outline what it should be. The main theme of this approach is that mid- and long-term socio-economic and political issues affect organisational reputations, credibility, and stakeholder relationships and should be more strategically identified, analysed, and managed. That is, the strategic communication imperative is for higher level practice that transcends day-to-day marketing communication because it secures dialogues with stakeholders about important emerging issues, and this potential resolution, well before they turn into crises.

The book uses theoretical concepts from the management, professional communication, and sociological literature to argue that strategic issues communication is a discursive social practice in which organisations, as social and political actors, contribute to dynamic issues debates in their non-market environments. There is a duality in this process: the parameters of public debates about socio-economic and political issues constantly change and these dynamics in turn influence how organisations continue to advocate their views on those issues.

So, this journey has led to a view that issues analysis, management, and communication is an explicit high-level strategic professional practice that transcends the day-to-day technical concerns of marketing communication. That is, while strategic communicators must be aware of current business issues and how to apply the technical tools of their profession to address them, their more significant and value-added role is mid- to long-term issues analysis, management, and communication. This goes beyond traditional discussions of strategic communication because its focus is on *why* a strategic approach should be taken to issues communication is vital, and what that involves. In doing that, the book makes a significant contribution to scholarly and practitioner understanding of strategic communication because it explains how issues debates influence initial and subsequent decisions about strategic directions.

ACKNOWLEDGEMENTS

It is impossible to look back over the experience of writing this book without recognising that it has only reached this point because a lot of people were prepared to talk, listen, and advise; too many people, from academic, professional, and personal networks, to list individually here. Yet all their contributions were valuable and valued.

Many academic and professional colleagues contributed to this project in a variety of ways, not the least of which was how they encouraged me to start and keep going. Among them: Dr Kate Holland, Dr Julie Freeman, Dr Sora Park, Professor Peter Putnis, Professor Jen Webb, Professor Robina Xavier, Dr Leanne Glenny, Dr Joanna Henryks, and Dr Katharina Wolf. I thank them all for their interest and encouragement. Tom Parkes, Rob Masters, and Marisa Gerussi are practitioner colleagues who just listened to me outline my concept from time to time. Dr Damian Grace, a philosopher and friend, gave valuable encouragement, advice, and friendly prods when this book was being translated from a thesis to what is here, including incisive comments at various stages of the draft. Above all, this book would not have been possible without the senior Australian practitioners who contributed to the research that informed this journey. I am especially grateful to Professors Warwick Blood, Deborah Blackman, and Judy Motion for the excellent comments and advice they gave me as supervisors of my doctoral project, the research results from which informed the arguments I make here. Professor Kerry McCallum, my principal doctoral supervisor, was unstinting in her encouragement, support, and wise counsel.

The Routledge team, led by Karen Hildebrand, strongly supported this work from the start. Lucy Batrouney and Sarah Pickles managed the writing process by giving me space to get on with it. I am thankful to this team for that. Stephen Lyons edited the manuscript with great skill, care and sensitivity.

I owe an enormous debt of gratitude to my late father, who valued formal education but did not have the opportunity to experience it, for always encouraging an 'independent mind.' I hope I have demonstrated some independence here and that he would have enjoyed reading this book even though, as a journalist, he may not have agreed with a word of it.

Finally, my family has always been unstinting with its encouragement and support whenever I say, 'I've got a new book to write.' My greatest thanks go to my wife, Dr Janine Mahoney, who not only knew what it takes to do this, but gave me the space and time to get on with it, prodded when it was needed, and withdrew when it was important to do so.

1
FACING UP TO ISSUES

An introduction

During the worldwide Covid-19 virus epidemic that began in 2020, millions of words were published about what caused it, how it could be stopped and cured, the effect it had on societies, economies, and politics, and when it might end. And more. Pandemic issues, and how they affected every country, consumed politicians, public health specialists, medical researchers, and people who contracted the disease or lost loved ones to it. Defeating the virus was complicated by people who denied it even existed and ignored warnings about wearing face masks, the need for social distancing, and maintaining personal hygiene. In the United States in particular the existence of the virus was challenged, and responses to it were enmeshed in politics as some State governments defied official national and scientific advice about Covid-19 management, mask wearing, social distancing, and city and school closures. Such defiance was usually based on political party allegiance and individuals' views about their rights to freedom under the US Constitution and the Bill of Rights. Former US President Donald Trump's failure to effectively guide the national Covid-19 response became a major issue for him in his final year in office and contributed to his defeat at that year's presidential election.

Worldwide, governments' principal communication messages in their responses to the pandemic have focussed on dealing with immediate issues: the difficulties of controlling the spread of the virus to ensure public health, and, when vaccines became available, the need for citizens to be vaccinated. There remain urgent issues about how to deal with, slow down, and ultimately prevent Covid-19 infections, and to effectively manage the vaccination of populations. Government representatives, mainly politicians in executive cabinet positions, supported by medical experts, faced questions about why death rates were so high in some countries, about hospital care capabilities, vaccine availability, claims vaccines don't work, dangerous side effects from vaccines, and

DOI: 10.4324/9781003177340-1

about schools closing or opening. They were continually asked to explain why, and for how long, cities or whole countries would need to shut down in attempts to defeat the virus, and about government compensation for economic hardship during lockdowns.

Pandemic-related issues, and myriad others caused by them, will confront world governments, medical providers and researchers, and citizens for years as the mid- to long-term health, economic, social, and political consequences from the disease become clearer, especially the lasting medical complications for some people. Governments, especially, will need to develop strategic approaches to communicating about these issues in addition to their almost daily briefings about the pandemic. In Australia, which had one of the world's lowest infection rates, one researcher argued that to understand the impact that Covid-19 could have in five years, experts needed to literally wait five years to look at the patient data (Roberts, 2021). And in the United States, a study reported that its results provided a roadmap to inform health system planning and development of multidisciplinary care strategies to reduce chronic health loss among Covid-19 survivors (Al-Aly et al., 2021).

In addition to long-term health issues likely from the pandemic, it is not yet known how working from home during the pandemic will affect the way in which people go about their daily lives post Covid-19: will they or won't they continue to work, even for some of the time, from home, or will there be a mass return to offices? How will office spaces cater for a full return of workers if social distancing rules still apply? What will the consequences be for societies and their economies from a full return to formal in-office work, or will people stay in home-based work? Will life ever return to a so-called pre-Covid-19 'normal'? In this context, as the United States approached more than 33% of its population having been given at least one vaccination injection by the middle of 2021, one American CEO wrote about her concern that people might not want to go back to working in their offices post the pandemic. Merrill (2021) cited PricewaterhouseCoopers' research that found fewer than one in five executives wanted to return to shared workplaces as they were before the pandemic. If this attitude continues, what workplace issues will organisational leaders have to deal with to resolve a problem of 'absent' executives?

Outside the specific issues that result from the pandemic, all organisations face emerging mid- to long-term concerns related to other social, political, and economic factors. Left unchallenged, emerging issues like these have the potential to impact on day-to-day business performance, or turn into crises. This is the strategic communication imperative for mid- to long-term issues identification and analysis and on which communicative action to deal with them should be based. This analysis and planning should occur well before issues impact on organisations, and be pursued in a context that reflects the goals, objectives, and timelines set out in organisational business strategies. If an organisation is not actively identifying and analysing longer term issues, and their potential impact on business performance beyond 'today,' especially those that could pose dangers to corporate reputations, organisational credibility, and stakeholder relationships, then it is not practising strategic issues management. In this concept, strategic communication is about the organisation, not the promotion of its products or services. A model for linking communicative action to effectively deal with emerging issues to strategic communication plans, and a new definition of strategic communication that clarifies its long-term role, are proposed in the book.

USING 'ORGANISATION' AND 'BUSINESS'

In this book, the term 'organisation' is used to describe commercial businesses, not-for-profits, charities, industry and professional associations, government agencies, and political groupings. All are engaged in 'business' in the broad sense that it is what they actually do: make goods, provide services, pursue profits, protect individual and collective interests and rights, lead countries, or manage economies.

This approach recognises that 'being strategic' is not a day-to-day technical, tactical action. Day-to-day technical communication is about how organisations deal with current business issues like sales declines, or re-structures, or crises like labour unrest or the consequences of a factory fire, or misbehaviour by staff, or how they promote speeches, events, personalities, and products, produce issue media releases and background brief journalists, or tweet, re-tweet, and post to Instagram, Facebook, and YouTube. That is not strategic, but communication using basic tools, no matter how much whizz-kid practitioners, political media advisers, journalists, and some academics, captured in by the wonders of social media, and their fondness for instant news media coverage as the capstone of professional practice, would like to label it otherwise. Senior US practitioners have suggested that the Covid-19 pandemic has provided a pivotal moment for communication professionals that would enable them to move on from the tactical alchemy that defines much communication practice. One senior communicator described this as an opportunity to 'get out of the media relations spin cycle and demonstrate the breadth and depth of our value' (K. Swim, cited in Strong, 2021).

All professional practice should reflect the context of an overall corporate communication strategy that defines goals and measurable objectives to address issues that organisations and their stakeholders face together. Deciding how, when, and why each tactical tool should be used with specific target audiences in equally specific situations is not an exercise in 'more is better' communication so common in modern professional practice. It should be carefully calibrated to match overall goals and objectives, directed at defined target audiences, and use the tactical tools that reflect those that audiences use. That means strategic communication practice needs to be understood in its own terms (Hay, 2002) beyond the traditional functional descriptions in the scholarly and professional literature of what communication strategy is and how it works.

So, corporate-level strategic communication is not some re-named variant of day-to-day tactical marketing communication. As an important, valid, and agenda-setting discipline in its own right, it is an organisational imperative, time defined in both its planning and implementation, and integrated with business strategy. Properly executed strategic communication deals with issues beyond the market, short-term financial performance, current political agendas, and the news media's latest fascination, although much professional practice and scholarly discussion about communication would suggest otherwise. The argument advanced in this book is informed by primary and secondary research which found that decisions by senior practitioners about strategy are primarily influenced by issues that affect organisational reputations, credibility, and stakeholder relationships, and that they are mostly willing to engage with opponents over issues, but are often driven by senior managers to pursue short-term tactical methods. Communication strategies would be more effective if they were planned, linked, and implemented in the context of mid- and long-term business planning time frames because building and maintaining, or repairing, reputations, credibility, and stakeholder engagement is not a short-term activity. It takes time to do this, and these issues cannot be resolved by tactical communication. That is, strategic communication does not deliver results 'today' because it is about changing awareness, attitudes, and understanding, and generating action.

Researching and writing a corporate-level strategic communication plan should primarily be driven by the need for organisations to contribute to, and thus influence, public discussion of socio-economic and political issues that affect relationships with their stakeholders, the impact on their reputations, and, ultimately, their ability to achieve organisational goals. This is equally true of issues raised by organisations themselves in an endeavour to build enhanced business environments and which become the subjects of public debate. There is a duality in this process as the parameters of public debates about issues constantly change and these dynamics in turn influence how organisations continue to advocate their views on public issues. This is especially so if making those decisions is conceptualised as a highly politicised and discursive social practice aimed at generating action (Hendry, (2002) principally to build and protect organisational reputations, values, and credibility, and to develop, maintain, and advance relationships with stakeholders, in the mid to long terms. Dealing with reputational and relationship issues requires consistent professional communication endeavours that link directly to mid- to long-term organisational aspirations, goals, and objectives. This in turn requires an understanding of what strategy really is, how it is influenced by external factors and internal debates, and how organisations, represented by their spokespeople or agents, are social actors when they engage with public issues debates. Hence, communication action should be planned to reflect business planning time frames, principally the three planning 'horizons'—the current, mid, and long terms—proposed by Baghai et al. (2000).

Applied to this planning model, tactical communication occurs in the current term, leaving the other two 'horizons' as the arenas for strategic communicative action based on longer term issues analysis. This time-defined notion of strategic communication appropriately applies not only to commercial business, but to public sector and not-for-profit organisations, as well as in a party-political context, because it is concerned with issues that occur at a level above the immediate tactical approach of public relations, public affairs, and corporate and political communication.

Facing up to issues using a strategic focus to identify and analyse emerging external socio-economic and political concerns is needed precisely because left unidentified, and thus ignored, or unchallenged, these issues can potentially damage an organisation's ability to go about its business, protect and grow its market share, and generate profits. Immediate marketing concerns of course impact on financial performance and many have 'strategic' dimensions in the sense that they determine how organisations will, for example, grow their customer bases, diversify their product offerings, consolidate supply lines, and reduce costs, thus enhancing financial performance. These concerns are likely to be identified and addressed as an organisation interacts daily with customers, suppliers, and competitors in a contemporary time frame. This is the day-to-day realm of marketing communication—advertising, direct selling, and the technical and tactical public relations and its various offshoots like public affairs and corporate communication. It is not the arena in which strategic communication and the management of potentially damaging emerging political, social, and economic issues play out. That occurs in a different context—the space where organisations interact with their stakeholders to reach a consensus about issues. Resolving these issues, for example, the long-term effects of Covid-19, industry regulation, industry policy, tariffs, government funding for education, subsidies for farmers, or the matters raised by activists pursuing specific interests like protection of the natural environment, and increased corporate taxation, requires organisations to engage with bureaucratic decision-makers, regulators, suppliers, politicians, industry associations, activists, and other issues definers, and often in public discourse. That is not the task of tactical and technical marketing communication focussed on the bottom line, no matter how much some scholars and practitioners want it to be so.

Increased activism about minority rights and ingrained misogyny and abuse of women in politics, business, sport, and government agencies are among the most significant issues organisations face. Negative reactions to electoral law changes in some US jurisdictions that limit access to elector registration and voting processes, which, for example, in 2021 saw businesses and sporting organisations withdraw activity from the State of Georgia, is an example of how failure to resolve issues impacts on an organisation's relationships—its day-to-day performance. In this example the organisation was a government, or more precisely the majority in its legislature, which ignored potential mid- and long-term political and economic impacts of its decisions to amend electoral laws. The resolution of issues like these cannot be achieved through technical and tactical communication in a market environment. It will take consistent, planned efforts to re-build reputations and stakeholder relationships and serious reform that follows significant issues analysis and organisational involvement in public issues debates.

Despite practitioners' nod to the need to plan professional communication strategically, they often fail to convince senior management of the requirement to address important public policy issues at a level beyond dealing with the mass news media's demand for immediate responses to a current issue. Public policy issues do not arise like some natural phenomenon. Some issues, of course, are consequences of how organisations should react to crises and natural disasters on their immediate ability to go about their business. But most public policy issues have socio-economic and political implications that are created by changes in an organisation's external non-market environment—the space where such matters are raised. In this space, described by Habermas (see esp. 1992) as the 'public sphere,' those changes occur when issues are debated, elaborated, and resolved. This is a dynamic process in which organisations should be actively involved, just as their opponents and other stakeholders are involved, despite the reluctance of some senior corporate executives to stray too far into commenting in public arenas. The need to participate this way in the non-market environment is the strategic communication imperative.

In facing up to issues before they reach the level of imminent threat to business success, organisations and their spokespeople, or agents, are social and political actors who employ discursive social practices when they engage in dynamic issues debates. Management, communication, structuration, and other sociological theories can help to explain how dynamic issues debates impact on organisations, and how the parameters of those debates change and in turn influence organisations' responses.

The point in play here is that socio-economic and political issue boundaries are not static. Issues are established as a result of social action by so-called issues definers and change as debate about them takes place. In this process, organisations as social actors define their positions on issues and alter them as more views enter debates about them. Each contribution to an issues debate alters its boundaries, even if by a small margin. In this sense, issues debates are dynamic, and their boundaries change as other social actors participate in a process that seeks resolution through stakeholders reaching consensus. It is in this context that 'strategic communication' practice becomes what it is meant to be: forward-focussed professional communication that deals with long-term organisational positioning via a framework from which other communication disciplines find direction.

Thus, strategic communication can be conceptualised as two unique, but inter-related, constructs: communicative action that (1) builds and protects organisational reputation, values, and credibility, and (2) maintains and advances relationships with stakeholders. Each involves communicative action that is focussed on long-term objectives dealing with non-current issues. That leads to an understanding of strategic communication as a high-level function that deals specifically with how organisations, as social actors, communicate about mid- to long-term public policy issues and manage stakeholder relationships. That explicit definition differentiates strategic communication from other professional communication disciplines.

Strategic communication concepts

Explaining why decisions are made to communicate in a particular way about specific issues is fundamental to understanding strategic communication. This is especially the case if making those decisions is conceptualised as a highly politicised and discursive social practice aimed at generating action, principally to build and protect organisational reputations, values, and credibility, and to develop, maintain, and advance relationships with stakeholders, in the mid to long terms.

Social, political, and economic issues related to these matters are raised and debated in an organisation's 'non-market environment' (Bach & Allen, 2010). Luoma-aho and Vos (2010) conceptualise the 'places of interaction' (p. 10) in which organisations and their stakeholders engage in these debates as issues are- nas. This external forum reflects the concept of a public sphere (Habermas, 1979, 1989) in which citizens engage in discussions to reach consensus about issues. The essential difference between the public sphere and the non-market envi- ronment is that Bach and Allen (2010) dealt with issue discussions in a specific context: how corporations and their stakeholders reach consensus about issues. Non-market environmental issues include debates about, for example, industry regulation, or industry policy, tariffs, government funding for education, subsi- dies for farmers, or the matters raised by activists pursuing special interests, the natural environment, taxation changes, and what journalists report. The resolu- tion of issues raised and debated in this external non-market environment nev- ertheless impact on an organisation's 'market environment' relationship, that is, its day-to-day business performance. Bach and Allen's (2010) construct provides a direct description of an issues arena that, from a professional communication perspective, illustrates the importance of issues analysis beyond tactical day-to- day market concerns. That is, the non-market environment is an appropriate description for the arenas in which issues debates occur.

Dealing with reputational and relationship issues is not a short-term, tactical pursuit. It requires consistent professional communication endeavours that link directly to mid- to long-term organisational aspirations, goals, and objectives. This in turn requires an understanding of what strategy really is, how it is influ- enced by external factors and internal debates, how the non-market environ- ment works, and how organisations, represented by their public spokespeople, are social actors when they deal with public issues. Hence, the argument here is that strategic communication should be planned to reflect the 'three hori- zons' business planning time frames proposed by Baghai et al. (2000). In this view, strategic communication can appropriately apply not only to commercial business, but to public sector and not-for-profit organisations, as well as in a party-political context, because it is concerned with issues that occur at a level above the immediate tactical approach of public relations, public affairs, and corporate and political communication.

Embracing theoretical approaches from other disciplines

Concepts from communication and other disciplines help explain how strategic communication decisions are made and how the practice can be more effectively planned and implemented. Scholars challenge academics (for example, Falkheimer, 2007; Lane, 2007) interested in the theoretical underpinnings and practice aspects of professional communication to further embrace theoretical approaches from other disciplines, especially management, to more effectively explain the role of professional practice. Others (for example, Bütschi & Steyn, 2006) called for scholars to produce new models, concepts, and theories relevant to 21st-century corporate communication by thinking outside the box, adopting risky research strategies and trying out new methods. Baines and Viney (2010) called for research to investigate how organisations control their strategic environments, especially their interactions with vital non-market stakeholders.

Strategic communication as a high-order, value-added function

Strategic communication can be conceptualised as two specific but inter-related constructs: communicative action that builds and protects organisational reputation, values, and credibility, and develops, maintains, and advances relationships with stakeholders. This communicative action involves a focus on longer term goals and objectives than those used to advance day-to-day organisational financial performance, which is essentially the role of marketing communication and tactical public relations. The significance of this view is that strategic communication can be regarded as a higher order value-added function for senior management. Plowman (2013) illustrated the importance of building that understanding when he noted that organisations attempt to implement strategic communication campaigns while 'struggling to even define the concept of strategic communication and its value to the organisation' (p. 556).

Despite a deep commitment to the idea of strategically planning and implementing organisational communication, a majority of practitioners are required by clients or organisations' senior management, usually described in professional communication scholarship as 'dominant coalitions,' to work tactically.

The description of senior management as a dominant coalition originated from the work of organisational theorists Cyert and March (1963). As part of their 'behavioural theory of the firm,' Cyert and March (1963) argued that decisions about goals are made by informal coalitions that comprise internal and external people associated with organisations and that goals change as membership of the coalition changes. For example, Cyert and March (1963) posited that in business, managers, workers, stockholders, suppliers, customers, regulatory agencies, and others comprised coalitions; in government agencies, coalitions include administrators, workers, elected and appointed officials, judges, and interest group leaders; and in not-for-profit organisations, coalitions include paid functionaries, volunteers, and donors. Drawing on Cyert and March (1963), Bowler (2006) argued that coalitions influenced goals through informal, rather than formal, channels and that an organisation's top management was 'typically, but not exclusively or necessarily of the dominant coalition' (p. 261). In a professional communication context, J.E. Grunig (1992) explicitly described the group of senior managers who control organisations as the dominant coalition. Public relations academics White and Dozier (1992) argued that dominant coalitions had the power to enforce decisions about organisational directions, tasks, objectives, and functions. Moloney (2006), a critical scholar, noted that while the function of public relations staff was one of agency, some may also be members of dominant coalitions and therefore 'act as controllers of that function and its staff' (Note 20, p. 178). In this organisational power context, Berger (2005) argued that the notion of a dominant coalition in organisations is 'a pivotal concept in mainstream public relations theory.'

Most senior practitioners look for ways to convince dominant coalitions of the importance of communication strategy in advancing organisational goals. In reporting their research on the theory and practice of stakeholder management, Ackerman and Eden (2011) illustrated the difficulty in doing this when they note that 'ideas developed in the abstract without the demands of practice (even when plausible) do not often gain the attention of practicing managers, and so cannot influence their decision making' (p. 194). The paradigm shift proposed in this book to more effectively align strategic communication planning with business plans would assist practitioners to operationalise strategic communication in a way that demonstrates its mid- to long-term value for dominant coalitions.

Strategy, issues, and professional communication

The notion of 'strategy' is embedded in all professional communication activity. A primary function of senior practitioners is to develop and implement the communication strategic plans that address issues that organisations, or consultants' clients, face. Strategic plans for public relations and other aspects of professional communication are viewed by scholars and practitioners as the mechanisms for ensuring a consistent approach based on agreed objectives. The strategic approach I propose means that long-term views are taken into account, organisations can be proactive, and potential difficulties and conflicts are considered (Gregory, 2009 b). In an integrated communication context, strategic planning includes coordinating activities and fine-tuning messages to maximise effectiveness (Lauer, 2001). All this is, or should be, integrated with an organisation's strategic business plan.

Definitions of strategic communication

Scholarly discussions of strategic communication argue that it operates at a level beyond a functional, tactical approach (Cornelissen, 2005) and that it embraces all organisational communicative interactions with stakeholders. Argenti and colleagues (2005) argued that strategic communication was the alignment of communication with an organisation's overall strategy, to enhance strategic positioning. In this view, strategic communication works in time frames beyond the immediate day-to-day activities of other professional communication disciplines. It is planned communicative action in which an organisation participates as a social actor (Hallahan et al., 2007) to advance its mission in its non-market environment—the external forum that is similar to Habermas' (1979, 1989) concept of a public sphere. It is in this environment that social, political, and economic issues are raised and debated. Examples of non-market environment issues are a government proposal to increase patient rebates for doctors' fees, or a new international trade agreement on agricultural exports, or a proposition that student fees for tertiary education should be increased. Debates about these issues would involve, respectively, doctors', medical insurance, and patient lobbies, farmers' groups and other food exporters, student associations, universities, and tertiary education staff associations.

Non-market environment issues like these are not resolved quickly but how they are eventually resolved impacts on an organisation's ability to conduct its business in its market environment. The market environment involves an organisation's relationship with suppliers, customers, and competitors. Consider a hypothetical consumer group's proposal to the Therapeutic Goods Administration (TGA) that the basic skin protection factor required in suntan lotions should be increased from 50+ to 60+. In pursuing their arguments about this issue, the consumer group, suntan lotion manufacturers, and politicians would publicly debate the merits of the proposal by engaging as social actors in their non-market environments. While it might not participate in the debate other than to provide facts, the issue would also play out in the Therapeutic Goods Administration's non-market environment. That is, the issue would not yet impact on how the TGA goes about its daily role, but the Administration would need to monitor the public debate because of potential regulatory implications. It may take a year to resolve the issue because of public debate and perhaps consultation by politicians and the TGA with activist groups, the industry, and health experts. If the suntan lotion manufacturers 'lost' the debate, the new regulation would impact on their market environment relationships with customers (price, availability, safety), suppliers (availability and price of raw materials), and on how they compete with each other (marketing, product promotion, price). The implementation of any new regulation would impact on the TGA's day-to-day (or market) relationships with its customers (the manufacturers) because of the need to ensure the new skin protection factor was applied to suntan lotions.

In their introduction to the first edition of the *International Journal of Strategic Communication*, Hallahan et al. (2007) described communicating purposefully to advance an organisation's mission as the 'essence of strategic communication' (p. 4). They argued that this was an approach that seeks communication solutions beyond traditional techniques of integrated marketing communication. Sandhu (2009) regarded strategic communication as multidisciplinary, purposeful, rational, and intentional communication requiring deliberate decision-making. Falkheimer and Heide (2018) described strategic communication as a fundamental management function and a practical specialisation that includes all forms of communication. J.E. Grunig (2006) has viewed strategic communication as a standardised bridging activity between organisations and their stakeholders. Zerfass and Huck (2007) argued that strategic communication prepares organisations for an uncertain future.

Cornelissen (2005) noted that the scope and involvement of strategic communication as a management function becomes more substantial when it stretches beyond a set of functional goals and tactics and responds to business needs and concerns. Plowman (2013) proposed a definition of strategic communication for the US Army in which communication between the organisation and its key stakeholders was managed 'on a long-term basis to meet measurable objectives in a realistic timeframe' (p. 549). Plowman (2013) argued that in a traditional public relations or public affairs sense, strategic communication would 'ideally occur' at the highest levels of an organisation and be carried out 'down through the lowest or tactical levels' (p. 550) and would consider long-term effects on strategic stakeholders while 'constantly scanning the organisational environment for issues that might affect the organisation' (p. 550).

Each of these brief definitions pursues a common theme that seeks to locate the practice beyond the short term dealt with by the tactical public relations/ affairs functions of day-to-day media relations, and attempts (in a political context) to manage the news process, product promotion, event management, or get the Chief Executive on talk-back radio, or tonight's television public affairs program. However, those definitions can be extended by arguing that at its core, strategic communication can be regarded more precisely as the channel through which organisations as social actors explicitly deal with mid- and long-term issues, especially those involving organisational reputation, values, and long-term stakeholder relationships. None of this can be achieved with a quick fix in the short-term time frames in which traditional tactical professional communication practice operates.

Professional communication and business objectives

A consistent theme in the literature about the role of communication in supporting organisational goals and objectives has been that it must be aligned to business objectives. J.E. Grunig and Repper, for example, discussed such an alignment in their 1992 commentary on the *Excellence Study*; Cornelissen dealt with it in 2005; Jones and Bartlett in 2009. J.E. Grunig (2009) returned to the theme in the context of applying social media to public relations practice and how this would enhance his concept of two-way symmetrical communication. In this positioning, strategic communication is deliberate practice that deals with significant issues that affect organisational success.

Significant issues are the economic, social, and political public policies about which organisations need to be concerned to achieve their missions and goals. Resolution of them requires a careful focus on early identification, and analysis of emerging issues, and implementation of planned communicative action over the mid to long term that reflects business strategy and directions to address them.

Hallahan et al. (2007) argued that the specific focus of strategic communication was on how an organisation presents and promotes itself through the intentional activities of its leaders, employees, and communication practitioners, and on how it functions as a social actor to advance its mission.

The idea that strategic communication involves intentional activity, and that an organisation functions as a social actor when promoting its mission, suggests that the process is dynamic. For that reason, communication strategy decision-making, development, and implementation can be viewed as discursive social practice, are thus dynamic, and as a result can be explained through the prism of Giddens' (1986) structuration theory. B.G. Smith (2013), for example, reflected this approach when he noted that structuration theory could help explain how individuals make strategic choices towards developing integrated communication, and how human interaction in this process is also influenced by structure, that is, Giddens' (1986) concept of duality. Durham (2005) saw structuration as a way of viewing communication practitioners, especially those in public relations, as potentially powerful social actors involved in dialogues of change and conflict.

Theoretical concepts

Scholars have applied theoretical paradigms, or models, from the physical sciences, sociology, philosophy, psychology, and management to the study of professional communication—and have been challenged to do more of this. In this way, for example, systems and complexity theories have been used to develop the situational and contingency theories of public relations.

In their *Excellence Study*, Grunig and colleagues (1992) sought to define the characteristics of high-quality public relations practice, much as Peters and Waterman (1984) did with their research into excellent company management practice. Professional communication scholars have adapted research from psychology, sociology, and management to explain how and why people communicate, and how they process and react to marketing communication and public relations messages.

Much of this scholarly work has led to defining, perhaps differentiating, public relations and its specialities with terms like 'corporate communication,' 'public affairs,' 'community relations,' 'stakeholder relations,' 'issues manage-ment,' 'financial and investor relations,' and 'crisis and recovery communication.' Many of these terms are attempts to define professional communication practice functions in ways that avoid the use of 'public relations,' of which they are argu-ably sub-sets. That occurs because of alleged negative connotations associated with public relations. However, scholars who first sought to explain the concept of strategic communication differentiated it from other communication speciali-sations by defining it as a high-order practice (see, for example, Sandhu, 2009; Zerfass & Huck, 2007; Hallahan et al., 2007; Cornelissen, 2005).

The theoretical concepts from the management, professional communication, and sociological literature which help explain this 'high-order' practice are:

- strategic communication advances organisational objectives by contributing to public debate about social and political issues that impact on their ability to achieve business goals and objectives (professional communication)
- decisions about how organisations deal with issues reflect both the outcomes of internal discussions (a discursive social practice) about their importance to the organisation, and the dynamics of public debates (management, sociol-ogy, professional communication)
- issues debates occur in an organisation's external non-market environment (management, professional communication)
- organisations are social and political actors when they contribute to public debates about issues (management, professional communication)
- issues are dynamic in the sense that debates about them constantly change as organisations and other social and political actors contribute to them (pro-fessional communication, sociology)
- there is a duality in this process because issues dynamics in turn influence how organisations continue to advocate their views on those issues (sociol-ogy, professional communication)

The non-market environment

The concept of strategic communication I propose is also grounded in Bach and Allen's (2010) argument that organisations have two distinct external environ-ments. The first is their immediate 'market environment,' defined by their rela-tionships with suppliers, competitors, and customers. This is the environment in which they do business and in which public relations activity directed at pro-moting products and sales as part of marketing communication is employed. The second is the 'non-market environment,' which Bach and Allen (2010) described as the relationships outside the market but which nevertheless affect an organisa-tion's ability to reach its business objectives. It is in the non-market environment that debates about public policy issues generated by activists, governments, regu-lators, and citizens occur, and are covered by the mass news media. For example, the resolution of debates about revisions to taxation codes, or the imposition of new regulations, or the adverse impact of industrial development on the natural environment, ultimately impact on how organisations go about their business even though the debates occur in a non-market context. Bach and Allen's (2010) concept provides a significant framework in which to locate an arena, or place of interaction (Luoma-aho & Vos, 2010, p. 10), in which mid- to long-term issues debates occur. Luoma-aho and Vos (2010) noted that social issues arenas are places for 'interaction about ideas' (p. 11).

Organisations as social and political actors

In the non-market environment, organisations are advocates, or social actors, who legitimately contribute to debates about issues that can potentially impact on their ability to achieve business goals and objectives. As social actors, organisations use communication strategy and techniques to influence issues debates. Bach and Allen (2010) argued that organisations must be social and political actors in the non-market environment whether managers 'like it or not' (p. 48). They argue that using participation in market debates as a strategic opportunity is important because,

> Politicians, regulators, nongovernmental organisations, and activists won't hesitate to impose new rules of the game on an industry, unless companies themselves become active participants in the process.
>
> *(Bach & Allen, 2010, p. 48)*

This is why Anderson (1992) regarded activists as strategic publics: they have the potential to constrain an organisation's ability to accomplish its goals and mission.

Hallahan et al. (2007) built on Habermas' (1979) view that organisations are significant social actors with an increasingly important role in debates about public issues, and that this role has transformed how modern society deliberates on those issues when they are purposeful, or strategic, in advancing their mission. They argue that strategic communication research should include examining how an organisation presents itself in society as a social actor in the discussion of public issues (p. 27).

Luoma-aho and Vos (2010) have conceptualised issues arenas as the places in which actors deal with dynamic issues. In this conceptualisation, actors are organisations and their publics.

Issues dynamics

Public policy issues debates in an organisation's non-market environment also impact on their strategic communication decision-making processes. This can in part be explained by contingency theory if issues are regarded as independent variables and decisions about strategic communication directions as dependent variables. This argument views issues as dynamic, meaning that they sometimes emerge unexpectedly, and that the ways in which they are framed, and impact on organisations, alter as other social actors join the debates about them. In this context, professional communication practitioners' primary and subsequent decisions about advocating an organisational position, or stance on an issue, reflect the dynamics of issues debates. Heath and Palenchar (2009) extended this idea by noting that issues dynamics are not simply those that occur when organisations and activist groups engage in debate: issues dynamics also occur in industries, between activist groups, and between government agencies (p. 120). They argued that in this

> array of players, issues managers are wise to be concerned about understanding the dynamics of the various publics and the dynamics that motivate them.
> *(Heath and Palenchar, 2009, p. 120)*

Hallahan (2001) viewed issues as complex, dynamic, and involving more than merely a dispute between two parties. In a reflection of classical issues management practice, Hallahan (2001) argued that to effectively deal with an issue, organisations and their managers need to develop an understanding of claims made, and the context in which a particular issue evolves.

The use of contingency theory in management and communication scholarship grew out of scholars' application of general systems theory to better understand organisational structures (Hatch & Cunliffe, 2006; Donaldson, 2006). Thus, organisations are complex systems involving dynamically interacting parts in which a change in one part can affect the behaviour of other parts (Beinhocker, 1999). Contingency theory also helps to model how organisations' constituent parts and external factors interact to achieve organisational goals and that these complex systems are path dependent (Hodge et al., 2003).

It is in this perspective that contingency theory informs how social, political, and economic issues act as independent variables that influence organisational decisions on strategic communication directions. That is, while communicators must deal with an organisation's short-term needs, the decisions they take about mid- to long-term strategy should be influenced by their analyses of the dynamics of issues yet to appear in their day-to-day practice.

Strategic communication as discursive social practice

Discursive social practice occurs in two issues management contexts. The first context is internal, when senior practitioners discuss issues analyses with other managers, or a dominant coalition to decide how the organisation should deal with them. The second is external when organisations advocate their views about issues to generate or contribute to, or resolve, public issues debates.

Writing in a management decision-making context, Hendry (2002) argued that strategy is a form of social practice in which the debate involved in decision-making is a central feature. This contextualises strategic decisions as an aspect of the organisational debates through which strategic thinking is linked to action (Hendry, 2002). That link is reflected in the definition of strategic communication advanced by Hallahan et al. (2007), who argued that it involved organisations acting as social actors who used persuasive, discursive, and relational communication.

Bach and Allen's (2010) view that organisations need to carefully manage key social, political, and environmental issues, and relationships with the actors who care about them, in their non-market environment, reflects how organisations engage in discursive social practice when they engage in advocacy. This is analogous with Heath's (2009) view that professional communication practice is essentially rhetorical action or 'suasive' discourse. Heath (2009) argued that a rhetorical perspective of communication acknowledges a two-way debate and that rhetoric, which he describes as strategic, is the ultimate social process that involves the expression of opinions, preferences, and behaviours that create and maintain community.

Hendry (2002) posited that senior managers invoke strategic decisions to influence the actions of colleagues. Hatch and Cunliffe (2006) viewed decision-making through a political frame in which organisational power takes account of the interests of the subcultures, factions, and debates in organisations. That means that where differences occur over goals and tactics, power and politics influence decision-making (Hatch & Cunliffe, 2006). This is what Burkart (2009) described as practical debate in which the object is to justify interests and decisions and in which value judgements are discussed. Hendry (2002) saw decision-making as part of an organisational debate. Second, he regarded strategy as a form of social practice (see Hendry, 2002, p. 957). Third, he linked strategic thinking to action. Hendry's (2002) argument is that a decision takes its meaning from the social practice and debate in which it is located and notes,

> In pursuit of their aims, strategists do all the things that feature in the traditional definitions: they evolve shared perspectives, create plans and enact ploys. Intentionally or otherwise, they participate in the social creation of patterns and the positioning of their organisation's product-market offerings, and they observe such patterns and positions in other organisations.
>
> *(Hendry, 2002, p. 970)*

This argument reflects issues of communication practice that involves research, environmental scanning leading to a situation analysis, and the strategic plan development and implementation decisions that follow. This is a discursive social practice in which communication planners identify, discuss, and analyse external and internal factors that have the potential to impact on their organisations. It is also inherently political, and it is often a reactive practice that follows the results of ongoing issues identification and analysis—Jaques (2009a, b) made the point about issues management being strategic.

Structuration theory and professional communication

Professional communication strategic plans are not static documents. They change as an organisation's circumstances, priorities, and goals change. Primary and subsequent decisions about an organisation's communication directions are affected by internal and external debates about issues that occur in its non-market environment. This process has a duality. Strategic communication decisions are based on issues identification and analysis and the actions that follow them are designed to influence public debates about issues. Those debates are never static. The changing definition and framing of issues in public debate, in turn, impact on how organisations deal with them. Structuration theory, advanced by the sociologist Anthony Giddens (1986), suggests an important theoretical frame for explaining this process.

Giddens (1986) described structuration as the process of production and reproduction of social systems via the application of generative rules and resources. In Giddens' (1986) view, 'structures' result from the 'actions' of 'agents.' The theory holds that structure both enables and constrains how individuals interact at the same time as those interactions set the structure that enables and limits them. Giddens (1986) argued that 'one of the main propositions' (p. 19) of the theory was that the production and reproduction of social action drew on the same rules and resources that were the means for system reproduction. Giddens (1986) called this a duality in social systems.

Durham (2005) argued that structuration theory provided a way of viewing public relations practitioners as potentially powerful social actors, in which the corporate workplace and its actions are 'connected to the world beyond the company walls' (p. 33). Falkheimer (2007) proposed structuration theory as a method for developing dynamic and process-oriented communication strategies. Falkheimer (2007) argued that when they were viewed from a structuration perspective, core communication processes were dynamic, ideological, temporal, and spatial, and were performed by all members of an organisation. Falkheimer (2007) argued that because structuration theory describes organisations as dynamic and transforming, it helps to explain the role of strategic communication. Hendry (2002) argued that structuration theory shows how a debate about strategic decisions can act at the agency level of intentional communication and thus 'provide a common foundation for the competing rational, action based and interpretive views of strategic decision making' (p. 971).

Structuration theory, then, allows a 'rich, composite but internally consistent picture of strategic decision making' (Hendry, 2002, p. 971). Structuration theory also provides a lens that helps to explain the impact of issues dynamics on strategic communication decisions. Olufowote's (2003) framework based on the four central elements of structuration includes examining situated routine social practices, the depth and stability of structures (because structures partly explain why routines sustain themselves), the ways in which agents interact with structures, and the interplay between actors and institutions. This enables the process in which decisions about communication strategy directions are made to be regarded as a structure that can be influenced by interactions with agents/actors—a discursive social practice that may produce unintended as well as intended actions.

If strategic communication can be conceptualised as a professional practice that deals with organisational reputation, values, credibility, and relationships with stakeholders in the mid to long terms, then it can be aligned explicitly with mid- and long-term business planning. That is possible because communicative action to promote, build, and maintain positive organisational reputations, values, credibility, and relationships with stakeholders requires long-term strategic action. An alignment of this kind extends the traditional view that communication goals and objectives should be grounded in the organisation's strategic plan by more precisely linking them to business planning time frames.

Thus, based on an investigation of how a cohort of purposively selected senior Australian communication practitioners responsible for making top-level strategic decisions understand and deal with issues in their organisations' external environments, I argue that senior practitioners' professional agency in decision-making about how an organisation should manage an issues debate is often undermined by demands from senior management for short-term tactical responses to issues. That suggests that strategic communication should be more precisely defined. In my view, that definition should posit strategic communication as a professional practice in which organisations as social actors explicitly deal with mid- to long-term external issues in their non-market environments, especially issues related to reputation and stakeholder engagement. That provides strategic communication with a definition that clearly locates it as a practice that can be directly aligned to the business planning approach described by Baghai et al. (2000). They argued that business growth for corporations could be managed across 'three horizons' simultaneously in order to distinguish between the embryonic, emergent, and mature phases of a business' life cycle. The horizons they propose are:

- **Horizon 1**: extending and defending core business. This horizon encompasses the businesses that are at the heart of an organisation and with which customers and analysts most readily identify.
- **Horizon 2**: building emerging businesses. In this horizon, management is concerned with the emerging stars of the company, because they transform companies.
- **Horizon 3**: seeding options for future businesses. Baghai et al. (2000) described Horizon 3 businesses as options on future opportunities.

Baghai et al. (2000) argued that planning for each should be separated to avoid a natural tendency for Horizon 1 immediacy to overshadow the need for the other two. The issue raised by Baghai et al.'s (2000) view is similar to a problem facing communication practitioners who are too often required to focus on short-term tactical solutions to deal with issues, rather than to work in longer time frames. The concept of horizons thus provides an important perspective on the time element in which strategic communication should be planned and implemented.

The planning model proposed here would first make strategic communication practice explicit to Horizon 2 (the mid term) to support organisational efforts to strategically enhance reputations, and to counsel dominant coalitions on the public communication aspects of regulatory issues, and lasting relationship management with stakeholders in the context of business building strategies. Second, the model would mean a communication focus on Horizon 3 (the long term) involving long-term public issues identification and analysis, strategic counselling, and associated long-term communication program planning.

Facing up to issues using this 'over the horizon' focus is a strategic communication imperative beyond the day-to-day market-based tasks of extending and defending the core business to increase profits. That imperative delivers on what being strategic in communication management really means. In doing that, it positions strategic communication as a corporate function that is integrated with strategic business planning and operations.

2

THE ALCHEMY OF PROFESSIONAL COMMUNICATION

In the canon that defines professional communication practice, researching and writing a strategic plan is an article of faith, the first step in a process designed to build a reputation, alter opinions, convince stakeholders to support a particular point of view, or generate sales. Strategic plans that deal with public relations, public affairs and lobbying, corporate and political communication are supposed to define problems, argue their importance to a client, recommend ways issues can be addressed, and set out the activities by which the strategy will be carried out, and how it will be later evaluated. The canon holds that these plans at least reflect organisational corporate, or business, strategic plans. Professional communication planned and implemented in this way is a high-order, value-added function.

In this professional world, 'strategy' is supposed to mean considering the long term by identifying and analysing current and emerging issues and potential difficulties, and proposing communication solutions. That in turn dictates which communication tools, for example, media releases, speeches by chief executives, briefing papers for politicians, posts on websites, social media engagement, and face-to-face meetings, will implement the 'strategic' plan. Organisations and communication consultancies appoint strategists; academics preach the tenets of researching and writing strategic plans to undergraduates; scholars define professional practice by whether it is strategic activity that interprets the outside world to an organisation and the organisation to its stakeholders, or simply the technical daily grind of writing, organising, tweeting, and liaising with journalists.

This description of the ideal world of professional communication poses a number of questions. Despite senior practitioners' nod to the tenets of planning communication in a strategic way, are they more focussed on tactical, day-to-day activities? Why? Are the professional communication concepts of 'strategy' and 'tactics' often blurred, confused, and misused? Do practitioners actually

DOI: 10.4324/9781003177340-2

consider the effects of mid- and long-term external socio-economic and political issues on their organisations' abilities to achieve business goals? In a professional environment increasingly dominated by social media activity, is it simply
too hard to avoid concentrating on technical, or tactical, communication while
under pressure from clients for immediate success? Which issues, or categories of
issues, influence the decisions senior practitioners make about the communication strategies they prepare? Do they actually link their communication strategies to organisational business plans, and, if not, why not? Would a revision to
the commonly accepted definitions of strategic communication help make the
practice better understood, and enable a more effective link with organisational
business planning?

The importance of dealing with issues was pointed out by Edward Bernays,
one of the founding scholars of public relations, as long ago as 1952 when he
argued that, far more important to the profession than the mechanics of its activities were the social, economic, and political problems that faced client relationships with their publics. In Bernays' view, even public relations textbooks ignored
dealing with issues of this kind. In its rush to embrace technology, modern professional communication has become a kind of alchemy in which the only issues
to worry about are those happening now. In this alchemy, a technical and tactical approach to solving problems dissolves any notion of real strategy; tactical
marketing communication takes precedence over well-thought-out long-term
communication strategies; any thought of identifying and analysing emerging
issues is deemed a waste of time and money.

Most of what passes for strategic communication in politics is also tactical,
and based on the alchemy proposed by media advisers from party backgrounds,
or journalism, who don't understand communication strategy but know how
to spin for the daily news media demand. The same approach is often used in
commerce, government agencies, industry associations, and in public relations/
marketing communication agencies, where practice seems to be, we'll talk about
strategy but, really, we'll do what the client wants.

A scientific approach to successful professional strategic communication practice is that it is based on research that informs a well-founded plan prepared by
practitioners who understand the importance of dealing with issues, especially
those related to organisational reputations, values, and stakeholder relationships,
in a strategic way. Such plans should be integrated with an organisation's strategic business plan, or strategy, if they are to effectively communicate views
about socio-political and economic issues that impact on its ability to achieve its
goals. In this view, strategic communication should involve activities that have
a clear purpose, are directed at long-term changes in stakeholder attitudes and
beliefs, utilise a wide range of tools and channels, and acknowledge that meaningful relationship and reputation outcomes, so important to achieving organisational goals, mean hard work and cannot be achieved with short-term alchemy.
Often, a well-researched, scientific approach is not achieved because practitioners are unable to address issues in a strategic way because senior management

decision-makers are not convinced that professional communication about important issues involves more than the alchemy of tactical action.

To be effective in supporting organisational business goals, the concept of strategic communication should more precisely define what it is and what it does compared to extant definitions. This concept would view organisations, whether public, private, or not-for-profit, as social actors who publicly pursue their perspectives on socio-economic and political issues in the non-market arena. The concept would define strategic communication in mid- and long-term time frames, and recognise that these issues are not resolved by instant technical alchemy. Perhaps more importantly, strategic communication would be located as a corporate-level activity, integrated with business planning, and as a function that is concerned about an organisation's overall reputation, values, and perceived credibility. This becomes the strategic communication imperative, an approach that can be operationalised by integrating communication planning and action with strategic business planning. That means organisations should take a longer term view about how issues can be resolved, based on research that tracks emerging and dynamic issues in external non-market arenas. In conceptualising these arenas, Luoma-aho and Vos (2010) used Actor Network Theory (ANT) to help explain the interactions between organisations and their stakeholders (actors). ANT is a controversial theoretical and methodological approach to social theory that holds that everything in the social and natural worlds exists in constantly shifting networks of relationships and that nothing exists outside those relationships. Despite its disputed nature, the concept is similar to what happens when organisations, as social actors, advance views in the non-market environment. Here, the parameters of issues debates change when the differing views of organisations, experts, opponents, regulators, and activists are challenged. In the ebb and flow of debate, issues remain unresolved until consensus is reached. None of this is resolved in current time frames, but it does require that basic technical professional practice tools are used to disseminate point of view.

Even though they acknowledge the need for strategic planning and implementation, practitioners remain at odds with senior management or clients who are not convinced of its importance as a high-order, value-added organisational function. Strong (2021) reported that 36% of respondents to the US 2021 JOTW Strategic Communications Survey had said that working with leaders who did not understand professional communication was one of the three main challenges they faced. This is a puzzling position for dominant coalitions as they recognise the importance of corporate-level strategic business planning. Thus, a senior, and distinguished, practitioner who participated in my research, noted,

> in a consultancy environment, clients [want] the here and now, and they're paying for the here and now, they don't want to be paying for the 'what if down the track,' and that's very difficult.

This presents a further problem: the long-standing inability of many senior communication practitioners to be formal members of all the forums in which organisational management decisions are made, and to provide expert communication counsel at those forums. This will not be resolved until strategic communication as a professional practice is more closely defined, and practitioners can prove it is effective by demonstrating its direct umbilical link to strategic, as distinct from current tactical, business plans. It may be that with this link, strategic communication, as I conceptualise it, becomes the compass for marketing, advertising, and technical public relations directions and planning. That would be its role if it was treated as a corporate function that was concerned about the overall, high-level communication goals and objectives.

Communication practitioners' views

So, what do practitioners think about linking strategy to business planning? How do they understand their organisations' external environments, and how do issues in those environments affect the decisions they make about strategic directions? My Australian, and European and Asia-Pacific region, research suggests some answers.

In 2020–2021, the findings of the European Communication Monitor (Zefass et al.) provided an answer to the first question. The 2020–2021 ECM reported that its researchers had been following how business strategy and communication were linked since 2007. This had been continuously ranked as a top three issue by more than 40% of ECM respondents until 2016, had performed strongly (37%) until 2019 but was less relevant to practitioners in the two following years. In 2020–2021, linking business strategy and communication was ranked fourth (30.5%) and was more important for companies (33.4%) and consultancies and agencies (31.4%) than for government (24.8%) and not-for-profit (29.6%) organisations. The top ranked strategic issue for European practitioners in 2020–2021 was building and maintaining trust (38.8%). This was more important for European governments (43.6%) and consultancies and agencies (41.1%) than for companies (35.9%) and not-for-profit organisations (34.4%). Along with dealing with sustainable development and social responsibility (ranked third at 31.3%), these were the only 'strategic' issues in the top seven in a list of 11 issues the ECM gave as the 'most important strategic issues for communication management until 2024.' The other four were, in reality, tactical and technical issues about new ways of creating/distributing content, strengthening communication support for senior management, dealing with the speed and volume of communication flow, and digitising communication processes with internal and external stakeholders.

In contrast, the 2020–2021 Asia-Pacific Communication Monitor (Macnamara et al.) reported that 'linking business strategy and communication' was the seventh most important strategic issue for communication management (25.5% of respondents) in that region. However, rated third most important was 'building and maintaining trust' (34.3%), and at fourth, strengthening the role of the communication function in supporting top-management decision-making. The top two issues were technical and tactical, rather than strategic: coping with the digital evolution and social web (38.1%), and using big data and/or algorithms for communication (36.9%). Fifth and sixth in the top seven 'strategic issues' were dealing with sustainable development and social responsibility (29.9%) and exploring new ways of creating and distributing content (28.2%). The APCM reported that building and maintaining trust is rated highest by companies (37.3% of practitioners) along with non-profit organisations (41.4% of practitioners). However, only one third of government communication professionals who responded to the APCM survey rated building and maintaining trust as a strategic issue. The APCM reported that this, and a high focus on coping with the digital evolution and social web, using big data and algorithms, and dealing with the speed and volume of information flow by government communicators, suggested government priority on the dissemination of information rather than engagement and two-way communication.

The data about reputation, sustainable development, and linking communication with business strategy illustrates communication practitioners' support for a strategic approach to communication practice. However, the inclusion of so many tactical issues in a list described as 'strategic' reflects the continuing grip that alchemy has on their practice.

The 2021 Communication Benchmark Report (Ragan, 2021) noted that, in the context of the Covid-19 pandemic, 42% of respondents had stronger relationships with other departments in their organisations, 26% were included in senior management discussions which included strategic decision-making, and 21% had better access to their chief executive officer. The 2021 US JOTW Strategic Communications Survey found that 21% of respondents reported to the Chief Executive Officer'(CEO), the chief marketing officer (20%) of the chief communications officer (CCO) (22%), but that many would prefer to be independent of marketing and report either to the CEO or CCO (Strong, 2021).

Research grounded in contingency theory found that 87 internal and external variables impact on practitioners' abilities to do their jobs (Pang, Yin, & Cameron, 2010). Among such variables were organisational reputation, values, and credibility, stakeholder (including employees) relationships, and regulatory factors.

Nevertheless, the 2020–2021 European and Asia-Pacific monitors' findings, and those from earlier research by Pang et al. (2010), reflect my research that indicates that senior Australian practitioners:

- support a strategic approach to issues management
- are willing to communicate with stakeholders in a range of contexts, especially those that involve organisational reputation

- identify and analyse external issues occurring in their immediate business environment, but do not always do this for mid- and long-term communication planning, and
- support aligning communication strategies with their organisations' business strategies

Summarising significant findings from the research

My research identified eight significant findings about how senior Australian communication practitioners who participated in this project understand their external environments and how this influences their decisions about strategic planning. These findings informed a proposed definition of strategic communication, and enabled me to theorise a way of linking communication strategies with organisational business planning. (See Appendix 1 for an outline of the research approach, participation demographics, and detailed results tables.)

De Bussy and Wolf (2009) found that strategic planning and counsel were regarded by Australian public relations practitioners as their second most frequent duty, after writing and editing. In view of this, it is not surprising that the quantitative and qualitative data suggest that respondents overwhelmingly support the role of communication strategies in advancing corporate goals and objectives in the mid and long terms. Most regard communication strategy as critically important or important and believe communication strategy should be aligned with corporate business plans, and should focus on organisational values and reputations, and on maintaining relationships with stakeholders about issues that are important to the organisation. Respondents list include emerging political issues, and the need for senior executives to build relationships with the government as matters that involve strategic communication. Most respondents do not regard their roles as being focussed only on achieving bottom-line financial results.

Values, reputation, and relationships

The attitudes of the group of senior Australian practitioners in this study about the importance of reputation, values, and credibility in their decision-making reflected arguments by management and professional communication scholars that organisations need to protect their reputations through a strategic approach to communication. Linking communication strategy and reputation was an important point for some respondents who added qualitative comments to their online survey answers. This reinforces a further finding that respondents attempt to be strategic in their approach to communication because building, sustaining, and enhancing organisational reputations and credibility, and promoting values, requires continuing long-term efforts.

Issues drive strategic communication

A constant theme was that strategic communication is concerned about advancing an organisation's interests by advocating its positions on external issues. This applied across all sectors. Most respondents said they engage in analysis of potential and emerging issues as ongoing practice. All respondents are concerned about how issues impact on current business activities; most also engage in issues identification for the medium term; less than half engage in long-term issues analysis.

Issues as organisational risk factors

While a majority of respondents engage in issues analysis as ongoing practice, many frame this as 'risk analysis,' usually because their organisations are concerned with identifying the impact of potential risk on broader business operations. Most practitioners identify potential damage to an organisation's reputation as a primary risk factor.

Willingness to engage in dialogue with opponents

The majority of respondents are willing to recommend that their organisations or clients enter into dialogues with opponents over issues, but their decisions to do this depend on the situation they are addressing. For example, for most a threat of litigation against their organisation would constrain their decision to enter into a dialogue. Most respondents would recommend engaging with organisational critics and opponents even if this would result in negative publicity, especially when the organisation's reputation is threatened. Respondents believe senior managers should engage with critics. The extent to which a stakeholder group is covered by the mass news media is not a significant variable that practitioners take into account when they consider whether to engage with a group.

A tendency to tactical practice

At interview, most respondents reported a tendency for clients and institutional management to demand tactical activity to deal with current issues. This was especially the case for practitioners working in state and federal government agencies when demands from ministers' offices often diverted their attention from strategy to day-to-day political issues. Consultants, too, reported that clients wanted them to focus on immediate issues. However, practitioners acknowledge a move to strategic issues identification and analysis and communication practice after clients and organisations faced a crisis, especially one dealing with a reputational issue.

Sectoral differences in issue priorities

Overall, issues related to organisational reputation, values, and credibility, and relationships with stakeholders, were the two most important issue categories that concerned respondents. However, the research data from this study suggest differences in primary issue category importance between practitioners in different sectors. For example, strategic communicators in higher education regard reputation, values, and credibility as the major issue category, while those in state government agencies view current Australian political issues as the major category. Practitioners in industry associations are primarily concerned about regulatory issues that affect their industry, while those in not-for-profits rate stakeholder relationship as the major category.

Gender differences

The senior practitioners who participated in this study differed significantly in their importance rating of issues on only one category: stakeholder relationships. Female respondents rated stakeholder relationships as the second most important issue category while males rated this as the fifth most important category.

Corporate social responsibility

Most respondents regard their organisation's involvement in projects that demonstrate a commitment to corporate social responsibility as strategic opportunities. However, respondents were less concerned about socio-cultural and natural environmental issues that might impact on their organisations.

The importance of communication strategy

Senior Australian practitioners overwhelmingly support the need for a communication strategy for their organisations or clients. Senior practitioners believe communication strategies should advance corporate goals and objectives in the mid and long terms, do more than enhance the organisation's bottom line, and be aligned with an overall business or corporate plan. Senior practitioners believe communication strategy should promote organisational values, maintain dialogue with stakeholders about issues that are important to the organisation, and that emerging political issues should be factored into business planning. They support the view that communication with stakeholders is important in creating a positive reputation and a majority of respondents to this online survey (68.1%) would recommend engaging in a dialogue with those opposed to the organisation's stance on an issue when faced with negative publicity. Most (87.3%) do not believe that engaging in long-term dialogue with stakeholders who criticise their organisations would be a waste of managers' time, and a majority (61.1%) say they engage with a stakeholder when reputation is threatened. Overall, these comments reflect arguments by Bach and Allen (2010) and Hallahan et al. (2007) that organisations should participate in discourses about public policy as social actors.

Almost all respondents (95%) regarded a communication strategy as important (30.4%), or critically important (64.6%). A communication strategy was neither important nor unimportant for two respondents, and two others regarded a strategy as either unimportant or totally unimportant. For one private sector respondent,

> Strategy is king. Anyone who leaves the dock without a plan deserves what they get.

This respondent wrote that the value of a strategic communication practitioner was as a 'trusted advisor' who is 'well across' issues that are relevant to the business from the political and economic environments to technological advances.

Another respondent described the importance of a communication strategy in this way:

> The best researched policy position is of little value if it isn't effectively communicated. Influencing public policy, particularly in this day and age, is all about communicating your position, not only to policy makers, but also to media and the broader electorate.

This was echoed by a practitioner at a not-for-profit organisation, who argued that a public profile was critical to achieving behavioural and attitudinal change. Despite the absence of a current strategy, this not-for-profit gave 'significant support' to communication. A practitioner at a federal government agency reported support for communication but noted this was seldom resourced at the project level.

Another respondent noted that the task was to use communication skills to help clients solve business issues and to enhance the positives of their business practices. A consultant with more than 20 years' experience noted in a qualitative comment in his survey response that this was done by first understanding a client's business plan and marketing strategy, then recommending a range of communication solutions. One business respondent with more than 20 years' experience argued that strategic communication should be part of all executive teams, report to the chief executive officer, and be accountable for strengthening an organisation's reputation.

Qualitative semi-structured face-to-face interview comments indicate that issues identification and analysis, leading to the development of a communication strategy, is not always normal practice because this is not always supported by senior management. One consultant explained this as:

> it's all very well to worry about what might happen in five years, but there are some clear and present dangers that we need to face right now, and what they are, let's get on top of them.

However, qualitative survey and interview responses also indicate that senior management support for issues analysis and strategy development is more likely after an organisation has experienced a crisis, particularly a crisis involving the organisation's reputation, or if it is required to deal with a significant public policy issue.

For example, one practitioner with 11 to 15 years' experience noted in qualitative comments that a focus on strategic communication by the private sector business for which she worked was only recent and had been 'born out of a reputational crisis.' Before the crisis, this organisation gave little importance to communication, but its importance has now significantly increased. A consultant said about 15% of clients sought help in issues analysis, but that those who had experienced a crisis were more likely to ask for this, and to engage a public relations consultant.

A private sector practitioner described a tendency 'to get started on the tactical side of things without giving due consideration to the key task of understanding [the need for] defining objectives.' Another reported that while communication strategies were critically important when managers were concerned about issues, little thought was given to communication at a strategic level on lower order issues.

Willingness to communicate on issues

Quantitative and qualitative data from the online survey and face-to-face interviews indicate that senior practitioners are willing to recommend communication with stakeholders in a wide range of potentially negative situations. For example, 68.1% of respondents disagreed or strongly disagreed with a statement that they would be 'less likely' to recommend dialogue with a stakeholder opposed to their organisation's stance on an issue. A majority (61.1%) said they usually engaged in a dialogue with a stakeholder who threatened their organisation's reputation. However, more practitioners, but still less than half the sample (44.5%), said they would be likely to recommend a dialogue with external groups with which the organisation had had past negative experiences, than those who would be less likely to do that (32%).

These responses suggest practitioners are generally willing to communicate with their organisations' opponents on issues but that their decisions to do so depend on the situation in which such dialogue would occur. One respondent described this as 'a more complex dichotomy' than the questionnaire allowed, and said that willingness to engage depended on the group and the issue.

Communication strategy and organisational reputation

Management scholars (for example, Argenti et al., 2005; Bach & Allen, 2010; Ghemawatt, 2010) have stressed the need for organisations to protect their reputations through a strategic approach to communication. Their views are echoed by communication scholars (for example, Grunig & Repper, 1992; McCarthy & Hartcher, 2004; Grunig, J.E., 2006; Gregory, 2009; Sandhu, 2009). Linking communication strategy and reputation was a theme for some respondents to the online survey reported here.

A female practitioner, who managed communication for a large private sector project, reported that the organisation had learnt that the absence of a communication strategy for the project for 'few years' meant 'the reputational price they paid was far greater than the price of getting an [communication] expert on board.' This comment was reflected by a private sector respondent who noted that a company decision to focus on a strategic approach to communication was 'born out of a reputation crisis.'

The role of strategic communication in protecting organisations' reputations was viewed by one respondent as including minimising a potentially negative reputation, engaging employees, creating an internal reputation with a potentially large group of advocates, and with clear measures and accountabilities around reputation.

A number of respondents described dealing with organisational reputation in terms of risk, rather than issues, analysis. For example, one public sector communicator noted that for his operational agency, potential reputational damage was identified as a risk that required a management plan. That plan involved rating the risk, providing 'treatment' for it, and reporting at least quarterly on progress with the plan. In this way the agency did not wait for a risk to become a crisis. The practitioner gave this example:

> one of our risks…is whether the community will lose the confidence in us to do our job effectively…So what's the treatment for that? We'll reinforce with the community how you do your job, why you do your job, what the results of doing that job are, communicate messages about how they can help…you do your job and so that risk doesn't arise.

At interview, a practitioner managing communication for a university reported being required to compile a risk register for his department, which fed into a similar document for the whole institution. Each issue listed in the 'corporate' register had a communication component. The register included the branding, marketing, and communication of 'the university's story' as a risk in terms of whether it was done well or not. A state government practitioner noted that she had instituted an agency-wide Issues Management Register which included about a dozen matters mainly around reputational risk. Many of these were in the register because a counterpart state or federal agency had experienced them, resulting in her chief executive asking, 'from my perspective that could tarnish us and questions could be asked here [so] how robust are our systems?' This led to the development of position papers that set out how the agency would deal with a particular risk, and protocols to ensure it didn't happen. A consultant noted that assessing risk for clients was 'about mapping out not just a particular issue but how that issue then links in with some of the other threats.'

Aligning business and communication strategies

In a reflection of the arguments of scholars (for example, Argenti et al., 2005; Cutlip et al., 2006; Guth & Marsh, 2006), a significant majority of respondents supported the notion that communication strategy should be aligned with overall business strategy (94.4%). Asked for their reaction to a statement that aligning communication and business strategies would not enhance their organisation's strategic position, 73.6% of the respondents who answered strongly disagreed. Another 20.8% disagreed with the statement. No respondent agreed in any way with the statement, although four respondents had no opinion either way. This reflects the finding that the majority of online survey respondents agreed (50.7%) or agreed strongly (42.3%) with a statement that strategic communication involved advancing corporate goals and objectives in the mid to long terms.

A private sector practitioner argued that in the business/communication strategy alignment, strategic communication should 'position the organisation [in] its core markets and strengthen the reputation of the business, brands and people.' One online survey respondent commented that working to a communication strategy ensured what was implemented was in line with the client/company's corporate business, operations and marketing strategies, and was 'also the only way to reconcile the communication outcomes against predetermined [key performance indicators].' A public sector respondent said their organisation's support for communication strategy was 'shifting,' but an effort was still required to ensure communication strategy was considered early in the process of business strategy development. However, some areas of this organisation still regarded communication strategy 'as no more than a media release' to announce things. Another practitioner said strategic communication was a 'new way of thinking' for their federal government agency but had become 'an integral part of the overall strategic plan.' A university practitioner said they argued for communication aspects to be included in whole-of-business decisions about the future of the institution because a long-term strategic communication plan could not be separate from the business of the institution.

A state government practitioner noted that in their agency, business and communication strategies were linked but that current political issues 'can actually draw us away from the strategy quite a lot' and easily override 'all your best laid plans [and] influence our day-to-day activities, and then actually change the path of them so quickly.' This practitioner noted that there was time to prepare strategies, but that time was not valued because as flatter organisational structures were implemented, managers between communication staff and the top levels 'aren't necessarily people who would prioritise communication.'

A consultant who works with federal government agencies argued that strategic communication was about making sure the organisation 'goes in the right direction, and that the comms [sic] is aligned with the organisation's objectives as well.'

Issues management and communication strategy

In professional practice, identifying and analysing current and emerging issues is a vital first step in communication planning (see, for example, Cornelissen,

2005; Cutlip et al., 2006; Gregory, 2009b; Mahoney 2011a, b; Mahoney, 2013). The issues identified in this process are independent variables that affect senior practitioners' decisions (the dependent variable) about strategic directions. So, what issue categories concern senior communication practitioners when they make decisions about strategic planning, and what are the contexts in which they research and analyse the issues they need to deal with?

Identifying potential and emerging issues as professional practice

Qualitative responses to my online survey on the need to analyse issues beyond a tactical focus reflected the views of Heath and Palenchar (2009) and Jaques (2009a, b) about the need for this practice to be regular and strategic. The majority of respondents (84.6%) described the identification of potential and emerging issues by their organisation as ongoing practice; 11.5% did this annually; 2.6% every two or three years. Surprisingly, one respondent did not know how often their organisation did this. A practitioner at an Australian university noted that identifying potential and emerging issues meant doing this 'nearly all the time' even though plans were only formally updated annually. A professional lobbyist reported issues identification was often more frequent than annually 'given the focus of our work on pre-empting and responding to issues.'

The importance of issues identification as ongoing practice was linked to reputation management by two respondents. A consultant noted that clients had greater awareness of the need for proactive issues management and that they better understood 'the link that reputation has with effectively handling shareholders and the need to prepare for possible issues.' A private sector business practitioner noted that prior to a reputational crisis the organisation did not 'scan the horizon at all.' One respondent summarised the importance of issues identification and analysis this way:

> Change is everywhere and it's fast and it's dramatic. You have to stay on top of things to add value. If you're not providing valuable information and advice, people won't pay your bills.

At interview, a consultant noted their agency had clients who did engage in long-term issues analysis, partly on the basis of global pressure and partly as a result of directives from parent companies. However,

> I'm philosophising here, but you know we're all mug punters and voters and none of us are, apart from Bernard Salt [the Australian demographer], none of us have the crystal ball, and we know probably that whatever happens we will get through and we'll cope.

One government communicator argued that if they were doing their jobs correctly, practitioners would have 'an eye or some resource devoted to looking at what's coming down the train track and what are the emerging issues.' For this practitioner, this approach was strategic and about the link between reputation and operational issues.

Issues management contexts

The concept of strategic communication suggests that the focus of this professional practice should be on dealing with issues over the mid and long terms (for example, Argenti et al., 2005; Cornelissen, 2005; Hallahan et al., 2007; Zerfass & Huck, 2007). Argenti et al. (2005) argued that while the focus of strategic communication must have a long-term orientation, practitioners must also meet short-term needs. This view was reflected by the responses of all those who answered this question (see Table A1.6) when they reported that they conducted issues analysis and management in the context of how issues impact on current business activities. Most (86.5%) also considered medium-term contexts, but less than half (45.9%) considered the long term.

The focus on the 'here and now' was explained by one participant in an online survey comment:

> Our clients tend to be focussed on the present and on the very short-term. This is to the detriment of their best interests as they experience and deal with change. We try to encourage longer-term consideration of opportunities and threats and by preparing them for issues and crises [and to] help their organisations (and individuals in management) to be more flexible and better able to survive difficulties. We believe that regular focus on the future enables better decisions to be made in the present and thereby to influence the kind of future they (and we) experience.

A state government communicator described their agency's approach to issues analysis as 'you can't just be thinking about what the current issues are, you have to have an eye for the emerging issues.'

One influence on issues management for most public sector communicators was the three-to-four-year electoral cycle. One state government communicator said they generally only identified issues that were likely to occur in the four-year electoral cycle of their State Parliament, although some budget bids were made on the basis of issues concerned with servicing stakeholders in a shorter term. For one federal government communicator, the issues management driver was the budget cycle.

A private sector communicator linked issues management contexts to the 'central' question of what the organisation was trying to achieve. Communicators had to be 'forever scanning the horizon and have a clear understanding of audiences, desired behaviours and objectives to make sure that you are adding value. It's why they pay you.' A consultant noted that a lot of issues management involved 'keeping an eye on' what governments were doing because, 'if there's an issue coming out of a government, whether that be local, state, national or even international, you know that's really where things are being driven.'

Tactical issues communication

Despite respondents' support for strategic communication planning and practice, many commented on the tactical approaches they were required to take as a result of client or management demands. Some were concerned about how pressure from clients or senior management to work tactically did not produce long-term results. One pre-eminent consultant described this as 'short-termism' that 'ran riot' through every business and government in which the focus was on the current two years. The consultant said some businesspeople 'think they're smart enough to deal with any issue that comes up in year three and beyond, and after that it doesn't matter because I won't be here.' The consultant said:

> 80% of what we do, even now … is still publicity about the client's fine product … It's not about strategy, it's not about forward thinking, it's not about futures thinking. I've tried at this level to get my people interested in futures … because it's the connection to issue and crisis management. It's the point of intersection with what we do in PR.

Another consultant said they operated tactically because clients demanded this. Clients were 'not necessarily looking for the strategic direction; they would much rather work on a month-by-month column inches approach, rather than a 12-month engagement strategic plan.' For this consultant, tactical communication was driven by economic circumstances; few had three-to-five-year business plans because there was no point 'in planning for the future if you're not going to be around for the future.' The consultant said:

> in a consultancy environment, clients [want] the here and now, and they're paying for the here and now, they don't want to be paying for the 'what if down the track,' and that's very difficult.

One consultant reported that clients tended to be focused on the present and on the very short term 'to the detriment of their best interests as they experience and deal with change.' For another consultant, communicators had lost 'the strategic war' to accountants and lawyers who they described as 'the decision-makers' who were becoming chief executives. These executives did not understand how communication could add value to the bottom line, were inherently guarded and risk averse, but could deliver a dollar value to the business.

Government communicators described a requirement for them to respond tactically to the demands of ministers or ministers' 'offices,' often from media advisers. One described this as 'something that can actually draw us away from strategy quite a lot, so it can very easily override everything that you do…all your best laid plans.' This meant that government communicators were,

> increasingly finding yourself chasing that media pressure and political driven agenda, and you can't go back sometimes to what you would have advised at the start with frank and fearless advice.

Another government practitioner argued that the public sector focus on tactical communication was because the value of communication was 'a pretty rude thing…keeping the minister happy.' That is,

> the minister's saying, get me out there, I want to announce that policy, and I want it covered, and I want the media interested, and I want it up in Facebook, and I want it here … to convince my parliamentary colleagues; I want to convince caucus and so on.

That meant that the communication 'front line steps up and gets all that done, [and] at the end of the day the minister smiles and says, well done chaps. It's pretty rude…and it's absolutely tactical, not strategic; this is tactical, basic stuff.'

According to another government practitioner, a factor influencing this tactical approach was the background many public sector communicators had in journalism as opposed to organisational communication. This meant they focussed 'on fire fighting and bushfires.' A consultant argued that the 'good' journalists they employed were strategically focussed, maintained good connections, were well read, and were often 'the frontline of defence because they smell stuff that other people don't in the wind.' They joined the organisation because they were 'tired of being negative…they want to move away from confrontation and into building things…forming relationships and taking a long-term view.'

An industry association practitioner viewed tactical communication in the context of 'never letting a chance go by' when reacting to political developments:

> you may have a strategy which has a 10-step approach on paper, but in the political world, as we all know, nothing is planned. If something happens, and it doesn't fit in to your strategic framework, you'd be stupid to let it go past without acting on it.

This view was reflected by a consultant who argued that issues management involved common sense and was based on accessibility to organisational management, accountability, honesty, and transparency. In many instances, issues managers had 'one minute to make up your mind, not a day, or a week or a month, or a year—you've got to trust your gut.' Another consultant noted it was 'a practical reality that people are dealing with the tactical' but said clients who wanted to focus on media relations were advised that doing that in the long term would fail because 'there is no strategic framework around it.'

For state and federal government practitioners, working in a tactical frame was a consistent theme, caused by instructions from ministers' offices that they react to the demands of the daily news cycle, and the reality that elections every three or four years (depending on the jurisdiction) did not provide time for a more long-term approach. The operational nature of one respondent's government agency meant a tendency to be focussed on the day-to-day impact of issues on reputation and operations, which the respondent described as 'tactical management.' Here, 'a focus on the strategic remains an ongoing challenge,' a point echoed by two other respondents who noted,

> experience shows that attempting to predict issues beyond the state or federal political cycle does not provide sufficient clarity to be useful.

and

> Beyond top level policy planning, State Governments in my experience tend to struggle with commitment to communication strategys [sic] & issues management beyond the hourly, daily, weekly, monthly media cycles, as well as 3-yearly election cycles.

At interview, a state government agency communicator said that, because politicians were driven by media influence, they were forced to respond on the record very quickly and could not escape this. This meant that government communicators increasingly found themselves,

> chasing that media pressure and politically-driven agenda, and you can't go back sometimes to what you would have advised right at the start with frank and fearless advice as the right way to go.

A consultant argued that some government communication had 'real short-term strategies' because practitioners in that sector 'don't have a lot of control, and sometimes the tail wags the dog fairly ferociously … I'm lucky not to have to work there, but I see it close at hand, and I don't envy them one bit.'

One federal public sector communicator explained why their large agency's communication was so tactical this way:

> The day-to-day thing takes over … and the size of the operation is a reflection of the daily tasks … they're huge and they're substantial, and they're all … absolutely in a short-term government framework. It really is the government's today, issues today, program today policy that we're working on.

Overall issue priorities

Scholars have previously identified nine categories of political, economic, and social issues that are important in issues management and strategic communication planning.

Participants in my research were asked to prioritise these issue categories on a scale of 1 to 10, where 1 was the most important category and 10 was the least important. A rating average automatically calculated by the Survey Monkey software was used to produce a priority ranking order for these categories. A rating average is calculated by dividing the sum of all answers to a question by the number of respondents. The construction of this question meant that respondents needed to indicate their highest priority by ticking '1,' and their lowest by ticking '10.' This meant the lowest rating average was the most important priority.

Issues related to organisational reputation, values, and credibility were given the highest priority (rating average: 3.54) by senior practitioners (see Table A1.7 in Appendix 1). The least priority overall was issues related to the natural environment that might impact on the organisation (rating average: 7.06).

Issue categories as influences on strategic communication

Argenti et al. (2005) identified regulatory imperatives, organisational complexity, and the need to improve credibility as strategic communication drivers. Do these drivers apply in Australian communication practice? Knowing this is relevant to identifying whether it is possible to theorise how strategic communication planning can be linked to the three business growth horizons described by the management scholars Baghai et al. (2000). Baghai et al. (2000) defined these horizons as:

Horizon 1: extending and defending core business. This horizon encompasses the businesses that are at the heart of an organisation and with which customers and analysts most readily identify.
Horizon 2: building emerging businesses. In this horizon, management is concerned with the emerging stars of the company, because they transform companies.
Horizon 3: seeding options for future businesses.

In this book, Horizon 1 refers to the current term, Horizon 2 to the mid term, and Horizon 3 to the long term.

How senior practitioners rank issue categories, or strategic communication drivers, in the contexts of Baghai et al.'s (2000) horizons for business growth is important. To do this, data from responses to issues management contexts were cross-tabulated with responses that generated rating averages for issue priorities. This process revealed only one change to the priority ranking of issue categories: in the current term, respondents rated 'current Australian political issues' as the second most important category, and relationships with stakeholders third. Overall, these two categories were rated equal second. However, the priority ratings for these two issue categories were reversed in responses about the mid and long terms. A standard deviation calculation of rating averages for each issue category confirmed participants were consistent in their responses.

Differences in issue priorities between industry sectors

Communication practitioners are employed by organisations in all sectors of the economy, including as consultants and professional lobbyists. An outcome for my research was to determine whether senior practitioners in different sectors, or as consultants, gave different priorities to issue categories. Knowing whether there is a difference between the issues that practitioners' focus on in specific sectors is important for explaining how and why they participate in issues debates. The research sought to identify differences between senior sector-based practitioners on issues that influence strategic communication decisions. A cross-tabulation of quantitative responses about issue priorities with those for organisation type found differences between sectors on the primary driver of their strategic communication. Issues related to organisational reputation, values, and credibility were the primary drivers of strategic communication for universities and lobbyists, while practitioners who worked as consultants and for not-for-profit organisations rated stakeholder relationships as their main drivers. Practitioners deciding strategic communication directions for industry associations rated regulatory issues as their primary drivers. Practitioners working in private sector businesses are concerned about emerging Australian political issues; those in state and federal government agencies prioritised current Australian political issues.

These results were not surprising. For example, industry associations exist to influence government decision-making about industry policies, many of which are directed at regulatory issues. Universities depend on their reputations, values, and credibility to attract research funding and students. Qualitative data reinforced the importance of current Australian political issues to the day-to-day practice of senior communicators in state and federal government agencies. This is a reflection of their reported reality that their professional practice was driven by the daily demands of ministers and/or their staff.

Gender and strategic communication

The research found virtually no difference between male and female practitioners' views about the importance of communication strategy for their organisations or clients. While a majority of respondents of both genders regard strategy as 'critically important' (66.7% of males; 61.5% of females), a greater percentage of female practitioners regarded it as 'important' (35.9% female; 25.6% male). This was due to three males regarding strategy as either 'totally unimportant,' 'unimportant,' or 'neither import nor unimportant.' Only one female rated strategy outside the 'important/critically important' response points. This respondent said strategy was 'neither important nor unimportant.' However, rating averages generated from the online survey's quantitative data revealed differences between the priorities male and female practitioners say drive their strategic communication decision-making.

For both genders, issues related to reputation, values, and credibility were the most important drivers they considered in their decision-making. However, senior female practitioners were more likely to rate stakeholder relationships the second priority in their strategic communication decision-making, while males rated this as their fifth priority. Males were more concerned about current and emerging political issues and ranked these as second and third most important drivers. Female practitioners regard current political issues as the third priority strategic communication driver and emerging political issues as their sixth. Surprisingly, socio-cultural issues, and those related to the natural environment, were rated the lowest two priority drivers.

A two-tailed *t* test was conducted on the results for stakeholder relationships as a driver of communication because the difference between genders in rating averages was the biggest of the five major drivers. The *t* test (p $\leq$ .05) showed that the difference between genders on the priority given to stakeholder relations was statistically different (*t* = 0.041). The two-tailed *t* test (p $\leq$ .05) showed no statistically significant difference between genders on the other drivers. Female respondents were more likely to regard communication strategy as 'important/critically important' (97.4% of females) than their male counterparts (92.3%).

Fewer female practitioners than male practitioners said they identified issues likely to emerge in the mid term (83.3% of female respondents compared to 89.5% of males). However, more female practitioners than males said they conducted issues management in the context of identifying issues likely to emerge in the long term (48.6% of females; 42.1% of males).

These results suggest female practitioners may take a more strategic view of communication than their male counterparts, a view supported in face-to-face interviews. This may be because in professional practice, building and maintaining relationships with stakeholders and developing and retaining organisational reputations and credibility are long-term tasks and most participants in the face-to-face interviews suggested female respondents took longer term approaches to communication than did males.

A female state government communicator noted that while this view might 'fit with a few stereotypes,' it was natural for women to be collegiate and to build collaborative relationships and that this was 'a valuable thing that adds to both business as well as [to] how we as communicators work.' This meant that 'ensuring those relationships will stand you through' no matter what day-to-day issues needed to be considered, was long term and 'definitely more strategic.'

A female practitioner at a federal government agency regarded stakeholder relationships as what strategic communication really encapsulates. This was explained as,

> in strategic communication anything I can sort … influence or meld into what I want to achieve is something that I value. So relationships with stakeholders would probably be very important to me.

A consultant regarded female practitioners as having 'a good strategic perception, a good strategic grasp, whereas men typically gloss over that and become
far more tactical in their approach.' A female consultant, who has also worked
at the top level of federal government communication, expressed surprise at this
result but noted there were more females in government communication areas.
Nevertheless, the practitioner noted that 'the [male] focus actually tends to be
on the very practical get it done, get it out the door, done and dusted, sort
of approach. So it becomes a very practical and un-strategic focus.' Two male
interviewees also expressed surprise at this result. One was 'staggered' at the
difference because 'I wouldn't have thought there would be at all.' The other, a
consultant, expressed surprise that, despite anticipating men and women would
have slightly different views, practitioners would not have relationships 'way up
there. I would have thought relationships were primary, whether you're a man
or a woman.'

   Another consultant noted that the only defining factor between the approaches
of men and women in their consultancy was that the men tended to be former
journalists while the women were not. This 'sometimes means...the guys in
the consultancy, the input that they give can come slightly more from a news-
oriented political landscape point of view, and sometimes the women may come
from a more humanist point of view.' At interview, a higher education practitioner put this point in the context of the influence male and female institutional
leaders had on communication. Male leaders tended to have a transactional view
of communication in which they devised what was needed to be said in a given
situation, and delivered that. On the other hand, female leaders wanted to engage
in a conversation to devise a message strategy. That meant that female leaders
asked more questions around 'who have we talked to about this, as opposed to
the males who have asked me, who do we need to tell?'

   A female state government practitioner expressed the difference between genders in the context of always regarding communicators as being advocates for
customers 'in some way, shape or form.' That meant in strategic discussions about
programs, or the direction of the business, part of her role was to comment,

> Well, from the customer's point of view, I don't think I'd be very happy
> with that sort of response. Can we just think a moment about how that
> might be perceived if we start communicating ... with a message that this
> is what our purpose is?

A government communicator with a range of private and public sector experience, who described himself as 'quite strong in the tactical and less strong on the
strategic,' classified the good female communicators he worked with at senior
levels as the opposite: 'If I was putting them into boxes, I would say the majority
of them would be strategic.' Another government communicator with private
sector consultancy experience noted that female practitioners were quicker to
recognise the dimension of the relationships they needed to establish to deliver

a strategy. Women were also quicker to recognise the potential penalties, and problems in stakeholder relationships when 'they're mapping out' a strategy whereas men

> are a bit more inclined to sort of deliver immediately, more inclined to put the stakeholders down the list sometimes in a more directive kind of way.

This point was reflected by a male industry association practitioner whose organisation has a significant political focus. He noted that, like a lot of people working in a lobbying environment, he tended to be impulsive and that 'the strategy may be there, but I'll jump in and fast forward…on that strategy where I have to.'

Influences on strategic communication decision-making

Senior practitioners' direct insights into how they understand their external environments are important in analysing their approaches to strategic communication decision-making. This includes how public policy issues influence their strategic decision-making and the issues with which they are most concerned. These influences can partly be explained by contingency theory. In this view, issues are independent variables that influence decisions (dependent variables) about how organisations as social actors (Hallahan et al., 2007) participate in non-market environment issues debates (Bach & Allen, 2010). My research therefore sought senior practitioners' agreement/disagreement with 22 statements about issues and their strategic communication practice using options on a five-point Likert Scale. These statements are independent variables that influence the decisions (the dependent variable) that senior practitioners make about communication strategy directions.

Reputation and values

Regester and Larkin (2005) noted that real or perceived threats to reputation could destroy an organisation's brand or image 'literally in hours or days' (p. 2). Thus, the need to safeguard an organisation's reputation was implied in substantial budgets for marketing, compliance, recruitment, public affairs, and communications. Heath and Palenchar (2009) linked organisational character and perceived legitimacy to the credibility an organisation has during debates about issues. Heath and Palenchar (2009) argued that the way in which organisational images are interpreted demonstrates the close connection between image or reputation (even brand equity) and socio-political issues. My research data support these arguments and indicate that senior Australian practitioners recognise the links between reputation and organisational character and the dangers of potential threats to clients', or organisations', reputations detailed by Regester and Larkin (2005) and Heath and Palenchar (2009).

The data suggest that the major issue categories, or independent variables, that influence respondents' decision-making are those that relate to their organisation's, or client's, reputation, the values those organisations represent, and their ability to build and maintain credibility. Overall, 97.2% of respondents agree/ strongly agree that communication with stakeholders is important in creating a positive reputation—75% strongly agree. Similarly, 94.5% of respondents believe promoting organisational values is an important part of strategic communication practice. The notion that strategic communication involves advancing corporate goals and objectives in the mid and long terms was supported by 93% of respondents. A significant majority of respondents (94.5%) rejected a statement that it was not important for their organisation to build and maintain open dialogues with their stakeholders.

At interview, one consultant described the results on reputation and values as 'a bit of realism…not a lot of academic attitude to what ought to be there, but a realistic view of what is actually there.' In additional comments to their survey response, a state government communicator noted the importance of employee engagement with organisational values and described this as 'becoming a critical issue for strategic communication.' The communicator noted that, 'even the best strategies can be broken by employees who don't demonstrate values or brand promise—undermines [the] credentials of the brand in a more impactful way than any outside stakeholders.'

Enhancing an organisation's financial performance

Although they say they are often required to work tactically, senior Australian practitioners do not regard their roles as focussed only on financial performance. They overwhelmingly disagreed with the idea that strategic communication should only be concerned with enhancing their organisation's financial performance (93.9% disagreed/strongly disagreed). However, they are divided on whether the economic stability of their organisation affects their dialogue with stakeholders: 43.1% said it did, 30.6% said it did not, and 26.4% had no opinion.

Despite this support for a longer term view of communication, respondents were aware of the requirements of executives and boards to deal with the bottom line. One consultant noted in an interview that chief executive officers and managing directors cared about only two things: the bottom line and 'seeing themselves in the paper.' Another consultant noted that while high-level executives

> understand the importance of the bottom line, [they] actually understand a little bit about future planning. So it's not too hard to convince them to adopt a more of a long term view.

Respondents' support for the notion that strategic communication involves advancing corporate goals and objectives in the mid to long terms (93%), reflects their focus on the long-term tasks of protecting organisational reputations, values, and credibility, and the importance of stakeholder relationships. The view that building and maintaining open dialogues with stakeholders about issues was not important was rejected by 90.3% of respondents. Just over half the respondents (52.8%) believe senior management should focus on dealing with mid- to long-term issues than day-to-day tactics.

Engaging with opponents

In a reflection of the view by scholars that effective communication is dialogic, respondents appear prepared to engage in dialogues with stakeholders who oppose their organisation's views on issues. A majority (87.3%) disagree/disagree strongly that long-term dialogue with those who criticised the organisation would waste managers' time.

Differences between senior practitioners' views about engaging with groups opposed to the organisation, or who were activists, or with stakeholders perceived as radical, were narrower than on other questions. More than two-thirds of respondents (68.1%) disagreed/strongly or disagreed that they were unlikely to recommend dialogue with those opposed to their organisation's stance on an issue when faced with potentially damaging publicity. Only a fifth (19.5%) of senior practitioners said they would not recommend dialogue. The remaining 12.5% had no view.

This suggests that while practitioners regard stakeholder engagement as important, many tend to be cautious about the circumstances in which they would recommend engagement. More senior practitioners believe organisations should engage with a stakeholder even when that stakeholder threatens the organisation's reputation (61.1%) than those who do not. However, almost one third of respondents (30.6%) neither agreed nor disagreed with engagement in that circumstance, suggesting they may not have thought about the possibility. Senior practitioners are less likely to recommend dialogue with stakeholders if their organisation had previous negative experiences with groups (44.5% would recommend dialogue, 32% would not, and 23.6% neither agreed/disagreed).

Almost 90% of respondents disagreed or disagreed strongly (89.3%) with a statement that it would be a waste of managers' time to engage in long-term dialogue with stakeholders who criticise their organisation.

Previous research (Reber & Cameron, 2003) found that a perception that a stakeholder group is radical can act as a variable that affects how organisations communicate. Only 20.8% of respondents agreed they would recommend a dialogue with a group perceived to be radical. While just over a third of respondents had no view on this, 45.9% strongly disagreed/disagreed that they were willing to engage in a dialogue in these circumstances. Nor would a majority of respondents (56.4%) engage with activists as this would mean legitimising activists' claims. However, more say they would recommend a dialogue with groups with whom their organisation had had past negative experiences (44.5%), than those who agree they would be less likely to do this (32%).

Political and regulatory issues and corporate social responsibility

A majority of respondents believe their organisations should factor current political issues into their business planning (91.5% of respondents to this question agreed/strongly agreed). These issues are given a high priority in their organisations', or clients', communication activity, according to 70.8% of those who answered this question. One industry association communicator described dealing with political issues as going 'into the battlefield, into the trenches and [having] lots of political fights.' A consultant put this in the context of industry associations protecting their members: 'and they're usually behind the eight ball, and they're usually too late because they haven't considered the issues.'

Practitioners are also concerned about emerging political issues and relationships with governments. Most respondents (91.5%) disagreed or strongly disagreed (52.1%) with a suggestion that their organisations did not need to factor emerging political issues into business planning. That result is reflected in respondents' rejection of the view that senior executives do not need to devote time to building and maintaining relationships with governments (94.5% strongly disagreed/disagreed with the view).

A majority (83.3%) say their organisations or clients are often concerned with issues related to government regulation. One consultant said in an interview that while their agency was interested in regulatory issues facing clients, it did not work as a lobbyist but helped clients to understand, or interpret, issues in a way that they could react through communication. A higher education practitioner noted that relationships with the local government over planning regulations were as important as those with donors, other governments, and funding bodies.

Overall, senior practitioners believe that demonstrating a commitment to the principles of Corporate Social Responsibility (CSR) is a strategic opportunity (78.2% agree/strongly agree; 2.8% disagree/strongly disagree; 18.2% have no opinion). However, respondents were more nuanced in their comments about how organisations viewed corporate social responsibility and some consultants mentioned client cynicism towards such programs. For example, one said that clients regarded CSR as 'almost…a by-the-by, and it's at best a necessary evil.' This view was reflected by one higher education interviewee who said:

> we make a lot of noise about the fact that this is driving our thinking, but ultimately I'm a bit a cynical and I say, well, often decisions are made for the pure economics of it, rather than for the social consequences.

One consultant argued that CSR was better termed 'Common Sense Really.' This was not a

> new fandangled thing … if we're proud of what we're doing we are genuinely operating in a CSR space. Not because we want to get up on some CSR ladder of the index, because our genuine intent is to do the right thing.

For this consultant, CSR should not be an outcome in itself, but part of the business culture because 'it's the right way to do things, it's the right way to treat people, it's the right way to treat the environment. And it will deliver good economic outcomes if you adopt that principle.' A higher education respondent said that because the university's key stakeholders did not regard it as a profit-making entity, there was a sense that 'the dividend paid is our community contribution. So doing the right thing rather the most profitable thing, it sits high in the institution.'

A majority of the companies one consultant worked with undertook corporate social responsibility activity from 'an internal culture point of view, very little about the perception from the outside.' However,

> It honestly depends on who your client is, and where they're coming from. We're lucky enough to have some clients who are very proactive in the CSR space, and rely on us for advice and guidance, but they're coming from exactly the right place. They're aligning themselves with their own culture, and they understand that good PR is about aligning the behaviour of an organisation with the expectation of its stakeholders.

This view was reflected by another consultant who noted that in the second decade of the 21st century more organisations knew what corporate social responsibility meant and quite a few focussed on it seriously. But

> when it comes to the crunch it's not as important as the other factors that drive the business, and a lot of them are still paying lip service to corporate social responsibility because they think, well we should be doing this, we've been told it's got to in an annual report, how would it really affect us?

Organisational complexity

Scholars have argued that organisational complexity is a factor that sometimes inhibits dialogue with stakeholders or regular analysis of external issues beyond the market environment (see for example, Reber & Cameron, 2003; Argenti et al., 2005; Porter, 2008; Bach & Allen, 2010). However, the senior Australian respondents did not regard organisational complexity as an issue affecting their ability to communicate. Of those who answered a question about organisational complexity and external issues analysis (74.6%), more (15.5%) had no view about this than said it was a difficulty (9.8%).

The possibility of litigation

Researchers in the United States found that the possibility of litigation sometimes inhibits practitioners' ability to do their jobs (Reber & Cameron, 2003).

The responses of senior Australian practitioners in this study reflected this finding. While almost half (47.9%) of the respondents did not have a view about willingly engaging in dialogue with parties to a lawsuit when litigation was pending against the organisation, only 15.5% agreed they would do this. The remainder strongly disagreed/disagreed with that they would be willing to engage in such a dialogue (36.6%).

At interview, one government communicator reported that the possibility of litigation sometimes constrained their agency's communication effort:

> It's really disappointing that the nature of our organisation is very risk adverse, and the other thing is, is that … we've got an old school sort of culture that exists within the department, so I think being able to change those attitudes and behaviour that already exist within this culture is really difficult. So, we do miss a lot of opportunities.

Another government communicator from a large service-delivery department said that most decisions about public communication were always put through a 'prism' of, 'what's the potential to offend them, what's the potential for them to sue, what's their potential to take action against the department in one way or another.' A respondent from a government agency often involved in sensitive operations with potential political impacts said the threat of legal action didn't prevent communication about important issues, but stressed the need for a cooperative approach with organisational lawyers to protect its legal position and reputation. An industry association communicator said the possibility of litigation was an issue they had to bear in mind but that 'we're fortunate though that it's not a daily concern for us, but we do push the envelope a bit, so we do have to be careful about how we…paint the activities of certain groups.'

A consultant argued that the potential for litigation mattered in counselling clients about action they should take but that getting lawyers and communication people 'going in the same direction' was sometimes extremely difficult. Communication people had to be 'very strong in those situations and say, "These are the implications. Now OK, you might have a court case, but would you rather have a court case or a business?" And it almost gets to that.'

Stakeholder media coverage as an influence on communication decisions

The extent to which a stakeholder group is covered in the mass news media does not seem to be a significant variable that practitioners take into account when they decide whether to engage with a target public. Less than half the respondents (44.5%) said they would engage with a stakeholder who had received substantial media coverage in the past—and 38.9% surprisingly had no view on this.

Relationships between influences on decisions about strategic directions

Data from the quantitative survey were cross-tabulated to investigate whether there were relationships between respondents' attitudes to strategic communication and the importance of issues that influence their decision-making.

The importance of communication strategy and issues management contexts

Respondents were asked their views on the importance of communication strategy and the contexts in which they conducted issues management for their organisations or clients. The importance of a communication strategy was rated on a five-point Likert Scale on which options ranged from 'critically important' to 'totally unimportant.' The three issues management contexts given to respondents were the current business environment, the mid-term business environment, or up to five years in the future, and the long term, or beyond five years.

The data for those who responded that a communication strategy was critically important, or important, were compared with those for 'Yes' responses about issues management contexts. Only four practitioners who answered the question about the importance of a communication strategy responded that it was totally unimportant, unimportant, or neither. These responses were not compared.

The comparison confirms senior Australian practitioners' focus on the current and mid terms. Whether they regard a communication strategy as critically important, or important, they say their priority is managing issues that impact on their clients' or organisations' current business environment, and then in the mid term. Less than half of those who regarded strategy as critically important (46.9%) or important (42.9%) undertook long-term issues analysis. At interview, one consultant described this focus in these terms:

> the majority of our clients' problems are immediate problems. You know, our industry is that of problem solvers ... we add value as well, but most of the time we're problem solving and [there is] an incredible value in that— clients come to trust us and rely on us.

Another consultant noted that 80% of their business was about publicity for clients' products: 'It's not about strategy, it's not about forward thinking, it's not about futures thinking.' A national industry association practitioner said issues management was normally done in the context of the election cycle, particularly when there was an expectation of a change of government, and because most of the issues the association faced were in any case short to medium-term issues. This organisation had committees that produced policies 'like the lava coming down the hill, slowly and surely.' However, the two-yearly change in the organisation's executive meant long-term planning was hard to maintain, so the focus was on the daily political climate in which 'you just know when to act and when to leave and when to respond.'

A government communicator with private consultancy experience noted that when practitioners argued for longer term issues analysis to enable organisations to be prepared, managerial objectives were quite often, 'No, let's worry about today.' The communicator said that in the consultancy sector,

> what you see is people come through the door looking for answers to today's problems. They don't come through the door saying, tell us where we're going to be in 10 years, and let's work towards that.

A respondent who consults to government clients, and who also has significant experience working in-house for government agencies, described the focus of public sector communication as always being on 'that instant immediate fire that they have to put out...and they'll let other things just burn away slowly.' Government communicators would 'always be looking to the next election' and would not be planning five years ahead. This consultant argued that government communicators recognised the need to be more strategic but 'it gets swallowed up in the imperative of the day-to-day media cycle' and that in the public service 'maybe one of three years is all you can do [for strategic thinking].'

Senior practitioners are more likely to identify and analyse issues expected to impact on business environments in the next five years than they are to predict issues that might occur in the long term, or beyond five years in the future. One said: 'I would say sometimes clients' business plans might go out past five years, but our advice I would never say goes beyond that.' Another consultant noted that it was crucial for communicators to look to the mid and long terms, but this did not happen often. Private sector clients looked for short-term outcomes for their investments, while those in local government were more likely to take a longer term view because their issues, for example, driving regulatory reform, took three or four years to resolve.

Issue category priorities and the importance of strategy

Respondents to the online survey were asked to rate the priorities they gave to a series of issue categories that concerned their organisation on a scale of 1 to 10 (where 1 was the most important priority and 10 the least important priority). These ratings were cross-tabulated with respondents' views about the importance of strategy. This confirmed the priority order for issue categories that concern practitioners in their decision-making reported earlier. Respondents who believe communication strategy is critically important/important gave their highest priority to issues concerning organisational reputation, values, and credibility. Stakeholder relationships and current Australian political issues were the next most important priorities, followed by the competitive business environment and regulatory issues. However, priorities varied slightly between respondents who regarded communication strategy to be 'important' and those who said it was 'critically important,' although the difference was not statistically significant (two-tailed t test, $t = 0.97$, $p \leq .05$).

The importance of strategy for organisation sectors

The research sought to discover whether practitioners in different sectors of the economy differed in their attitudes towards strategic communication planning. This was tested in two ways. First, quantitative data giving details of the participants' organisational sectors were cross-tabulated with questions about the drivers of strategic communication. Second, respondents' views on the importance of communication strategy were cross-tabulated with that for the sector in which they worked.

Practitioners overwhelmingly rate communication strategy in the 'Critically important/Important' range. However, the data suggest that professional lobbyists, consultants, and those in commercial businesses are more likely to view strategic communication as critically important for their clients than are practitioners in other sectors.

Importance of strategy and issues identification time frames

Any attempt to propose how communication strategy can be aligned with business planning requires an understanding of how often practitioners identify and analyse potential and emerging issues. Research respondents were asked to nominate on a five-point Likert Scale the time frames in which they analysed issues. The result was cross-tabulated with responses to the five-point Likert Scale about the importance of strategy (see Table 2.1).

Some interviewees indicated that issues identification and analysis were not always their normal practice. However, 91.3% of total respondents engage in regular identification and analysis of potential and emerging issues. Of the 63 respondents for whom issues identification and analysis is 'on-going practice,' communication strategy is either critically important or important. This suggests a strong link between decisions about communication strategy directions and issues analysis.

Influences on communication decisions and issues management contexts

Participants' level of disagreement with 12 statements related to the strategic communication drivers identified by Argenti et al. (2005) were correlated with those for issues management contexts, that is, whether they conducted issues management in the current, mid, and/or long terms (see Table 2.2).

TABLE 2.1 Percentage of respondents who agree with drivers and issue management time frames

	Issues management time frames					
	Current		Mid Term		Long Term	
	%	%	%	%	%	%
Strongly agree/agree with statement	SA	A	SA	A	SA	A
Communication with stakeholders important in creating positive reputation	75.0	22.2	78.3	20.3	78.3	20.3
Promoting organisation's values important for strategic communication	38.9	55.6	39.1	55.1	39.1	55.1
Management should focus on mid to long terms rather than day-to-day	11.1	41.7	11.6	40.6	11.6	40.6
Current political issues given a high priority	33.3	37.5	33.3	37.7	33.3	37.7
Strategic communication involves advancing corporate goals in mid to long terms	42.3	50.7	42.6	50.0	42.6	50.0
Organisation usually engages in dialogue with stakeholder who threatens its reputation	15.3	45.8	15.9	44.9	15.9	44.9
Organisation often concerned with issues related to government regulation	51.4	31.9	52.2	30.4	52.2	30.4

Key: SA = Strongly agree; A = Agree

Table 2.1 reports percentages showing respondents' level of *agreement* with statements that might influence their decision-making cross-tabulated by the issues management contexts in which they take those decisions.

TABLE 2.2 Percentage of respondents who disagree with drivers and issue management time frames

	Issues management time frames					
	Current		Mid Term		Long Term	
	%	%	%	%	%	%
Strongly disagree/disagree with statement	SD	D	SD	D	SD	D
Dialogues with stakeholders about issues that affect the organisation are not important	79.2	15.3	81.2	13.0	81.2	13.0
Senior execs don't need to spend time building relationships with governments	80.6	13.9	81.2	13.0	81.2	13.0
Organisation too complex for regular issues analysis beyond market environment	16.9	57.7	17.6	58.8	17.6	58.8
Organisation does not need to factor emerging political issues into business planning	52.1	39.4	54.4	36.8	54.4	36.8
Long-term dialogue with critics is a waste of managers' time	31.0	56.3	30.9	55.9	30.9	55.9

Key: SD = Strongly disagree; D = Disagree

Table 2.2 reports percentages showing respondents' level of *disagreement* with statements that might influence their decision-making cross-tabulated by the issues management contexts in which they take those decisions.

This strongly confirms respondents' focus on organisation reputations, values, credibility, and stakeholder relationships irrespective of the context in which they conduct issues identification and analysis, or the importance they place on strategy. Practitioners rejected the view that dialogues with stakeholders about issues that affect an organisation are not important, and they equally strongly believe that senior executives need to spend time building relationships with governments. This is an important recognition because governments and their agencies are social actors in organisations' non-market environments. Respondents also believe that managers would not waste time engaging in long-term dialogue with organisational critics, and that organisations need to factor emerging political issues into business planning.

Keys to the strategic communication imperative

Despite international and Australian research showing that senior practitioners support a strategic approach to communication, and that it should be linked to business strategy, it seems few are able to achieve that. As a result, practitioners tend to pursue a tactical focus, mostly at the behest of dominant coalitions or clients.

In Australia, this means practitioners do not always engage in the vital first step in strategic communication: issues identification and analysis for mid- and long-term campaign planning. As a consequence of their inability to convince dominant coalitions of the need to take a strategic approach to issues debates, most practitioners are required to use tactical communication to deal with current issues, especially those working in state and federal government agencies. Respondents report that in government agencies this happens because demands from ministers' offices often divert senior practitioners from dealing with strategic issues to work on day-to-day political issues. Consultants, too, reported that business sector clients wanted them to focus on immediate issues.

Australian practitioners say they are willing to communicate with stakeholders in a range of contexts, especially those that involve organisational reputation.

Australian practitioners strongly support the role of communication strategy in advancing corporate goals and objectives in the mid and long terms, and view strategic communication as being concerned with advancing an organisation's interests by advocating its positions on external issues. A majority of respondents engage in issues analysis as ongoing practice, but many framed this as 'risk analysis' and most identify potential damage to an organisation's reputation as a primary risk factor.

While the majority of practitioners are willing to recommend that their organisations or clients enter into dialogues with opponents over issues, their decisions to do this depend on the situation they are addressing. For most, a threat of litigation against their organisation would constrain their decision to enter into a dialogue. Most respondents would recommend engaging with organisational critics and opponents even if this would result in negative publicity, especially when the organisation's reputation is threatened. Respondents believe senior managers should engage with critics. The extent to which a stakeholder group is covered by the mass news media is not a significant variable that practitioners take into account when they consider whether to engage with a group.

Organisational reputation, values, and credibility, and building and maintain relationships with stakeholders were the most important issues for the senior Australian respondents in my research. However, there are differences in primary issue importance between practitioners in different sectors. Senior female and male practitioners also differ significantly in the importance they give to stakeholder relationships. Female practitioners rated stakeholder relationships as the second most important issue category while males rated this as the fifth most important category. In a stakeholder relationship context, most respondents regard their organisations' involvement in corporate social responsibility projects as strategic opportunities, but they are less concerned about socio-cultural and natural environmental issues that might impact on their organisations.

It is curious, given these findings, the strong academic focus on researching strategic communication, and practitioners' support for strategic approaches to their practice, that the modern normative approach to professional communication remains as tactical alchemy which does not resolve long-term issues. It seems little knowledge transfer from strategic communication research to professional practice has happened. In Australia, for example, the tactical focus was reinforced by practitioners who responded to a survey asking for their continuing professional development priorities (Mahoney, 2019). Courses on strategic communication planning were rated highest (47.4% of respondents rated it extremely relevant to their careers), followed by those covering measurement and evaluation (40.9%). This suggests a significant proportion of practitioners are working without relevant knowledge. The tactical focus was reflected in practitioners' top six ratings of technical training relevance to their careers: using social media (23.7%), content creation (24.3%) and negotiation skills (19.6%), internal communication (19.1%), influencer engagement (17.1%), and data analysis (15.9%). In addition, the findings reported in the 2020–2021 editions in the European and Asia-Pacific Communication Monitors show a dominance of tactical topics in ratings for the most important 'strategic' issues for communication management.

One of the principles for producing a communication plan is that this is undertaken less often than tactical planning. Most often, campaign strategies are written for a 12-month period, but they are rarely rigid and are often revised as circumstances change. Tactical action to deliver campaign messages is included in a plan to describe the communication pathways and tools to be used to deliver information to target publics. The 2021 Ragan Benchmark study reported that 35% of practitioners undertook strategic planning on a one-to-three-month schedule, while 23% did this weekly (Silber, 2021). Findings like these also suggest that tactical approaches to 'strategic' communication dominate professional practice.

Perhaps this is why in professional communication alchemy, the reagents that combine in the beaker of tactical practice are producing bubbling outputs needed to satisfy C-suites, but they are hardly strategic. Social media applications, and efforts directed at attaining news media coverage, are of course important. However, my heretical view is that they are technical and tactical tools used in market environments to deliver short-term outputs rather than to pursue meaningful longer term issues management outcomes. This fleeting role in a market environment is not a planned, extended, and consistent dialogic communicative effort to build and maintain an organisation's reputation and credibility, and to foster meaningful stakeholder relationships. That cannot be done within a few days. Modern professional communication alchemy also does not advance corporate interests in the mid and long terms, nor advance an organisation's positions on external issues. Despite the glow it gives C-suites, this alchemy cannot produce the elusive gold of successful outcomes that deliver on measurable communication strategic goals and objectives that are aligned with corporate business strategies.

The tension between strategic and tactical approaches, illustrated by the research cited in this chapter, can be resolved if dominant coalitions are convinced strategic communication delivers tangible results. Equally important is for senior management to understand how strategic outcomes, based on planned long-term dialogic communicative action about emerging socio-economic and political issues, will enhance organisations' market success and protect corporate reputations. This is the strategic communication imperative that both dominant coalitions and practitioners must accept for issues management success, and that provides rich territory for scholarly exploration.

For decades scholars and practitioners have written about the need for communicators to have the clichéd 'seat at the table' so they can be involved in high-level corporate decision-making. As the 2020–2021 European Communication Monitor data illustrate, some practitioners have achieved this, but many still seek closer alignment between business and communication strategies. That this has not happened despite scholars and practitioners arguing it should, suggests communicators have not found the key that would convince dominant coalitions of the imperative to do it. The key to resolving this is two-fold. First, there is a need for a definition of strategic communication that explains its dialogic role and the time horizons in which it should work. A definition that does this clearly differentiates strategic communication from the tactical alchemy that commonly uses the components of marketing communication to deal with sales promotion, publicity, personal selling, and product advertising. In doing that, the definition would help avoid the tendency for practitioners to inflate what they offer by describing every plan for using tactical communication tools as 'strategic.' Academics might find that a revised definition would enable a tighter focus for their research, and eliminate their habit of labelling so many tertiary communication courses as strategic when they are patently not. Second, practitioners need a planning model that senior managers understand. That should involve demonstrating exactly how a strategic communication plan flows from, and integrates with, a strategic business plan. This should transcend the time-honoured salute to communication strategy supporting corporate goals and objectives to demonstrate how strategic communicative action actually deals with current issues, as well as those that are likely to confront long-term business proposals. Exploring those two keys, and proposing solutions, is the focus of what follows.

3
THE NATURE OF STRATEGIC COMMUNICATION

The major theme of this book is that strategic communication operates as a practice beyond the tactical, day-to-day considerations of marketing communication because it is concerned with identifying, analysing, and addressing important socio-economic and political issues that occur in organisations' non-market environments. When they do this, organisations are social actors advancing their views on issues. In this role, strategic communication can be conceptualised as the specialisation that sets the directions for all other organisational professional communication. It is, as a former academic and senior international advertising expert, Richard Buddle, once put it in a personal discussion, the strategy you have before you have a strategy. In that role, strategic communication is a high-level corporate activity specifically concerned about organisational reputation, values, and credibility, is integrated with business planning, and recognised for its value-added function.

Such a heretical view may be challenged by professional communication scholars and practitioners who might argue that public relations and its associated specialities already have this strategic role. Yet it was principally scholars who research and teach in these specialities who sought to define strategic communication and differentiate it from the normative concepts of professional communication when they launched the *International Journal of Strategic Communication* in 2007, and who, based on their research, contribute to that journal's ongoing discussions of the concept.

No matter how well-founded a strategic communication plan might be, and in spite of their acknowledgement of the need for communication strategic planning and implementation, practitioners are often prevented from acting strategically by senior management or clients who have not been convinced of its importance as a high-order, value-added organisational function. This occurs even though senior managers and clients recognise the importance of strategic business plans

DOI: 10.4324/9781003177340-3

to the organisation's success. This apparent neglect of the strategic communication imperative by senior management will continue until the concept of strategic communication is more closely defined, and practitioners have a model that sets out a mechanism for effectively integrating it with long-term business planning processes. Finding that mechanism was a result of my research aimed at identifying, from their direct personal insights, the factors that influence a cohort of senior Australian professional communication practitioners when they make decisions about strategic issues communication. That primary research, and work by other scholars on similar subjects, informed the arguments presented here, especially that current conceptualisations of strategic communication need to be extended to locate it more precisely within definitions of strategy, and as an essential, integrated element of mid- and long-term business planning. Such an extended conceptualisation will help to extend scholarly discourses about strategic communication and, hopefully, provide professional practitioners with arguments to convince senior management to take the practice more seriously.

Strategic communication has a specific alignment with an organisation's overall business plan to enhance strategic positioning. Communicating at this level is important for private, public, and not-for-profit sector organisations and involves participating in issues debates that occur in an organisation's non-market environment (Bach, 2007; Bach & Allen, 2010).

The role of strategy in professional communication

Scholarly definitions of a 'strategy' encompass the idea that it is a plan designed to achieve particular long-term organisational management, or professional communication, aims (Mintzberg, 1994; Cutlip et al., 2006; Hill & Jones, 2008; Frandsen & Johansen, 2010; King, 2010; Machiori & Bulgacov, 2012; Montgomery, 2012; Rumelt, 2011; Wilcox & Cameron, 2012; Macnamara & Zerfass, 2012). The concept of strategy as 'the art of war' becomes a metaphor in planning for business competition and engaging in issues debates (see, for example, the discussion in Quinn, 2003, at pp. 11–15). This metaphor derives from the title of a military treatise written by the ancient Chinese sage, Sun Tzu. The Chinese character fa is translated in the title of the treatise as 'Art' but, while it has a primary meaning of 'law' or 'method,' Sun Tzu regarded it as 'doctrine' (Griffith, 2011). Tzu's doctrine for conducting a war included 'five matters' a general needed to consider in waging war: organisation, control, assignment of appropriate ranks to generals, regulation of supply routes, and the provision of principal items used by the army (Griffith, 2011). Tzu's five matters resonate with the elements of strategic management and communication plans that set out goals, objectives, and the actions and resources needed for success. Tzu argued,

> There is no general who has not heard of these five matters. Those who master them win: those who do not are defeated.
>
> *(Sun Tzu, cited in Griffith, 2011, p. 95)*

Tzu's advice that mastering what is needed to implement a strategy enhances the chances of success applies to business management and communication planning in the sense that working out what needs to be done, and how that should be pursued, is at the core of strategic decision-making. In strategic communication practice, that means identifying and understanding the issues facing an organisation, planning activities to advance the organisation's views about them, and detailing how success will be measured.

Strategy as intentional action

The idea that making decisions about strategy is a discursive social practice is reflected in the focus of the critical realism ontology of scholars who regard 'strategy as practice' and has been inspired by pragmatist philosophy and the work of Mintzberg and Giddens (Frandsen & Johansen, 2010). Strategy is 'something people do' and a social practice (Marchiori & Bulgacov, 2012, pp. 201–202). Standard conceptions of strategy include that it is 'a deliberate move towards a desired end-state' (King, 2010, p. 19) and involves intentional decision-making about power or change (Frandsen & Johansen, 2010). Common to all definitions of strategy is the

> idea of *directed* and *planned activities* within the organisation as a whole, or within specific area or at specific levels of the organisation to reach a specific goal or specific objectives.
>
> *(Frandsen and Johansen, 2010, p. 298, emphases in original)*

Montgomery (2012) argued that a 'great' strategy was not a dream, nor a lofty idea, but a bridge between the economics of a market, the core ideas of a business, and action. To be sound, that bridge 'must rest on a foundation of clarity and realism, and it also needs a real operating sensibility' (Montgomery, 2012, p. 3). And Montgomery (2012) described strategists as 'meaning makers' for organisations, 'voices of reason,' and operators (p. 1).

In a management context, strategy is a way through a difficulty, a response to a challenge, and an approach to overcoming an obstacle; a coherent action backed by an argument; and not a long list of things to do—which are tactics (Rumelt, 2011). In this view, strategy is

> coherent action backed by an argument. And the core of the strategist's work is always the same: discover the crucial factors in a situation and design a way to coordinate and focus actions to deal with them.
>
> *(Rumelt, 2011, p. 8)*

Gregory (2009b) noted that there is considerable discussion about what strategy means, but argues it 'is dictated by, and springs from, the issues arising from

[an] analysis of the problem' (p. 188). In this sense, a problem might be how an organisation will generate business growth, or how it will repair a damaged reputation, or how an activist group will go about convincing a government to increase environmental protection measures for a wilderness area, or how a government agency will attempt to convince young people to stop smoking cigarettes or using a mobile phone while driving.

Strategic plans for professional communication

The concept of 'strategy' as an overall plan designed to achieve measurable outcomes is embedded in all professional communication planning. It should be a primary task of senior practitioners to develop the communication plans that set out how organisations will address issues they face. These are widely described as strategies and there is a significant scholarly and professional literature about the process of researching and writing them. Strategic plans for professional communication are viewed by scholars and practitioners as the mechanisms that deliver consistent and coordinated approaches to organisational communication based on agreed goals, objectives, and messages. These plans describe how objectives will be achieved; provide guidelines and message themes; and 'offer a rationale for the actions and program components that are planned' (Wilcox & Cameron, 2012, p. 154). Communication strategies are designed to achieve particular outcomes: to promote an organisation's views, or to make something happen, as in a public policy change, and require long-term planning (Cutlip et al., 2006). A planned strategy means that the long term is considered so that organisations can be proactive by addressing potential difficulties and conflicts (Gregory, 2009). Macnamara and Zerfass (2012) reflect this when they noted that the broad meanings of 'strategic' as long term and focussed on the 'big picture' mean that the interests of key stakeholders as well as those of the organisation need to be considered 'if the organisation is to continue to operate successfully' (p. 291).

Henry Mintzberg, who is often cited in scholarly discussions about communication strategy for his insights into what it is, and for his critiques of the way in which it is applied, argued that 'strategy' is a word 'we inevitably define one way yet often use it in another' (Mintzberg, 1994, p. 23). In a management planning context, Mintzberg (1994, pp. 23–29) offered five definitions of strategy as a

- plan, or direction or course of action into the future, a path to get from here to there
- pattern, or consistency of behaviour over time
- position, or the determination of particular products in particular markets
- perspective, or an organisation's way of doing things
- ploy, or a specific manoeuvre to outwit and opponent or competitor

In this view, strategy is 'a set of related actions that managers take to increase their company's performance' (Hill & Jones, 2008, p. 3). Strategic planning is ongoing, and implementation involves taking action at functional, business, and corporate levels to 'execute a strategic plan' (Hill & Jones, 2008, p. 19).

A communication strategy should reflect all five of Mintzberg's (1994) definitions. A communication strategy is a plan concerned with locating an organisation in its external environment (position); it seeks to do that through a consistent approach (pattern) to promote an organisation's perspectives or the way it views the world; and it is certainly a ploy to provide an organisation with advantages over its opponents in debates about public policy issues.

Exactly how communication practitioners understand and work with strategy, issues, management, and leadership is unclear, and research suggests that some organisations are reactive in strategic planning, and engage in damage control (Frandsen & Johansen, 2010). That is, they approach issues from a tactical communication perspective, not with the long-term orientation Argenti, Howell, and Beck (2005) suggested characterises strategic communication.

In a public relations context, Cutlip et al. (2006) noted confusion about what strategy and tactics mean. They define strategy as the 'overall game plan' and tactics as the methods used to implement a strategy (p. 315). Cornelissen (2005) also differentiated between communication 'strategy' and 'tactics' when he noted that strategic communication is more substantial when it stretches to corporate and business unit level concerns. Deciding what is 'strategic' and what is 'tactical' is a familiar task for professional communicators. Communication practitioners are guided by technical definitions and accepted processes and communication strategy, or plan, structures (see for example, Cutlip et al., 2006; Gregory, 2009; Mahoney, 2013; Seitel, 2011; Wilcox & Cameron, 2012; Wilson & Ogden, 2008). Seitel (2011) viewed strategic communication planning as an essential part of management. Wilson and Ogden (2008) argued that strategy is a well-coordinated approach to reaching an overall goal and that communication is strategic when it helps an organisation to accomplish overall goals in a consistent manner. Wilson (2001) noted that being strategic in communication practice means contributing to achieving an organisation's mission and goals and systematically planning with them in mind. Wilcox and Cameron (2012) said that systematic strategic planning prevents haphazard, ineffective communication. This strategic function requires close alignment with key organisational leaders, meaning that public relations, for example, should take on a more strategic role (McDonald & Hebbani, 2011). Strategic planning includes coordinating activities and fine-tuning messages to maximise effectiveness (Lauer, 2001).

A consistent theme in the literature about the role of communication in supporting organisational goals and objectives has been that it should be aligned with, and reflect, an organisation's strategic business plan, or corporate strategy (see, for example, Argenti et al., 2005; Cornelissen, 2005; Gregory, 2009; Jones & Bartlett, 2009; Mahoney, 2013). J.E. Grunig and Repper, for example, dealt with such an alignment in 1992 in their commentary on the Excellence Study; J.E. Grunig (2009) returned to the theme in the context of applying social media to public relations practice and how this would enhance his concept of two-way symmetrical communication. Cornelissen (2005), who defined corporate communication as a complex management function that crosses functional boundaries to harness the strategic interests of an organisation, noted that this activity uses planned actions that follow from the overall corporate strategy.

Definitions of strategic communication

Those most directly concerned with defining and explaining strategic communication are scholars who teach and research public relations and its specialisations. They have applied the idea of strategic communication practice not only to corporations, but also to not-for-profit organisations and government agencies. It is, for one scholar, a field of practice 'beyond the traditional scope of the public relations function' (Zerfass, 2009, p. 69). For others, strategic communication is defined not as practice, but 'the study' of how communication is used purposefully to achieve organisations' missions (Frandsen & Johansen, 2017, cited in Falkheimer & Heide, 2018, p. 57). Yim (2021) recognised the reality of the definitional discourse about strategic communication by describing it as a 'still-evolving' concept (p. 69).

One aspect of the scholarly focus on strategic communication has been to investigate how management theories might inform a better understanding of how professional communication practice works. Zerfass (2009), for example, argued that institutional theory provided a valuable way of researching the future of strategic communication. Sandhu (2009) also argued that institutional theory provided a higher level of abstraction for explaining strategic communication as an organisational function than that provided by traditional rationalist models of strategic management, especially those oriented by the Excellence in Public Relations and Communication Management study reported by J.E. Grunig and Repper (1992).

The use of strategic communication as a descriptive term for differentiating this aspect of professional practice from other specialisations, such as corporate communication, public affairs, business communication, and public relations is relatively new (Hallahan et al., 2007). In their introduction to the inaugural edition of the *International Journal of Strategic Communication* in 2007, Hallahan and colleagues described strategic communication as an emerging paradigm that emphasised the strategic application of communication to how organisations function as social actors to advance their missions. They argued that the purposeful nature of strategic communication was critical because it focused on how the intentional activities of leaders, employees, and communication practitioners present and promote an organisation.

While scholarly discourses in the *International Journal of Strategic Communication* and other publications cover traditional definitional ground, they also advance academic and professional understandings of why the practice differs from other forms of professional communication. Other scholars, for example, Argenti et al. (2005), argue that strategic communication is the alignment of communication with an organisation's overall strategy, to enhance strategic positioning. Another definition differentiates the practice from marketing communication by holding that strategic communication operates at a level beyond a functional, tactical approach and embraces all organisational communicative interactions with stakeholders (Cornelissen, 2005). This view is echoed in Falkheimer and Heide's (2018) discussion about what strategic communication actually is when they propose it is not the same as planned communication, which is tactical and

> not related to the overall goal of an organisation, but rather to tactical goals at a mid-range level, such as the sale of products or services or getting citizens involved in taking care of newly arrived refugees.
>
> *(pp. 56–57)*

Falkheimer and Heide (2018) suggested that strategic communication is a conscious activity aimed at reaching an organisation's overall long-term goals, not, as for tactical communication, a tool for disseminating information and facilitating internal organisational discussions.

This definitional dialectic suggests the critical key to understanding its role in the professional communication canon is to accept that a strategic approach deals with matters beyond the tactical commercial communication requirements of the market. That strategic approach means dealing with emerging issues. Holtzhausen (2010) hinted at this in a proposition that communication strategists are committed to discussing how strategic communication

> affects debate in the public sphere; of how the ability of communicative entities, from large corporations to celebrities and everybody in between, can assert their right to communicate publicly, while balancing this right with the interests of the public.
>
> *(Holtzhausen, 2010, p. 75)*

In raising the public sphere, Holtzhausen (2010) made the important link between the dynamics of issues debates and how those kinetic forces are affected by strategic communication activity. It is in the public sphere, or a non-market environment, that debates about the impact of socio-economic and political issues on organisations occur. Strategic communication, then, works in time frames beyond the immediate day-to-day activities of public relations, and the demands of news and social media outlets. As Hallahan and colleagues argued (2007), it is concerned with long-term considerations of how organisations can participate as social actors to advance their goals and objectives by advocating their views in debates about public policy.

J.E. Grunig (2006) proposed that strategic communication, which he described as a bridging activity between organisations and their stakeholders, should be standard procedure, or, institutionalised. That point reflects the notion of two-way symmetrical communication (see, for example, Grunig,

2001), the practical applications of which Lane (2007) has argued are insufficiently considered by scholars and practitioners. In a 2009 discussion of two paradigms for public relations practice, J.E. Grunig provided a strategic management view of communication as it relates to campaigns designed to generate behavioural outcomes. In the first, practitioners working in a 'symbolic, interpretive' paradigm of marketing communication generally believed publics could be persuaded by messages that change their cognitive representations. This approach devoted excessive attention to the tactical role of communication in negotiating meaning by emphasising messages, publicity, media relations, and media effects. Grunig's (2009) contrasting 'strategic management, behavioural' paradigm built relationships with stakeholders and facilitated two-way communication and dialogue and included a framework of research and listening, as a result of which 'messages reflect the information needs of publics as well as the advocacy needs of organisations' (J.E. Grunig, 2009, p. 9).

Hallahan et al. (2007) moved beyond traditional approaches to strategic communication definitions and argued,

> Strategic communication differs from integrated communication because its focus is how an organisation communicates across organisational endeavours. The emphasis is on the strategic application of communication and how an organisation functions as a social actor to advance its mission.
>
> *(p. 7)*

In their view, strategic communication 'is about informational, persuasive, discursive, as well as relational communication when used in a context of the achievement of an organisation's mission' (Hallahan et al., 2007, p. 17). They gave four reasons for viewing strategic communication as a unifying framework to analyse professional communication by organisations:

- First, the ability of communicators to differentiate between traditional communication activities and their effects is rapidly disappearing.
- Second, important changes in public communication are being driven by technology and media economics.
- Third, organisations use an expanding variety of methods to influence the behaviours of their constituencies—what people know, how people feel, and the ways people act—relative to the organisation.
- Fourth, strategic communication recognises that purposeful influence is the fundamental goal of communications by organisations.

Sandhu (2009) reflected this approach in describing strategic communication as multidisciplinary 'intentional' communication that requires a purposeful actor, and rational and deliberate decision-making. In this view, strategic communication is dependent on institutions which both constrain and enable its practice, an idea that resonates with Giddens' (1986) structuration theory that, in brief, seeks an alignment between action and structure.

Argenti et al. (2005) noted that many companies take a tactical and short-term approach to communication with key stakeholders that is 'not only non-strategic but may be inconsistent with the corporate strategy or even implode it' (p. 83). In their view, strategic communication should be aligned with the company's overall strategy, to enhance its strategic positioning. They note that strategic communication must have a long-term orientation in which practition-ers must 'meet short-term needs but stay focused on the long-term issues' facing organisations (p 89). Zerfass and Huck (2007, p. 108) argued that strategic com-munication 'prepares organisations for an uncertain future.' In her argument that strategies are not only planned but also emerge from communicative interac-tions, King (2010) noted that strategic communication has a complex role in the competitive business environment.

In Cornelissen's (2005) view, the scope and involvement of strategic commu-nication as a management function becomes more substantial when it stretches beyond a set of functional goals and tactics to corporate and business unit levels. In their critical management function, strategic communication practitioners need to respond to a business' needs and concerns (Cornelissen, 2005). In other words, strategic communicators' concerns with other communication disciplines and their associated tactics are directed at how they advance top-level strategic goals and objectives, rather than in implementing tactics (Cornelissen, 2005).

Among communication management functions described by Van Ruler and Verčič (cited in Tench et al., 2009) are,

- counselling the members of an organisation on matters of values, norms, and issues important to society
- coaching the members of an organisation to respond communicatively to societal demands
- conceptualising and planning communication with important publics to gain public trust

Each of these management tasks applies communication techniques to long-term issues communication planning and preparing senior executives to play the role of social actors that Bach and Allen (2010) said they must, and ground strategic communication in Hallahan et al.'s (2007) view that it is intentional communi-cative action.

De Bussy (2013) addressed the tension between the views of Hallahan et al. (2007) about strategic communication and J.E. Grunig's (2009) public relations strategic management behavioural paradigm that he argues builds relationships with stakeholders, in his exploration of the concept of strategic public relations management. Hallahan et al.'s (2007) view had 'over-emphasised' strategic com-munication as a paradigm for understanding public relations because they were 'by no means equivalent concepts' (De Bussy, 2013, p. 89). In addition, Hallahan et al.'s (2007) 'undue focus' on persuasion as the role of strategic communication would 'downplay the importance of engaging with stakeholders and publics' (De Bussy, 2013, p. 83). De Bussy (2013), writing about strategic public relations management and stakeholder theory, argued that the strategic communication and relationship cultivation dimensions of public relations could be complementary if primacy was given to relationships.

In summary, definitions of strategic communication posit that it is planned and purposeful practice by private, public, and not-for-profit sector organisations to enhance their strategic positioning. But these definitions do not adequately differentiate strategic communication from other professional, but essentially tactical, communication practice. They use 'strategic' in a way that suggests its real time-defined meaning is generally understood. Thus, they avoid clarifying strategic communication's essential long-term orientation, an approach that would recognise the nature of what 'strategic' really means. It is in this time frame, and when it is closely aligned with overall business strategy, that strategic communication can effectively and legitimately engage organisations as social actors to advocate positions in debates about issues that affect their ability to achieve strategic objectives. That is, its focus is beyond immediate day-to-day needs and on potential longer term issues and stakeholder relationships.

Engaging with stakeholders

The notion that strategic communication is a long-term practice in which organisations, as social actors, debate public policy issues that have potential to impact on their ability to achieve business objectives, means engaging with stakeholders. The attitudes of these people and organisations towards socio-economic or political issues can affect how an organisation achieves its objectives, or, alternatively, they can be affected by the organisation's actions and views. Engaging with stakeholders about issues enables representation and debate as 'a strategic attempt to increase loyalty and commitment and to decrease resistance rather than seeking genuine decisional input' (Deetz, 2001, p. 39). In this context, strategic communication is not concerned with generating immediate results as are other communication disciplines such as, for example, advertising and the day-to-day mass news media-centric, product promotion, event management, and crisis communication aspects of public relations that are implemented to meet short-term needs (Argenti et al., 2005).

Planned mid- and long-term communicative action in which organisations operate as social actors to address emerging issues that can affect an organisation's ability to achieve its mission and objectives is, then, the essential core of strategic communication. That differentiation from other forms of professional communication practice operationalises a constructionist realism view of strategic communication as a sense-making practice to develop interpretations of the organisation's views on issues and present them to internal and external stakeholders (Raupp & Hoffjann, 2012). When stakeholders refer to these interpretations, for example by themselves participating as social actors in an issues debate, the organisation's environment, which was factored into the original sense-making, is in turn transformed (Raupp & Hoffjann, 2012). This perspective of strategic communication reflects the concept of duality embodied in Giddens' (1986) structuration theory.

In this interpretivist and sense-making role, strategic communication occurs in an organisation's non-market environment (Bach & Allen, 2010) and deals with factors external to its core day-to-day business, but which can nevertheless shape the dynamics of an organisation's operating environment. Non-market environment factors include social, political, economic, and cultural issues that involve all the relationships an organisation has beyond those with its customers, suppliers, and competitors, the resolution of which affect its ability to reach business objectives. For example, non-market relationships involve those with governments, regulators, activists, non-government organisations, citizens, and the mass news media (Bach & Allen, 2010). The concept of a non-market environment reflects Habermas' (1987, 1990) description of the public sphere comprising communicative networks in which citizens engage in discussions to reach consensus about issues (Habermas, 1987).

Because the non-market environment is the public arena in which organisations and their stakeholders raise and debate issues, a discussion of the concept of stakeholders helps to understand their importance to strategic communication goals and objectives.

Defining stakeholders

It is axiomatic that the external socio-political, economic, and cultural issues an organisation deals with are raised in its non-market environment by one or more of its stakeholders. To do this, stakeholders often use mass news media and/or social media networks as channels, in the context of an extant issues debate, or in an attempt to start a debate. Phillips et al. (2003, p. 479) described the term 'stakeholder' as powerful. The real or perceived power of stakeholders is a concept behind the stakeholder 'model,' or 'theory' (proposed in 1984 by the scholar, R. Edward Freeman), to explain approaches to strategic management. Stakeholder theory is often used as a theoretical base for analysing and explaining professional communication (see, for example, Berman et al., 1999; Clement, 2005; Fassin, 2009 & 2012 in a management perspective; Ledingham, 2003; Plowman, 2013).

For these reasons it is important to consider stakeholders and their role in issues debates in the context of a discussion about the nature of strategic communication.

The inclusion of versions of Freeman's (1984) stakeholder model in the research and commentaries of management and communication academics means scholars in these disciplines generally understand, and broadly define, stakeholders in a similar way. In this general understanding, stakeholders are broadly defined as people or groups who are important to an organisation's success because of their shared interests in issues. Smith (2012) positioned this common interest in issues as a 'central focal point' around which organisations and their stakeholders build relationships (p. 841). Smith (2012) argued that

> [r]elational states are defined by this connecting point and attitudes and behaviours are directed towards it.
>
> *(p. 841)*

In their discussion of stakeholder inclusiveness in strategic communication management, Steyn and de Beer (2012) relied on a public relations definition of stakeholders as people or groups who are affected by the decisions or behaviour of an organisation, or who can affect an organisation by their behaviour. Fassin (2009), writing in a management context, defined stakeholders as 'any individual or group that maintains a stake in an organisation in the way that a shareholder possesses shares' (p. 116). Fassin (2009) noted that Freeman's additional qualification that a stakeholder 'can affect or is affected by the achievement of the organisation's objectives' has become the most accepted definition (p. 116). Moloney (2006), a critical public relations scholar, used this qualification to describe stakeholders as 'others who do or can affect an organisation, and who are or can be affected by it' (p. 11). Gregory (2009a) noted that stakeholders were not just those management believed had a legitimate interest in an organisation, 'but those groups who decide for themselves that they will take a stake in the organisation' (p. 24). Choo (2009) used a similar definition but emphasises that stakeholders can influence an organisation as the first point in his definition (see Choo, 2009, p. 228).

Some academics, principally those who teach public relations, and practitioners, may be happier to segment an organisation's stakeholders into more relevant and precise target publics (see for example, Illia et al., 2013; Choo, 2009; Gregory, 2009b; Mahoney, 2013). Thus, one might argue that 'stakeholder' is not necessarily the appropriate term when communicative action need not always be directed at all stakeholders all the time, but to discrete, segmented publics for a particular situation in order to achieve a specific objective via targeted tactics. Choo (2009) noted that the distinction between stakeholders and target publics is not a 'sharp' one and that the terms are sometimes used interchangeably (p. 228). However, Choo (2009, p. 228) argued that

> stakeholders are potential publics, the critical factor being the arrival of a problem or issue. The risk to the organisation is that when such a problem or issue arises, stakeholders organise to become publics and are able to affect the interests of the organisation.

This is an important distinction for strategic communication and how it is planned to address specific issues, goals, and objectives. By identifying from an organisation's stakeholders, the specific people or groups (publics) who have a specific interest in a specific issue, communication strategists are able to more precisely focus their efforts to better understand attitudes towards those issues, engage in meaningful dialogue, and build and continually manage relationships. Ledingham (2003, p. 181ff) used a similar principle to propose relationship management between an organisation and its target publics as a 'general theory' of public relations. That general theory holds that building and sustaining organisational-public relationships 'requires not only communication, but organisational and public behaviours, a concept central to the relationship management perspective' (p. 194). The theory holds that communication is a strategic tool that builds and maintains transactional, dynamic, and goal-oriented organisation and public relationships 'driven by the perceived needs and wants of interacting organisations and publics' (p. 195). In this sense, the plural term 'publics' is a discipline-specific synonym for the collective term 'stakeholders' used in the management literature.

News media as stakeholders and journalists as target publics

Most professional communication and management scholars include the generic term 'media,' as in news media, in their lists of organisational stakeholders. Bach and Allen (2010), for example, firmly positioned the 'media' among stakeholders included in a non-market environment.

The mass news media and individual journalists become stakeholders in organisations' non-market environments because of the dual role they play in issues debates. The first role is the mass news media's ability to set an issues agenda when journalists decide what to cover, and the angles, or frames, they use to report the issue (see for example, Hallahan, 1999; Scheufele, 1999; Entman, 2007, Reese, 2007; Weaver, 2007). Second, mass media perspectives and frames draw attention to the attributes of matters covered in the news as well as to the matters themselves (Weaver, 2007). In a news sense, agenda setting defines problems worthy of public and government attention (Entman, 2007).

Professional communication practitioners who understand this dual role also use news framing techniques when they attempt to promote an organisation's views on an issue.

However, as with stakeholders in general, it is important to segment 'the media' into specialist journalists relevant to a situation, as in defining the 'media' as sports reporters for a sports story, political commentators for politics, and economic writers for economic topics. However, writing in a management context, Phillips (2003) questioned whether the news media and competitors could be regarded as stakeholders because advancing the interests of the news media and competitors was not the purpose of an organisation.

The general term 'news media' in a stakeholder context does not ignore the powerful role that the application of social media plays in issues debates. In a news reporting and commentary context, the term 'social media' describes a set of functional tools—'tactics' in the public relations lexicon—which may or may not be used by journalists to publish their news stories and commentary. In any event, the general term 'news media' includes online sites that report, comment on, and analyse news and public issues as extensions of television and radio stations, and newspapers, often with social media applications attached to them, and the personal applications individual journalists use.

The stakeholder model

The concept of using stakeholders to construct a model as a lens through which to view and analyse organisational management was first proposed in 1984 by the scholar R. Edward Freeman. The stakeholder model has been adopted in professional communication research and teaching to illustrate the network of relationships that an organisation needs to manage in pursuit of its mission and goals.

As a management scholar, Freeman (1984) dealt with stakeholders in terms of their relationships with companies in what Phillips (2003) described as a ground-breaking discussion. Freeman explained his 1984 model in the context of a company being related to seven stakeholder groups: suppliers, employees, shareholders, customers, government, competitors, and civil society. Freeman revised the model in 2013 to include financiers (for shareholders), customers (for clients), competitors, government, local community organisations, NGOs, pressure or special interest groups (such as environmentalists), and the media (Clement, 2005; Fassin, 2009).

Clement (2005) noted that scholars have also classified stakeholders in two categories: primary and secondary. Primary stakeholders are those whose continuing participation is 'critical to the survival of the corporation' (Clement, 2005, p. 256). Issues raised by these stakeholders—shareholders, employees, customers, suppliers—can have a substantial impact on an organisation, often an immediate one. Secondary stakeholders, for example, governments, NGOs, and activists, can be influenced by the organisation but do not have commercial transactions with it (Clement, 2005). These stakeholder classifications closely reflect the classic public relations roles of target publics: primary publics are those directly affected by an issue or situation; secondary publics are not directly affected by the issue or situation but can influence primary publics. For example, the primary public for a university's recruitment campaign is potential students; secondary publics are those who can influence a potential student's decision, such as their parents who will decide whether they can afford for the potential student to enrol in the university, or teachers who provide detailed information about the institution.

In developing his refinement of Freeman's (1984, 2003) stakeholder management model, Fassin (2009) noted arguments by management scholars for an extended classification of stakeholders beyond the primary and secondary categories. These include Phillips' (2003) classifications that describe stakeholders as direct or indirect, generic or specific, legitimate or derivative, strategic, moral, core, environmental, or classifications based on attributes of power, legitimacy, and urgency (see the discussions in Phillips, 2003, pp. 28–34; Fassin, 2009, pp. 116–118).

Fassin's (2009) argument that Freeman's (1984, 2003) stakeholder model had issues of vagueness and ambiguity led him to suggest a refinement that he called the 'stake' model. Heath and Palenchar (2009), who write as professional communication scholars, described a stake as something one person or a group has that is of value to another person or group whether it is tangible or intangible, material or immaterial. Heath and Palenchar (2009) noted that a stake

> is something each party desires from a relationship. Stakes can be transferable. They can be roughly divided into three types: instrumental, symbolic, and relational. A vote in Congress is instrumental; a behaviour was enacted. Customer goodwill is symbolic; it is earned by the moral and ethical conduct of a business. The management of the arrangement of stakes is relational.
>
> *(Heath and Palenchar, 2009, pp. 16–17)*

Fassin's (2009) 'stake' model adapted Freeman's (1984, 2003) framework but introduced the concepts of stakewatchers, or interest groups, and stakekeepers, or regulators, and argued that his refined model better reflected the distinct activities of stakeholders in one of three groups:

> the stakeholder who holds a stake, the stakewatcher who watches the stake, and the stakekeeper who keeps the stake.
>
> *(Fassin, 2009, p. 128, Fassin's emphases removed)*

Later, Fassin (2012) redefined 'stakeholder' as 'stakeowner' to avoid definitional confusion with the original term 'stakeholder.' Fassin (2012) also added a new classification, 'stateseeker' to identify those who seek to have a voice in an organisation's decision-making. Fassin (2012) further defined his stake model by describing stakeowners as genuine internal stakeholders who have a real stake in an organisation; stakewatchers as pressure groups that influence the organisation; and stakekeepers as those who 'impose external control and regulations' on organisations (p. 89).

In an important point that suggests the vital link between stakeholders and strategic communication, Fassin (2009) argued that his refined model improved conceptualisation of organisations, their environments, and the interrelationships between them. Fassin (2009) included 'the social political arena' as part of an organisation's environment (p. 116). The stake model would 'facilitate the strategic analysis needed to better manage stakeholders' (Fassin, 2009, p. 128).

Fassin's (2009, 2012) approach to segmenting stakeholders into what might be described as 'action categories' has two important consequences. First, Fassin's (2009, 2012) classification enables strategic communication planners to develop refined sets of specific publics based on their interest in the organisation and their likely positions on issues. For example, a list of activist publics classified as stakewatchers on a local issue related to the physical environment might include environmental and community groups, the local city council, individual politicians and other opinion leaders, specialist journalists, and residents in the area, each with negative or positive attitudes towards the issue. Second, understanding what holding, seeking, watching, or keeping a stake actually means in a given situation, and how those social actors operate in an issues debate, is at the core of issues analysis and strategic communication planning. Making decisions about action that needs to be taken to participate in a public issues debate includes considering the views of stakeholders, however classified, and how their views in turn impact on building and maintaining relationships with them.

Stakeholder management

A theme of both management and communication scholarship has been how organisations establish and maintain relationships with their stakeholders. For example, business scholars Barone et al. (2013) used Habermas' (1987) concept of an ideal speech situation, in which all parties to a dialogue have equal power of expression and equal ability to be heard, to propose a stakeholder engagement model for corporate social responsibility in the context of business accounting. Management scholars Ackermann and Eden (2011) explored how concepts from the stakeholder management literature could help management to increase the robustness of their strategies. They argued that managing the interface between an organisation and the often-competing demands of its many stakeholders was one of management's most important tasks during strategy making. Their research, from which they developed a Stakeholder Management Web, followed three themes: identifying stakeholders who 'really are in' the situation being addressed; exploring stakeholder dynamics involving multiple and interdependent interactions between stakeholders; and developing stakeholder management strategies. In addition, they based their research on the view that 'stakeholder management needs to be carried out *in relation to the goals of the organisation*' (Ackermann & Eden, 2011, p. 181, their emphasis). Although he was writing in the context of the US healthcare cost debate, J.M. Smith (2013) made a salient point about stakeholders that can apply to all organisations: they need data, which he termed 'actionable information' (p. S1). In their 2003 defence of stakeholder theory, Phillips el al. (including R.E. Freeman), argued that,

> Managing for stakeholders involves attention to more than simply maximizing shareholder wealth. Attention to the interests and well-being of those who can assist or hinder the achievement of the organization's objectives is the central admonition of the theory.
>
> *(Phillips et al., 2003, p. 481)*

In his discussion of stakeholder reciprocity, Fassin (2012) argued that, viewed from a strategic perspective, stakeholder management, with its 'underlying business ethics component,' urged organisations to consider how their actions and decisions impacted on their stakeholders (p. 83). This meant a focus on the fair treatment of employees, customers, consumers, and stockholders, and transparency in dialogues with other stakeholders in civil society, especially in approaches organisations take towards pressure groups.

De Bussy (2013), a communication scholar, was critical of stakeholder theorists for their 'apparent failure' to appreciate the significance of communication to relationships between organisations and their stakeholders (pp. 89–90). In a defence of J.E. Grunig's (2006) view that strategic public relations management cultivated 'high-quality, long-term relationships with publics or stakeholders' (p. 85), De Bussy (2013) argued that stakeholder theory 'appeared blind' to this 'crucial contribution' (p. 89). De Bussy (2013) argued,

> Stakeholder theory is...currently incomplete both as a theory which explains the nature of organisational relationships with stakeholders and as a roadmap for management practice. The 'missing link' is communication, specifically dialogic communication.
>
> *(de Bussy, 2013, p. 90)*

Luoma-aho and Vos (2010) note that interactions between organisations and their stakeholders are increasingly moving from the traditional stakeholder model centred on an organisation to one in which issues are addressed in

> multiple arenas in which the organisation may not be in the centre but needs multiple strategies to communicate with various stakeholders.
>
> *(Luoma-aho and Vos, 2010, p. 17)*

In this concept, the ideas and interests of organisations and their stakeholders are discussed in issues arenas on the basis of each having an equal stake in the debate (Luoma-aho & Vos, 2010, p. 10). In these authors' view, this approach differs from the organisation-centred traditional stakeholder model because it involves multiple strategies for interactions with stakeholders in various issues arenas in a dynamic global environment.

Communication environments

So far, this chapter has traversed the role of a strategy in professional communication by viewing it as planned, intentional action that engages organisations as social actors in public issues debates that have the potential to impact on their business performance. Extant definitions of strategic communication have been explored along with the idea that engaging in public issues debates involves interaction with organisational stakeholders, or the people who are interested in the organisation or are affected by its decisions. How and why organisations engage with their stakeholders are important aspects of both management and professional communication practice because they create the 'central focal point' (Smith, 2012, p. 841) around which relationships are built.

It now becomes important to consider the external environment in which strategic communication is practised, and the factors which influence decisions about the issues it needs to address.

Habermas and communicating in the public sphere

Political, sociological, management, and communication scholarship has used the 20th-century German philosopher Jürgen Habermas' (1987; originally written in German, 1969) concept of a public sphere as a theoretical base from which to research and interpret aspects of society. Habermas held that it was in a public sphere that citizens expressed and formed opinions.

Although Habermas' critical scholarship meant he was sceptical of some interests represented in the public sphere, his 1987 concept, and 1992 revision, provides a prism through which strategic communication's role can be viewed to build an understanding of organisations' non-market environments.

For Habermas (1987), the 'core' of a public sphere comprised communicative networks in which citizens engage in discussions to reach consensus about issues. For example, such discussions include the rational debates about political matters that take place in a public sphere. Bentele and Nothhaft (2010) described the public sphere as a 'kind of supra-institution' that emerges from, and is sustained by, interactions between individuals, organisations, and institutions who pursue arguments through the use of strategies. Habermas (1992) later defined this as the 'political public sphere' in which communication enables a 'discursive formation of opinion and will' by citizens of a state (p. 446).

Habermas (1990) distinguished between strategic action and communicative action in social interaction in a public sphere. He viewed strategic action as an attempt by one actor to influence another through the threat of sanctions, or the 'prospect of gratification in order to cause the interaction as the first actor desires' (p. 58). By treating each other strategically, actors try to 'reach their objectives by influencing their opponents' definition of the situation, and thus his decisions or motives, through external means' (Habermas, 1990, p. 133). In Burkart's (2009) explanation of this, Habermas means that strategic action is success-oriented in that a person's behaviour is oriented 'exclusively towards intended consequences' (p. 148).

On the other hand, Habermas (1990) argued that communicative action meant an actor sought to rationally motivate others by relying on the binding or bonding effects of a speech act. That is, actors are prepared to 'harmonise their plans of action' only on the condition of an existing, or yet to be negotiated, agreement 'about definitions of a situation and prospective outcomes' (p. 134).

Burkart (2009) noted that in this case, actions match the intentions and inter-ests of opponents, and communication is only used for building understand-ing, not to influence others. Burkart (2009) argued the difference between Habermas' definitions of strategic and communicative action is a 'somewhat mis-leading differentiation because it implies that consensus-oriented acting cannot be considered as success-oriented' (p. 148). However, Habermas (1990) argued that 'the actors are assumed to have the ability to act purposively and an inter-est in carrying out their plans' when they engage in strategic or communicative action (p. 134).

While Habermas later moderated his ideal view of the public sphere, he was critical of the roles of corporations and interest groups in the public sphere (Calhoun, 1992). He viewed the public sphere

> as a setting for states and corporate actors to develop legitimacy not by responding appropriately to an independent and critical public but by seek-ing to instil in social actors motivations that conform to the needs of the overall system dominated by those states and corporate actors.
>
> *(Calhoun, 1992, p. 26)*

Habermas (1992) questioned whether members of civil society, in competition with the media power of 'political and economic invaders,' had realistic chances of influencing changes in the spectrum of values, topics, and reasons channelled by external influences in a mass media dominated public sphere. Nevertheless, ethical strategic communication practice by business, government, not-for-profit groups, and other organisations does not rely on sanctions to influence people but is focussed on rational motivation in order to reach consensus about an issue.

Communicating in the non-market environment

The purposeful nature of strategic communication is critical because its focus is on how organisations use the intentional actions of their leaders, employees, and communication practitioners to present and promote themselves (Hallahan et al., 2007). This includes relationship building and using networks.

Strategic communication is located in a complex professional practice zone that is beyond the traditional approach to communication planning and action because it regards organisations as social actors who engage in deliberate and purposeful attempts to influence opinions about the organisation. It is this notion that an organisation should engage in public debates about issues that affect it—an overtly political action—that differentiates strategic communication from other professional communication disciplines. Additionally, strategic com-munication is planned, or should be planned, specifically to address emerging mid- to long-term non-market issues that involve socio-economic and political factors advanced by issues definers such as activists, regulators, governments, NGOs, and citizens. The other professional communication disciplines tend to be tactical, in the sense that they operate in the current term to deal with immediate matters, and technical because they use communication tools to engage in sales promotion, or advertising, or rapid responses to news media questions, or to inform target publics about an organisation via social media applications. In this role they are dealing with the immediate day-to-day concerns of customers, suppliers, and competitors. Technical, tactical tools are, at times, used to promote overtly political communication, for example when an organisation comments on proposed government policy, or an industry group initiates an advertising campaign against a tax or regulatory policy.

Holtzhausen (2010) argued that public issues debates would be more successful strategically if they involved open, dialectic communication. That view reflects Habermas' (1990) rational motivation and Heath's (2001) argument that professional communication (public relations in particular) is essentially a rhetorical practice that

> seeks to advance marketplace and public policy discourse by pursuing relational excellence (organisational responsibility) and discourse that lead to the co-creation, co-management, or co-definition of meaning (zones of meaning) that reconcile strains and alienation and foster mutually beneficial relationships.
>
> *(Heath, 2001, p. 35)*

The ability of businesses to achieve their objectives is affected by the way in which they shape their operating environment by dealing with the socio-economic and political issues that impact on them and increasingly affect the bottom line (Bach & Allen, 2010). Businesses are not simply economic agents but 'social and political beings' who cannot escape the reality that a plethora of actors seek to influence them through laws, regulations, social pressure, activism, and 'efforts to shape the public perception of business' and that 'smart executives... engage with their social and political environment, helping to shape the rules of the game and reducing the risk of being hemmed in by external actors' (Bach & Allen, 2010, p. 42).

This engagement occurs in an organisation's non-market environment and its primary focus is on issues and organisational values (Bach & Allen, 2010). In dealing with issues in a non-market environment, organisations need to become social actors 'whether managers like it or not' because

> [p]oliticians, regulators, non-governmental organisations and activists won't hesitate to impose new rules of the game on an industry, unless companies themselves become active participants in the process.
>
> *(Bach & Allen, 2010, p. 48)*

This is why Argenti and colleagues (2005) called for corporations, especially, to recognise a strategic communication imperative that involves developing a long-term corporate communication plan just as they have long-term market-ing and budget plans. That imperative recognises all actors in issues debates that pursue strategies and strategic communication to gain access to the public sphere and then to 'convince people that their point of view on a topic is right' (Bentele & Nothhaft, 2010, p. 105). This is the essential role of organisational social actors participating in debates occurring in their non-market environments. The point holds for a commercial business arguing its case on a taxation matter with bureaucrats and politicians, a not-for-profit group seeking funding support, or a government agency dealing with issues related to policy areas it administers.

Another description of the spaces in which organisations and their stake-holders deal with multiple common issues is issues arenas, conceptualised by Luoma-aho and Vos (2010), a public space similar to a non-market environment. However, Luoma-aho and Vos (2010) argue that practitioners and academics should focus on identifying the different issues facing organisations, and issues dynamics, before 'trying to define stakeholders and their preferred ways of com-municating' (p. 20). In their view,

> [t]oday, it is issues and topics, not organisations that are at the centre of communication.
>
> *(Luoma-aho and Vos, 2010, p. 4)*

This concept is a paradigm shift from an organisation-centred focus on relation-ship management towards 'monitoring and dialogue on issues arenas that are outside the organisation's control' (Luoma-aho & Vos, 2010, p. 15), and reflects the need for a long-term approach to issues identification and communication planning.

Factors that influence strategic communication

The idea that communicating in non-market environments means organisations are social actors debating public policy issues that have the potential to impact on their ability to achieve goals, leads to a consideration of the kinds of issues that concern communication strategists in their planning.

Issues identification and analysis to understand the opportunities and threats issues pose is essential to strategic communication planning, especially to iden-tify issues likely to emerge in the mid and long terms. Lauzen (1997) described this approach as a unique contribution to issues management which has become a sophisticated discipline that informs strategies for dealing with a wide range of public issues (Jaques, 2009a).

However, it is necessary to briefly explore the broad categories of issues that concern strategic communication counsellors. Scholars have argued communi-cation on issues moves along a continuum from pure advocacy to accommoda-tion according to the stance an organisation takes on a particular issue (see Pang, Yin, & Cameron, 2010). Research grounded in contingency theory found that

87 internal and external variables impact on practitioners' abilities to do their jobs (Pang, Yin, & Cameron, 2010). Among such variables are organisational reputation, values, and credibility, stakeholders (including employees), relationships, and regulatory factors.

Scholarly discussion of issues identification, analysis, and management is usually confined to business contexts in which 'business' is used in its broadest sense. However, issues management is also a function for communication professionals in government agencies, non-government organisations such as universities, and in the not-for-profit sector. More broadly, in their counselling roles, senior strategic communicators in all sectors of the economy advise management about organisational responses to political issues, reputation protection, crises, and long-range organisational positioning. That is, social, political, and economic issues can potentially impact on an organisation's reputation, values, and credibility, and its ability to achieve its objectives. This is the core point of Bach and Allen's (2010) argument that organisations need to carefully manage key social, political, and environmental issues, and their relationships with the 'actors' who care about them. For example, an emerging issue about a proposal to regulate and price carbon emissions would need to be monitored by, say, electricity producers and analysed for its potential impact on their business costs. Actors who care about an issue like this include the regulatory authority, politicians who support or oppose the proposal, competitors, employees who may fear job losses as a result of the resulting additional corporate costs, activists who support the issue, and specialist journalists who report and comment on environmental and business issues. Bad behaviour by sporting stars potentially damages the reputations of their teams, and the national and international organisations that manage their sports, just as corrupt or criminal behaviour by public servants damages a government agency's reputation, or similar behaviour by a company director damages a corporation's reputation.

Organisational reputation

Among the primary issues that concern senior communication practitioners are those associated with organisational reputations and values. Cornelissen (2005) described reputation as a 'perceptual construct' that is often extended and associated with organisational behaviour, and is formed by multiple stakeholder groups who evaluate multiple characteristics of the organisation. Such constructs and evaluations are grounded in organisational behaviour and demonstrations of corporate values, often through professional communication activities because they play an important role in creating a strong image and reputation for an organisation (McCarthy & Hatcher, 2004). In this context, Tench et al. (2009) described public legitimation and licence, each related to reputation and corporate values, as the main concern of communication management.

Cornelissen (2005) noted that as a strategic management function communication is 'charged with…guiding and managing reputations and relationships with important stakeholder groups' (p. 100). Thus, organisations build, maintain, and protect their reputations by engaging in discussions with stakeholders about issues they share.

The global financial crisis in the first decade of the 21st century delivered significant lessons to corporations and their communication advisers about seriously engaging in re-building and maintaining the reputations and credibility damaged by that international economic disaster. To communicate effectively now in a world pandemic, as then in an economic crisis, organisations need to understand what Argenti et al. (2005) described as three 'drivers' of the strategic communication imperative: regulatory factors, organisational complexities, and the need to increase credibility. They noted that new government regulations imposed after previous corporate crises meant a need for business, in particular, to revisit communication strategies and practices to ensure they were consistent as organisations grew. Ghemawat (2010), writing later and in the context of how business should approach the post-global financial crisis era, echoed this with an argument that identity and reputation were among five strategic re-alignments organisations would need to make. Ghemawat (2010) argued that as governments had taken on expanded roles as investors, customers, regulators, and tax collectors after the crisis, corporate diplomacy was an important strategic consideration. Ghemawat (2010) argued that in this environment, 'the insistence that the marketplace should completely dictate outcomes is unlikely to win friends and influence people. CEOs and other executives will need to spend more time managing government relationships' (p. 60). Luoma-aho and Vos (2010) argued that organisations' reputations reflect the interactions between actors in issues arenas. In this view, 'conversations and arenas left without organisational participation may threaten organisational reputation' (Luoma-aho & Vos, 2010, p. 11).

Being able to communicate meaningfully about reputational matters means being competent at identifying and analysing issues that impact on reputation before they emerge.

Organisational values

Organisational values are the beliefs on which the organisation bases its policies and actions. Peters and Waterman (1984) found that in the companies they described as excellent, explicit attention was paid to values. They concluded that clarifying the organisation's value system and breathing life into it were the greatest contributions a leader could make. Companies they described as excellent were clear about what they stood for, and were serious about value shaping, leading Peters and Waterman to question whether it was possible for a company to be excellent without clarity on values. In a commentary about programs to reintroduce corporate values during the 1990s in the wake of corporate re-engineering, Nash (1995) noted that it was hard to package morality without provoking a countercultural reaction of aggressive cynicism or quiet withdrawal. Corporate ethics statements, among responses to the troubled times of the 1980s, were often conceived in 'glorious isolation' by board chairs or a few top managers, and 'cast in a legalistic format, only to be shoved into a back file drawer by the few managers who actually retained them' (Nash, 1995, pp. 8–9). Values statements suffered similar fates and had little effect on corporate culture. Any attempt to influence the values of a firm required a range of coordinated efforts, from the chair's personal interest and commitment, through to discussion, debate, widespread dissemination, monitoring and communication channels for surfacing questions, arbitrating grey area problems or non-compliance, enforcement, and rewards.

Another aspect of organisational values as a factor in strategic communication decision-making includes those shareholders perceive to contribute to reputation. Shareholders are increasingly drawn from a broad social and economic base (McCarthy & Hatcher, 2004). This broadening of the shareholder base, coupled with greater activism against the corporate world, in particular, means a wider spectrum of values will be used to examine organisational responses to crises, especially by consumers who are part of what Stengel (2009) described as a responsibility revolution.

Building and maintaining credibility is a reputational issue that includes scrutiny of executive behaviour, especially scrutiny by the mass news media that leads possible negative news coverage that in turn impacts on stakeholder, especially shareholder, opinions of organisations. The same holds for activists who use non-market environments to raise and debate credibility issues, and regulators who police corporate behaviour. For example, the mass media appears to assume that executives have control over the actions of an organisation and should be held accountable for their ethical and moral lapses (An & Gower, 2009).

Also among organisational values is the focus they put on corporate social responsibility (CSR). Research by Jones and Bartlett (2009) demonstrated the strategic value of CSR for organisations in terms of relationship management rather than the communication-output perspective commonly given to it.

Relationships and change

The literature on communication during corporate restructuring, and how this affects relationships with stakeholders, provides insight for strategic communicators involved in external and internal issues management and decisions about strategy. That literature has a common theme: the need for leaders to set the values and objectives of their organisations (see for example, Beer & Eisenstat, 2004; Kotter, 1995; Laroche, 2004; Lewis, 2000; Nash, 1995; Peters & Waterman, 1984; Roper, 2005). Freitag and Picherit-Duthler (2004) argued that more research is needed to develop frameworks, models, and constructs for communication during change. Organisational change is often a response to external economic and political factors, and is complex, difficult for both those who implement it and employees who are affected by it, and often creates resistance and resentment (Christen, 2005; Dakin, 1989; Kotter, 1995; Lewis, 2000;

Recardo, 1995; Taylor, 1999). Communication with internal and external stakeholders during change is high on the list of factors that predict success, second only to participation by the main stakeholders (Gillis, 2004; Ströh, 2006).

Ströh (2007) argued that the complexity sciences suggest that building and maintaining stakeholder relationships is fundamental to effective change. Gregory (2000) also dealt with complexity and organisational change by arguing that very small incremental and insignificant changes create disturbances in systems which, through their own increasing dynamics, start major change. This means organisations should consider mutual causality where small multiple changes cause ripple effects which can magnify in an uncontrollable way (Gregory, 2000). In a communication sense, this means that seemingly insignificant comments and actions can escalate rapidly into hot issues and crises with what Gregory (2000) described as their own uncontrollable lives. The myriad health, political, economic, and social issues that emerged during the Covid-19 pandemic demonstrated the force of that view.

The role of chief executives as communicators in a change environment is important to the success of restructuring (Alexander, 2006; Barrett, 2002; Economo & Zorn, 1999; Gregory, 2000; Kotter, 1995; Lewis, 2000; Mahoney, 2006; Recardo, 1995). Alexander (2006), for example, examined how chief executives communicate with external stakeholders and argued that organisational leaders need to be competent communicators and understand communication practice at a high level to manage the range of interests and publics that impact on business goals.

In a commentary about the Peters and Waterman's excellent companies, Wilson (1994) noted that open and honest communication is a key element of business success for those companies, and observes that one of the five attributes they display is relationships with all their stakeholders built

> on respect, trust, and human dignity, not on profit or personal gain. Its philosophy will foster winning for all parties, rather than ensuring corporate success at the price of the failure of others. The focus will be on people, and they will be treated as competent adults capable of solving problems if provided the resources, support, and environment in which to do it.
>
> *(Wilson, 1994, p. 341)*

The four other attributes are long-range vision, commitment to community not just profit, strong corporate values that in some way emphasise the importance of people, and a cooperative approach to management problem solving (Wilson, 1994).

Regulatory factors

Argenti et al. (2005) argued that a significant driver of strategic communication is government regulation of industry. Debates about issues related to the effects of regulation on industries and individual organisations occur in the non-market environment. Examples of this are the Australian mining industry's 2010–2013 campaigns against the introduction of the so-called mining super profits and carbon taxes, and responses to them from various political parties and other interests. Similar issues debates occur about, for example, environmental, workplace safety, imports and exports, and refugee policy, all of which relate to how activity is to be regulated. Research by Kang and Cheng (2008) found that legal and regulatory factors affected issues management. These issues were also included in Pang, Yin, and Cameron's (2010) list of 87 internal and external variables that impact on practitioners' abilities to do their jobs.

Communicating with employees

An essential element of strategic communication planning is the design of effective ways of communicating with employees about organisational directions, structures, plans, and issues. The importance of effective employee communication is illustrated by the attention it is given in research into organisational change. Kotter (1995) argued that change needs to be rooted in social norms and shared values and described two important factors in achieving it: a conscious attempt to show staff that the new approach has helped improve performance; a need to take sufficient time to ensure that the next generation of top management 'personifies the new approach' (Kotter, 1995, p. 67). Baghai et al. (2000) argued that when employees are pursuing a common goal (of growth), work can become more exciting, purposeful, and fulfilling. This has an important dimension: employees who understand and support organisational directions, issues, and change are potentially strong supporters in external environments.

Researchers in a number of disciplines have studied organisational change and employee communication which is associated with it. Psychological researchers have, for example, examined employee reactions to change; scholars in the management and public relations disciplines have identified the ways in which management techniques and employee communication can assist in generating staff support for their change objectives (Barrett, 2002; Beer & Eisenstat, 2004; Dakin, 1989; DiFonzio & Bordia, 2002; Gillis, 2004; Grunig, J.E., 2001; Hamel, 1996; Jordan, 2004; Kegan & Lahey, 2001; Kotter, 1999; Laroche, 2004; Lewis, 2000; Pascale & Sternin, 2005; Ströh, 2006, 2007; Wood et al., 2004).

Pascale and Sternin (2005) proposed that companies use 'positive deviants' or 'secret change agents,' as champions of change in organisational restructuring. These employees, who are on the periphery of their organisations, are innovators whose practices and behaviours 'enable them to better find solutions to problems than others in their communities' (Pascale & Sternin, 2005, p. 74). In Hamel's (1996) view, pro-change revolutionaries in every company should be given a voice in strategy-making. Other researchers have developed what they call a 'strategic fitness process' to help corporate leaders have honest conversations with employees about strategic directions, including painful truths about what is wrong with the organisation, to enhance the capacity of organisations to change (Beer & Eisenstat, 2004). This fitness process, which involves a task force appointed by senior management to discuss issues with staff, enables senior managers to reduce cynicism, increase trust, and develop commitment.

Future challenges

Zerfass (2009) argued there were two scenarios for how strategic communication would develop as a discipline – in his context, post the early-2000s global financial crisis. In the first scenario, once economies recovered from the crisis, strategic communicators may no longer be able to influence dominant coalitions about issues of corporate social responsibility as the demands of maximising profits may focus corporate communication on product publicity. The second scenario meant that strategic communication may return to a normative concept in which managing relationships and reputations will be less valued than traditional ideas of public relations, advertising, and business communication. This is also true for the post-Covid-19 pandemic era as communicators find their value-added dual roles as issues managers and boundary spanners identifying and analysing non-market issues is overtaken by an economic need for corporate recovery. The urge for dominant coalitions to ignore the future and return to a focus on short-term, tactical, and technical communication alchemy will be strong. But communicators need to promote the strategic communication imperative of keeping reputation, credibility, stakeholder relationship, and regulatory issues on their non-market environment watch lists. Along with residual pandemic-related issues, these will still have the potential for significant harm to organisations unless they are the focus of a long-term research-based approach to issues management. Even if they are heeded in their dual roles as issues managers and boundary spanners, strategic communicators will likely find that barriers to success will be formidable and resonant with the challenges of post-crisis communication. For those engaged in political communication this will mean not only repairing credibility, but dealing with anger, negative word-of-mouth, account acceptance (Coombs & Holladay, 2009), and damaged reputations. Just as in the post-economic crisis, these challenges will need to be analysed against a background of calls for increased openness and transparency from organisations in all sectors (Waters, Burnett, Lamm, & Lucas, 2009) as a result of previous organisational reputational defaults.

Zerfass' (2009) normative second scenario for strategic communication suggests the practice needs to be more explicitly defined as a mid- to long-term practice in which organisations and their spokespeople are social actors who advance views about public policy issues in their non-market environments. Strategic communication defined in this way is also important for private, public, and not-for-profit sector organisations, because it provides an over-arching corporate-level plan that guides their participation in public issues debates in their non-market environments. In this construct, strategic communication is established as the professional practice that engages with stakeholders about organisational issues concerning reputation, values, and credibility. To do that it should use all the technical communication tools available to practitioners, including face-to-face communication, but in ways that implement strategic directions, not simply apply daily tactics to engage news and social media for marketing communication purposes.

This view of strategic communication would locate it in academic convention as a discipline in its own right, to be taught as such, with links to issues and business management content, and a focus on research rather than practical how-to-write strategies. There is nothing wrong with learning the practical processes involved in writing a communication strategy. This is essential knowledge. It should be learnt as part of a process that illustrates how research determines which are strategic, and which are tactical, situations in market and non-market environments. In this concept, strategic communication and issues management are likely more appropriate as postgraduate study and professional development courses for practitioners. No doubt practitioners and scholars will argue that this is already the case, but they need only look critically at their own work to see that despite their nod to strategic concepts, they do not always practise, nor research, it.

4

IDENTIFYING, ANALYSING, AND MANAGING ORGANISATIONAL ISSUES

A popular theme in science fiction is the notion that a butterfly flapping its wings in a Brazilian rainforest changes the weather in Europe. This so-called butterfly effect is a metaphor for concepts embedded in chaos theory, especially to explain how small changes in a system's environment may influence the way the system behaves. Management scholars use this principle when they adapt systems, complexity, and contingency theories to understand and explain organisational structures and management. The butterfly metaphor also translates to the impact that social, political, and economic issues that are raised and debated in an organisation's external non-market environment have on strategic communication decision-making. But unlike science fiction, those energetic Brazilian issue butterflies have a real kinetic, continuing influence on high level, strategic decisions beyond day-to-day concerns. That is, issues management is what Heath and Palenchar (2009) described as a struggle for issue ownership in an organisation's non-market environment. In their view,

> how an issue is resolved and in what communication context, including collaborative decision making, depends on how it survives in society itself. As much as we might like for all issues to be resolved through collaborative decision making among the key players, we also know that how an issue plays out in such sessions is never separate from how that issue is surviving in popular discussion.
>
> *(p. 226)*

But what is an 'issue'?

Scholars define issues as disputes between two or more people (Hallahan, 2001), or as 'unsettled matters,' or points of conflict between an organisation and one

DOI: 10.4324/9781003177340-4

or more of its publics (Cornelissen, 2005, p. 26). Other scholars say issues are 'controversial inconsistencies' caused by gaps between the expectations of corporations and those of their stakeholders or target publics, or as political and social problems (Dougall, 2008, p. 4; Regester & Larkin, 2005; J.E. Grunig & Repper, 1992). Organisational issues are also described as external matters that could 'positively or negatively affect [an organisation's] prosperity or survival' (Moloney, 2006, p. 37). In this 'quicksand of duelling definitions' about what an issue is, three distinct constructs have emerged (Jaques, 2012, p. 37). These constructs view issues in the contexts of dispute, expectation, and impact themes, which have broad scholarly and professional agreement.

Organisations, their stakeholders, and other constituencies, may be concerned about the same issue, but rarely share the same perspective (Dougall, 2008). Issues are strategic because they 'compel' an organisation to deal with them as a result of a conflict between two or more identifiable groups (Van Riel & Frombrun, 2008, p. 203). Bigelow et al. (1993) drew on the earlier work of other scholars (Ansoff, 1980; King, 1982; Mintzberg et al., 1976; Bucholtz, 1988; Mahon & Bigelow, 1992) to note that public issues are developments that will impact on organisational performance. This means they are important for resource acquisition and the ability to meet objectives. Dougall (2008) noted that issues management 'divine[s] and determine[s] the existence and likely impacts of these contestable points of difference' (p. 4) for organisations.

Hallahan (2001) argued that the origins of issues could be traced to the moment a person identified a situation to be problematic, that is, when it posed negative consequences for one or more people. Such situations were attributed to the unfair or risky actions of others and emerge only when people share problems through communication, and analyse, define, delimit, and label problems.

For Hallahan (1999, 2001), interpretations of how a problem or concern is understood, or explained, are at the heart of most issues and how disputants vie to have their preferred interpretation dominate. That is, issues involve disputants airing differing views in attempts to influence others by 'altering their knowledge, attitudes, or actions' (Hallahan, 2001, p. 29). Such disputes usually arise over the allocation of resources or the treatment or portrayal of groups in society and frequently mean an extensive public discussion. That argument reflects J.E. Grunig's and Hunt's (1984) view that publics form around issues. In an issue context, publics are defined by Hallahan (2001) as groups with which an organisation wants to form a relationship.

It is these points about disputes over differing views, how stakeholder relationships are built, and organisations and stakeholders having an interest in the same issues, that create a core principle underpinning strategic issues communication. That is, emerging stakeholder opinions need to be identified in professional issues analysis, so that organisations can take rational decisions on how to react to those opinions.

Issues emerge when publics/stakeholders raise problems they believe need to be resolved in their interests (Pang, Jin, & Cameron, 2010). That reflects Heath and Palenchar's (2009) argument that an issue is not what everyone believes but what some people strongly believe. In this view, people who strongly believe in something exert pressure for their views to be heard in public policy debates. Van Riel and Frombrun (2008) hold that the sooner a potential threat of an issue to an organisation's ability to achieve its business goals is recognised, the more likely the organisation is to take action on that issue. In Heath and Palenchar's (2009) view, debates about issues are routine in business management and communication practice and that the positive or negative outcomes of these debates can affect how organisations are managed. Thus, an issue is worthy of attention when it can have an impact on an organisation. This view should be extended to include the potential for socio-economic and political issues likely to emerge over the mid- and long-terms to impact, either negatively or positively, on an organisation's performance.

So, issues occur in an organisation's external environments when there are inconsistencies between its views on a socio-economic or political subject and those of one or more of its stakeholders. They are about disagreements that occur in public, and they are often debated by the population, addressed by governments, and reported in the news media (Hallahan, 2001). Organisations are compelled to deal with issues because of the potential impact they could have on their operations, even the organisation's survival, and on their stakeholder relationships. Dealing with them is a strategic practice. Issues are raised by people who strongly believe they should be resolved in their interests. Similarly, organisations raise and publicly address issues when they hold strong views about them and believe they should be resolved in the organisation's interests.

Having defined issues it is necessary to explore the concept of an organisation's non-market environment, the external public space where social and political issues that do not have an immediate market impact are debated, and how organisations are social and political actors when they express views on those issues.

Issues, non-market environments, and social actors

The principle that organisations behave as social and political actors when they deal with external issues in their non-market environment is key to understanding the role of strategic communication as a practice distinct from tactical, technical communication. That is, it is longer term practice that actively engages organisations in both public and private debates about issues that concern them, and means organisations use communication in a strategic way that is not the normative, market-based communication to which they, and, often, their professional practitioners, are accustomed. It is practice that attempts to influence the course and resolution of issues, and public policies, that can potentially harm organisations. Part of this is the need for organisations to understand and consider issues that are important to the wider world (McGrath et al., 2010). Engagement of this kind, and expressing points of view in issues debates, involves organisational functions that manage reputation with external stakeholders, political lobbying, and government, community, and media relations (McGrath et al., 2010). This means an organisation is involved in issues debates as a social and political actor.

The non-market environment

Management scholars have long investigated the impact of social, economic, and political pressures on the commercial market and how these affect business success and management strategies. In a seminal work, updated in 2008, Porter (2008) argued that external forces shape industry competition and strategy through the effects of market dynamics which cause the bargaining power of suppliers and buyers, threats to business viability from new entrants or substitute products, and rivalry between existing competitors. Emerging socio-economic and political issues in non-market environments are similar external forces which professional communication practitioners should identify and analyse as part of the link between strategic communication and business planning.

Professional communication scholars have focussed on the impact of social, economic, and political issues on organisations and how debates about those issues are managed (see for example, McGrath et al., 2010 and Wolfe et al., 2013, for discussions about this point). Bach (2007) placed these debates in the context of competitive advantage being built or lost outside the commercial market and argued that an organisation thus needed to maintain relationships not solely with those who comprise its market environment, but also with governments, regulators, NGOs, the media, and society at large whether it wanted to or not. Bach argued there were

> huge opportunities for companies here, but also immense dangers for those focused purely on the market side. Anyone can be affected by non-market forces and in very consequential ways.
>
> *(Bach, 2007)*

Bach (2007) argued that most organisations dealt with government affairs mostly in a reactive way that used a combination of lawyers and public relations staff. However, non-market forces were not going away and required a broader mix of people dealing with these forces, who were both reactive and proactive. Later, Bach and Allen (2010) argued a more proactive approach was needed to carefully manage key social, political, and other issues, and relationships with the actors who cared about them, in a broader environment. Bach had previously noted in this context that

> [n]on-market matters, such as reputation, the ability to work with NGOs, the capability to foresee relevant government actions and even to shape policy—these are all having an immense impact at a time when most companies are not even thinking about nonmarket strategy.
>
> *(Bach, 2007)*

In a reflection of earlier scholarly work (for example, Baron, 1999; Bach, 2007), Bach and Allen (2010) explained two external organisational environments in which organisations interact with their stakeholders (see Figure 4.1 for a graphic representation of the concept).

The market environment involves relationships that do not unfold within markets, but nevertheless affect an organisation's ability to reach its business objectives. Non-market environments are organised around issues and how they are debated and resolved in this environment shapes dynamics within markets.

What happens in both environments involves stakeholder relationships and communication. Therefore, what happens in those environments should be of concern to communication practitioners, who need to devise different strategies and tactics for each, and scholars, whose research should explicate what each means for corporate communication. The principal difference between the two is that the currency of exchanges in the non-market environment is information, not money (Bach & Allen, 2010). Non-market exchanges are essentially political. This is why it is important for senior communication practitioners to understand the concept of issues debates occurring in their organisations' non-market environments: information is the currency of their professional practice. The differences between the two environments that Bach and Allen (2010) list are that money, leadership, flexibility, predictability, and value characterise the market, while the market environment is characterised by information, coalitions, consistency, uncertainty, and values.

Baron (1999), writing in the context of US business and its efforts in the political system to build legislative majorities for policy changes, argued that

FIGURE 4.1   Organisational market and non-market environments. Adapted from Bach & Allen, MIT Sloan Management Review, Spring 2010

Figure 4.1 illustrates the concepts of organisations' market and non-market environments by showing the relationships organisations have in those contexts.

corporate and/or industry action in the non-market environment meant affecting the outcome of an issue by providing information, coalition building, and lobbying directed by a non-market strategy.

Communication and non-market issues

The primary focus of communication about issues in a non-market environment is to deal with 'the handful' of social and political issues that really matter to an organisation and is ultimately about the organisation's values (Bach & Allen, 2010). The importance of this focus is reflected in Baron's (1999) view that non-market strategies could open market opportunities when, for example, a firm worked for the creation of a trade agreement, or for the elimination of restrictions on entry to a regulated industry such as telecommunications. Similarly, non-market strategies could benefit a whole industry by reducing costs for that industry. This argument supports Bach and Allen's (2010) view that resolving non-market issues shapes market dynamics.

Some issues have immediate impacts on an organisation's business and need to be addressed immediately to avoid a crisis. They also have mid- and long-term implications and, sometimes, communicating about them occurs in a continuum in which there is no stark divide between market and non-market issues. Yet issues identification and analysis, if consistently applied, should have identified the potential for such issues to emerge over time and create market environment difficulties.

AN ISSUES CASE: AUSTRALIA AND THE COVID-19 VACCINES

Australia and New Zealand survived the first years of the Covid-19 pandemic with low infection rates and, compared with Europe and North America, miniscule death rates. This success was mostly attributed to rapid action by political leaders who closed borders and instituted quarantine regimes for travellers, and, especially in Australia, highly coordinated responses by state and federal leaders through a 'national cabinet.' Australians also generally did as they were told during the initial national lockdown phase: they stayed home from work, school, and university, shopped only when necessary, and most wore masks when outside their homes if health directions required them to.

After its success in controlling the pandemic, the Australian national government faced severe political and media criticism during 2021 over its Covid-19 vaccination rollout. The government widely publicised that it had bought tens of millions of doses of several vaccines early, and the Prime Minister, Scott Morrison, claimed that this strategy 'puts Australia at the front of the queue' (Hartcher, 2021). But the vaccine rollout stumbled, insufficient doses were in the supply chain, many medical centres were given only a limited number of doses each week, and an opinion poll found more than half of its respondents, 52%, thought the rollout was too slow (Hartcher, 2021). The blame for this was levelled at the national government. One unnamed senior public health expert described the rollout as 'a rolling omnishambles of disappointedness' (Hartcher, 2021). The rollout was complicated by the aversion of many to being inoculated by one of the vaccines said to cause blood clots and other side effects. Mixed messaging on this potential problem, and about the timing, and speed, of the rollout from state and federal ministers and public health officials, caused confusion about who, when, where, and why people needed to be vaccinated. The early co-operation with State Governments waned severely and became an issue with which the national administration had to deal. As Australia suffered new outbreaks, including of variations in the virus, in 2021, the national government faced criticism for failing to bring Australians home from overseas (especially from India) while allowing politicians and celebrities easier entry to the country. Additionally, as quarantine is a constitutional responsibility and power of the national government, criticism grew about its handling of virus isolation procedures. Basically, these were left to the States.

Issues like these, including mixed messages from the national government about which vaccines were appropriate for which age groups, do not seem to have been predicted in planning for the vaccine rollout. Communication planners should have been asking what issues were likely to emerge on each of these matters as soon as the national government began its wider planning. It seems this did not occur in sufficient depth. However, like so much political communication around the world, it appeared the national government was more concerned about immediate-term news media opportunities. This led to perceptions it had not thought-out effective communication responses to emerging, and potentially damaging, issues that should have been identified had a significant effort at mid- to long-term issues identification and analysis been pursued.

In discussion about why market and non-market strategies should be integrated, Baron (1999) noted that the latter involved organisations being effective and responsible participants in the public processes that lead to issue resolution. These processes are competitions between opposing interests actively attempting to build, in a US context, a legislative majority that supports their preferred alternatives, for example, for or against increased regulation in a particular industry. This view of non-market strategy reflects the role of issues analysis and management in which an important first step is determining the interests who are aligned with, or opposed to, an issue. That should lead to a communication strategy tailored to the realities of the politics of the institutional arena in which the issue will be addressed, and that is designed for a non-market environment. The notion of building a legislative majority, or convincing opinion leaders and decision-makers of the merits of a particular point of view, also touches on issues framing because 'nonmarket strategy targets both the agenda-setting stage and the voting stage' (Baron, 1999, p. 31). Thus, in the western liberal democracies, lobbyists, organisations, primary definers, and industry associations contribute to debates about regulatory change that might have been initiated by activists, or a regulatory authority, or from the report of an official investigation into an aspect of the overall economy or an industry. The aim of each of these social actors is to have their point of view on the proposed change accepted.

Social and political actors

Social actors are people or groups who participate in social practices, such as debates about public issues. In a discussion of how they are represented in social practices, van Leeuwen (1996) noted that social actors can be portrayed as either active or passive. When social actors were represented as active, they were regarded as dynamic forces in an activity, while passive social actors were at the receiving end of an activity. Deephouse and Heugens (2009) noted that social actors pursue solutions to issues by attempting to influence other actors who have more resources 'to remedy the issue' (p. 543). Organisations are advocates, or social actors, who legitimately contribute to debates about issues where that can potentially impact on their ability to achieve business goals and objectives.

Martin and Osberg (2007) posited three roles for social actors: those engaged in social entrepreneurship, social service provision, and social activism. While they were concerned specifically with defining social entrepreneurship, they viewed social activism as attempting to 'create change through indirect action, by influencing others—governments, NGOs, consumers, workers...to take action' (p. 37). Martin and Osberg (2007) viewed social actors in the context of the 'exalted tradition' (p. 38) of Martin Luther King, Mahatma Gandhi, and Václav Havel.

On the other hand, Hallahan et al. (2007) and Bach and Allen (2010) regarded social actors in a different political dimension. Hallahan et al. (2007) used Habermas' (1979, 1989) view to argue that it is increasingly important for social actors and organisations to be deliberate and thoughtful in their communication to be heard. Bach and Allen (2010) described companies as social and political beings, not just economic agents, and noted that companies cannot escape the plethora of actors who formally influence them through laws and regulation, and informally through 'social pressure, activism, and efforts to shape the public perception of business' (p. 42). They argued that 'smart' executives,

> engage with their social and political environment, helping shape the rules of the game and reducing the risk of being hemmed in by external actors.
> *(Bach and Allen, 2010, p. 42)*

For Deephouse and Heugens (2009), organisations adopt issues because key decision-makers are concerned about the social and political conditions in which their organisations operate.

As social actors, organisations use communication techniques to influence issues debates. Bach and Allen (2010) argued that organisations must be social and political actors in the non-market environment whether managers 'like it or not' (p. 48) and that using participation in non-market debates as a strategic opportunity is important because,

> [p]oliticians, regulators, nongovernmental organisations, and activists won't hesitate to impose new rules of the game on an industry, unless companies themselves become active participants in the process.
>
> *(Bach & Allen, 2010, p. 48)*

Bach and Allen's (2010) view that corporations are beginning 'to stretch the competitive playing field' from a focus on the market and are 'turning to social and political issues from mere nuisance to strategic opportunity' (p. 48), may reflect business strategy, but whether that includes issues identification and analysis by practitioners from a communication perspective, linked to business planning, is unclear.

Hallahan et al. (2007) built on Habermas' (1979) view that organisations are significant social actors with an increasingly important role in debates about public issues and that this role has transformed how modern society deliberates on those issues when they are purposeful, or strategic, in advancing their mission. They argue that strategic communication research should include examining how an organisation presents itself in society as a social actor in the discussion of public issues. In doing this, issues managers also need to make assumptions about the views of other political and social actors in this environment (Wartick & Rude, 1985). This 1985 view is a recognition of the need for more complete issues identification and analysis.

Luoma-aho and Vos (2010) used Actor Network Theory (ANT) to help explain the interactions between organisations and their stakeholders (actors) in their concept of issues arenas. ANT is a sociological theory that attempts to explain interactions in large, less-fixed environments and posits that 'every act of establishing something is linked with the different factors influencing it, such as its surroundings, regulations, other people, technology etcetera' (Luoma-aho & Vos, 2010, p. 9). This involves power relationships in networks of actors (Callon & Latour, 1981). Callon (1999) noted that ANT was developed to analyse situations 'in which it is difficult to separate humans and non-humans' (p. 183). Issues debates in organisations' non-market environments, issues arenas, are just such situations. It is worth noting that ANT has been criticised by some organisational scholars. Whittle and Spicer (2008) noted that ANT has been used to describe organisations as networks of social, technical, textual, and naturally occurring networks 'brought together in more or less stable associations or alliances' (p. 612). However, Whittle and Spicer (2008) argued that because ANT elevates the status of non-human actors, it degrades the meaning of political action which, in the context of the argument set out in this book, involves debates about public policy. Nevertheless, human actors and their networks are engaged in what Luoma-aho and Vos (2010) described as a struggle of power where all players have their own agendas and strategies as they participate in public policy issues debates in non-market environments. Baron (1999) raised concerns about whether it is appropriate for firms to use non-market strategies for influencing public decisions. However, Baron (1999) argued that society had two responses to such concerns. First, society could rely on competition from opposing preferences to mitigate the influence of both sides, and second, regulate non-market actions by requiring disclosure of such actions, a step many liberal democracies have taken through the introduction of lobbyists' registers.

The argumentative context: framing and understanding issues

It is axiomatic that organisations and their stakeholders seek to influence the course of debates about issues that concern them (see, for example, Van Gorp, 2007). Proponents attempt to set an issues agenda by presenting a point of view about issues in the way they want them to be interpreted by others. So, it is important that professional communication practitioners understand issues agendas, issues framing, and how people take meanings from issues debates.

A rich academic literature has dealt with agenda setting and framing as aspects of media effects theory with a particular focus on news framing. Issues agendas are set in the public arena when journalists decide what to report, and on the angle, or frame, they use to cover the issue. Frames are the ways in which journalists and others shape, structure, categorise, and define news and 'generally operate to snag related ideas in their net in an active process' (Reese, 2007, p. 150). But agenda setting is more likely to be practised by issues definers and other social actors in overt efforts to have their views reported by journalists.

Entman (2007) argued agenda setting was 'another name for successfully performing the first function of framing: defining problems worthy of public and government attention' (p. 164). Entman (2007) noted three types of agenda setting claims to

- highlight the causes of problems
- encourage moral judgements and associated affective responses
- promote favoured policies

McCombs (2004) described agenda setting as a robust and widespread effect of mass communication that resulted from specific content in the mass media. In this view public opinion evolves as mass media and public attention to issues fluctuates over time. For McCombs (2004), the most important aspect of the evolution of public opinion is the intense competition between issues for a place on mass media and public agendas. McCombs (2005) further argued that agenda setting had significant consequences because it shaped people's attitudes and opinions about issues.

Van Gorp (2007) regarded news frames as persuasive stimuli, or invitations to read a news story in a particular way, so that a specific definition of an event, the causal and treatment responsibility for a societal topic, and a moral judgement of a person, come more easily across the receiver's mind. This is a central point in understanding the importance of the role of the mass news media journalists as specific stakeholders in a non-market environment. But, in issues debates, news reporters' stakeholder role is limited that of a tertiary public that is in reality a communication mechanism for relaying views to intended target publics, despite their role in framing an issue. Relevant target publics are those directly affected by an issue. Thus, for effective campaign planning, journalists are not target publics, or audiences, in the same way as the primary stakeholders with whom an organisation seeks to engage in a dialogic issues debate. On the other hand, there are journalists, employed as specialist opinion writers, or to cover specific topics, who become secondary target publics with whom an organisation needs to communicate on relevant socio-economic and political issues. Commentators in this role are those who cover, for example, politics, economics, the environment, trade and foreign affairs, medicine, crime, courts, and sport. In this context they may not be directly affected by an issue, but they have a professional interest in it and use their columns in which to express opinions. In short, a sports reporter is not interested in covering an economics story unless it has direct relevance to the sport they report. This is an important, perhaps cynical, distinction that communication practitioners and dominant coalitions often ignore when they distribute information to 'the media,' without any differentiation of journalists' particular roles, in the belief that it is all that is needed to convince other stakeholders of an organisation's views. Making this point does not negate the importance of media coverage of an issue, nor of the role of news frames, because readers and viewers need to know such information. But it does reinforce the strategic communication planning requirement that relevant target publics be identified along with the ways in which they prefer to receive their news. Most often this is from internet-based applications and news sites, making it vital that the channels accessed by specific target publics are included in a strategic plan.

So, key to creating an issues agenda and effectively contributing to ensuing debates is to produce material that relevant target publics will read and understand. Doing that includes producing material that helps journalists interested in the issue to report in the context of a recognisable news frame. Thus, in issues management practice,

> Defining issues through the process of framing...becomes a pivotal concern. Issues can be framed as significant or insignificant to the public

interest but more important can be defined in terms of how people should think about an issue.

(Hallahan, 1999, p. 227)

While framing is used to influence an issues agenda (Hallahan [1999] described this as an integral part of agenda building), framing analysis has an important role in issues identification, analysis, and management. Framing analysis can help an organisation to understand how stakeholders navigate information by providing a way of deconstructing mass media narratives (Heath & Palenchar, 2009). That is, framing analysis elaborates how information is packaged by the mass news media and how that information is presented or portrayed (Blood & Holland, 2004). Weaver (2007) noted that media perspectives and frames drew attention to certain attributes of matters covered in the news as well as to the matters themselves.

Determining how issues are framed, by whom, and how a frame impacts on an issue dialogue, is a vital element in issues management and 'neither an idle matter nor the matter of only one party' (Heath & Palenchar, 2009, p. 223). This view is shared by Hallahan (1999), who described framing as a 'valuable concept for issues management' (p. 227).

Entman (2007) defined framing as the 'process of culling a few elements of perceived reality and assembling a narrative that highlights connections among them to promote a particular interpretation' (p. 164) to shape audiences' interpretations and preferences through priming. Further,

> frames introduce or raise the salience or apparent importance of certain ideas, activating schemas that encourage target audiences to think, feel, and decide in a particular way.
>
> *(Entman, 2007, p. 164)*

Earlier, Entman (1993) suggested that frames defined problems, diagnosed causes, made moral judgements, and suggested remedies, but not always in the one text, and argued that frames highlighted 'some bits of information about an item that is the subject of communication, thereby elevating them in salience' (p. 53). These discussions of framing are important in the context of issues analysis and management, especially the point that a frame,

> determines whether most people notice and how they understand and remember a problem, as well as how they evaluate and choose to act upon it. The notion of framing thus implies that the frame has a common effect on large portions of the receiving audience, though it is not likely to have a universal effect on all.
>
> *(Entman, 1993, p. 54)*

Introducing a special edition of the *Journal of Communication* that focussed on news framing, agenda setting, and priming effects, Scheufele and Tewksbury

(2007) argued that framing was based on an assumption that audiences would be influenced in their understanding of issues by how news reports characterised them. They noted that sociologists and other scholars argued that people constantly struggled to make sense of the world and their life experiences and applied interpretive schema (Goffman's, 1974, 'primary frameworks') to meaningfully process, classify, and interpret new information.

For public relations scholarship and practice, Hallahan (1999) defined framing as a message property that limits or defines its meaning by shaping the inferences people make about messages and reflects judgements made by message creators. Issues framing as one of seven he identified as applicable to public relations. (The other six are the framing of situations, attributes, choices, actions, responsibility, and news.) In Hallahan's (1999) argument, framing occurs when advocates attempt to communicate with members of affected or sympathetic groups, either directly or through the news media.

Vasquez (1996) conceptualised public relations as 'a communication and negotiation process' that attempts to 'negotiate the organisation-public relationship through the construction of frames of information that define and redefine the relationship' (p. 72). The frames used in an issue development process involved 'naming, blaming and claiming' through arguments, cases, and multiple agenda items as well as explicit and implicit messages about an organisation's values, images, and issues (p. 72).

Framing occurs at both a macro and micro level. At a macro level, framing 'refers to modes of presentation that journalists and other communicators use to present information in a way that resonates with existing underlying schemas among their audience' (Scheufele & Tewksbury, 2007, p. 12). In this way, frames, especially those used by journalists, become tools for presenting complex issues in an accessible and efficient way because they 'play to existing cognitive schemas' (Scheufele & Tewksbury, 2007, p. 12). Hallahan (1999) argued that news story framing almost invariably corresponds to at least one group's schematic understanding of an event and that journalists will 'purposefully strive to frame stories in ways that resonate with what journalists perceive to be the largest segment of their audience' (p. 228). As a micro level construct, 'framing describes how people use information and presentation features regarding issues as they form impressions' (Scheufele & Tewksbury, 2007, p. 12). Van Gorp (2007) also described two framing dimensions: first, how news is shaped, and second how an audience adopts frames and sees the world in a similar way to journalists.

Influencing public policy issues debates

The framing levels described by Scheufele and Tewksbury (2007) and Van Gorp (2007) are important in issues analysis and management. The point here is that macro level framing by proponents for both sides of an issue, and how those views are reported in the mass news media, is the primary influence on the course of public policy issues debates. It is framing and agenda setting that establish the parameters around which an issues debate occurs to create what Heath and Palenchar (2009) labelled as the 'argumentative context' (see pp. 221–225) of public policy issues debates. Thus, strategic communicators need to use analyses of macro level framing in research for their strategy decision-making to determine which interests support, and which oppose, their organisation's positions on issues in this argumentative context. Perhaps there will also be times in which interests who are neutral towards, or have no views about, an issue need to be identified in the expectation that they may be convinced to support the organisation's attitude.

In an example that helps to explain how macro level framing works, Van Gorp (2007) noted that scholars regularly argued journalists' autonomy and interpretations were partly shaped by power forces outside news media organisations. This occurred, for example, in dialogic interaction between social movements and the news media. Van Gorp (2007) described power forces as frame sponsors, 'interest groups, spin doctors, advertisers, and so forth' (p. 68). Frame sponsors use news conferences or government announcements to strategically try to generate media coverage in accordance with 'their' frame in attempts to direct journalists' perceptions and frame selection when they report an event (Van Gorp, 2007, p. 68). Such framing results from 'prior strategic decision-making' about how and when frame sponsors announce their views (Van Gorp, 2007, p. 68; see also Hallahan, 1999). For example, Van Gorp (2007) noted that frame selection for media releases was a deliberate attempt to convince receivers of a point of view as much as to inform them, even though journalists may report a counter frame, or even ignore those of frame sponsors. The 'persuasive power of frames' is enhanced when news media report identical frames because 'the media appear to address the audience with a single frame' (Van Gorp, 2007, p. 68).

Research by McCallum (2011) and Bakir (2006) illustrated macro level framing in public policy issues debates, especially about the influences of policymakers on media coverage. In her study of the relationship between media attention on Australian Indigenous issues and health policy, McCallum (2011) argued that an integral part of policymaking was the backdrop provided by media coverage and that policymakers in turn played a crucial role in the way issues were reported by the news media. Discussing the cultural dimension of framing, Bakir (2006) argued that media exposure impacted on policy in two ways: it shaped public perceptions of risk, and policymakers' perceptions of public opinion. Bakir (2006), writing in the context of risk communication and its impact on public policy agenda setting, noted that agenda setting research assumed that media coverage of an issue influenced 'which issues are discussed and prioritised in society' (p. 68).

In his constructionist view of framing, Van Gorp (2007) noted the distinction between framing by the news media and framing through the news media. Both are important for issues management, and planning strategic communication, because identifying the former enables analysts to understand who issue proponents are, and how journalists interpret proponents' views in non-market environments. The second distinction is a goal of professional communicators when they try to effectively use the mass news media as a channel for presenting their organisation's views to stakeholders in non-market environments. On the one hand journalists shape news content 'within a familiar frame of reference and according to some latent structure of meaning' and on the other an audience sees the world in a similar way to journalists when they adopt the frame (Van Gorp, 2007, p. 61).

An important result of micro level framing, or how people use information as they form impressions about issues based on what they take from news media reporting, is how stakeholders then participate in issues debates, or even withhold their views. In this way the framing process becomes interactive and prone to counter frames (Van Gorp, 2007). This means that media frames, audiences' and media makers' cognitive levels, frame sponsors' discourses, and a given culture's 'stock of frames' (Van Gorp, 2007, p. 64) interact to create the essential argumentative context of an issues debate in a non-market environment.

A concern that experimental framing research concentrated on one-sided communication led Chong and Druckman (2007) to argue that issues debates involved political competition between frames. Chong and Druckman's (2007) theory of competitive framing effects helps to explain the dynamics of issues debates and the complexities of issues analysis and management. Issues dynamics and complexities mean that

> virtually all public debates involve competition between contending parties to establish the meaning and interpretation of issues. When citizens engage an issue…they must grapple with opposing frames that are intended by opinion leaders to influence public preferences.
>
> *(Chong and Druckman, 2007, p. 100)*

Luoma-aho and Vos (2010) reflect the role of public affairs, a professional sub-set of public relations, when they argued that organisations need to actively participate in various issues arenas so that they are major players involved in co-producing outcomes. While this point resonates with the concept of dialogic communication, the underlying assumption is that when an issues arena is identified early, the organisation has a better chance of becoming one of the major actors in an issues debate (Luoma-aho & Vos, 2010, p. 18).

Here is the point about contestable issues frames that influence the strength or weakness of a debate, and mean that issues are discussed in various ways, with bias, and in varying degrees of depth. This reinforces Heath and Palenchar's (2009) point about issues debates taking place in argumentative contexts. That is, issue proponents use their own frames to convince others of the validity of their points of view, a communicative task directed at influencing how people understand an issue—or their personal zone of meaning.

Zones of meaning

Knowledge about how stakeholders take, or might take, meanings from organisational views on issues should be vital to planning strategic issues communication. Knowing what people already understand about an issue, or how they are likely to react to an organisation's views, assists in objective-setting, and in selecting the communication pathways on which messages will be delivered via the communicative tools that best suit how target publics access information. That is, for example, deciding whether a communication pathway like LinkedIn will reach a primary target public, and the communicative tool (a simple post, a detailed brief about an issue, or a copy of a speech) that should be used on that pathway.

When he theorised rhetoric as the essence of public relations, Heath (1993) approached issue contestability from the perspective of professional communication creating meaning about organisations, their stakeholders, and relationships that identify them and their prerogatives. Heath has consistently posited a rhetorical approach to understanding public relations (see for example Heath, 1993, 2000, 2001, and 2006) and argued that public relations

> is not just about communication, it entails communicating about something, something that its sponsors believe deserves to be said. The act of this communication, as well as its content, creates meaning.
>
> *(Heath, 1993, p. 144)*

Engaging in rhetoric to influence stakeholders' views about an issue could also be posited as the essence of strategic communication because issues debates involve creating meaning about, or understanding of, proponents' points of view. Heath (2006) viewed this as 'responsible advocacy' in which ideas are refined, facts and values are promoted and weighed, and interests consider and balanced as part of what he described as 'the essential means and rationale for collective decision-making' (p. 108).

Such communicative action involves tasks that are mid- to long-term endeavours. For example, Henderson (2005) noted that organisations, activists, and interest groups use issues management communication in attempts to manage the political environment by contributing to the construction of social reality about issues. Managing a political environment does not happen in a short-term, tactical time frame even when issues debates are covered daily by the mass news media. Issues management communication requires 'smart strategic planning' to advance the meanings 'organisations create and the implications of that meaning for the relationship between them and their stakeholders' (Heath, 1993, p. 150). Put another way, issues debates traverse organisational and personal zones of meaning about, or understandings of, issues. This perspective is important for understanding strategic communication as a form of social influence that treats persuasion as an interactive, dialogic process in which points of view are publicly contested (Heath, 1993).

Zones of meaning relate to how issues are understood and discussed as politicians, activists, and the news media compete to 'define, prime, make salient, and support' issues in a multi-tiered society (Heath & Palenchar, 2009, p. 226). Earlier, Heath and Palenchar (2000) described zones of meaning as patterns of shared meaning that could be identified via survey instruments. Zones of meaning are tiered. Those at the top tier know more about an issue, help to frame it, and prime others to take an interest in it. People in the top tier may be able to make substantial statements about an issue while those at the next level might know something about the issue, and those in the bottom tier might only know key words about the topic and react with 'slogan-like positions' (Heath & Palenchar, 2009, p. 226). That is, some people might understand an issue in detail while others know nothing about it.

Identifying a stakeholder's zone of meaning on an issue enables analysts to understand how stakeholder beliefs and attitudes can positively or negatively affect the future of an organisation by the way 'stakes are granted or withheld' (Heath & Palenchar, 2009, pp. 89–91). Such understandings are vital for effectively planning contributions to issues debates because they enable frame sponsors to be carefully identified and for stakeholders to be meaningfully segmented into target publics who are more likely to be sympathetic to a message.

Understanding stakeholders' zones of meaning about an issue requires practitioners to research demographics, knowledge, awareness, cognitive involvement, and communication patterns. This in turn enables them to work out how to effectively respond to issues in ways that meet stakeholder understanding of the issue, expectations, and need for information about the organisation's point of view.

Issues management as a professional practice

The US public relations practitioner Howard Chase coined the term 'issues management' in 1976 after reflecting on the influence that external forces exerted on corporations through the 1950s and 1960s (Issue Management Council website, n.d.). Chase believed internal experts could identify and alert organisations to emerging issues thus creating time in which an organisation could better respond, and avoid confrontation. He proposed a five-step issues management model that involved

- issues identification
- issues analysis
- issues change strategy options
- issues action program
- evaluation of results

In the 1970s, companies engaged in issues management to help define strategies to counter activist group pressure for stricter controls on business (see for example, Wartick & Rude, 1985; Regester & Larkin, 2005; Dougall, 2008; McGrath et al., 2010). Issues management was adopted as a strategic planning tool and implemented as a way for companies to deal with their critics (Regester & Larkin, 2005). Although it began as an 'unabashed corporate concept' (Jaques, 2012, p. 42), it has been adopted by non-government organisations, legislatures, and government agencies to promote and implement public policy, a use which is

> particularly evident when governments mobilise issue management tools and processes in relation to controversial issues...or respond in the aftermath of [crises].
>
> *(Jaques, 2012, p. 36)*

Thus, the overarching goal of issues management for organisations in the private, public, and not-for-profit sectors should be to resolve issues by identifying and understanding incompatibilities between zones of meaning about issues.

Defining issues management

The analysis and management of issues is a sophisticated discipline used to develop strategies for a wide range of public issues (Jaques, 2009a). Gillions (2009) defined issues management as a strategic planning function that used communication skills to influence public policy. Van Riel and Frombrun (2008) nominated early detection of issues that can 'potentially become a threat to the organisation' (p. 203) as the first step in issues management. That is, proactive issues management identifies threatening issues so that an organisation can 'influence their course and avoid escalation into a crisis' (Jaques, 2012, p. 38). Analysing emerging trends and issues prepares organisations to respond to them in a timely and appropriate way (Guth & Marsh, 2006). Earlier, J.E. Grunig (1992) described issues management as a process in which organisations anticipate issues before the public makes them an issue. Guth and Marsh (2006) adopted a similar view when they argued that like-minded individuals coalesce into a public when an issue affects a variety of groups and is seen to be evolving.

Early identification of issues is the essential precondition of issues management because if a potential issue is not detected nothing can be done about it (McGrath et al., 2010). Luoma-aho and Vos (2010) argued that issues should be identified before stakeholders are identified. They argue that the changing dynamics of organisational environments need continuous monitoring because it is important to find a balance in a relevant issues arena.

Issues management is

> a means for linking the standard public relations and public affairs functions and the management function of the organisation in ways that foster

the organisation's efforts to be outer directed and reflective, as well as to have a participative organisational culture.

(*Heath and Palenchar, 2009, p. 12*)

Blending these functions when an organisation seeks harmonious relationships in its external environments, which a variety of issues and stakeholders can make complex, is vital (Heath & Palenchar, 2009). They argued that strategic issues management can help organisations to be proactive, instead of merely reactionary. In this way issues management becomes a strategic planning process (Dougall, 2008) with the ultimate objective of expedient resolution of disputes in a way that benefits all parties (Hallahan, 1999). However, 'controlling' issue prominence in the news media, or in a public policy agenda, is the objective of effective issues management if a dispute cannot be resolved (Hallahan, 1999, p. 227).

Public affairs and issues communication

How organisations plan and manage responses to social, economic, and political issues is a topic of considerable academic focus. Ghemawat (2010), for example, suggested that one of five adjustments to corporate strategy directions post the 2008–2010 global economic crisis should be communication activity focussed on organisational identity and reputation, especially given the all-time low in the general reputation of business caused by that crisis. In a view relevant to a post-Covid-19 world, Ghemawat (2010) argued senior executives should spend more time managing relationships with governments as a result of their role as investors, customers, regulators, and tax collectors. Meznar and Nigh (1993) posited that a firm's legitimisation and survival could 'hinge' on its ability to adequately manage social and political stakeholder relationships. For Brønn and Brønn (2002), strategic issues management assists organisations to anticipate and respond to changes in their external environments and to identify and understand the 'forces that are at play…and how they shape [the organisation]' (p. 248).

Managing organisational participation in public policy issues debates is usually described as public affairs, broadly defined as policy and political discussions and interactions on public issues (Macnamara, 2012). Such interactions take place in the Habermasian concept of the public sphere which describes how public opinion should be formed in a civil society (Moloney, 2009, p. 447). This happens in a particular social, political, and economic context: 'accelerated pluralism, where organisations and groups seek advantage for their values, behaviours and material interests over their competitors' (Moloney, 2009, p. 460). Such activity follows monitoring of an organisation's business environment issues management through a combination of government relations, professional communication, and corporate citizenship strategies to 'influence public policy, build a strong reputation and find common ground with stakeholders' (Public Affairs Council, 2014).

That is, public affairs is essentially about political action by organisations as social actors who seek to influence public policy in their favour (see Moloney, 2009, pp. 442–444). Among the benefits of public affairs activity are protecting organisations from perceived threats of new policies or regulations, or from adverse comments by politicians, protecting reputation, and lessening the possibility of adverse action being taken by governments or regulators (Thomson & John, 2007).

Many scholars position public affairs in the non-market environment and study how organisations apply the practice whether they are a commercial business, non-government organisation (NGO), activist group, or government agency (Turnbull, 2001; Griffin et al., 2001; Harris & Moss, 2001; Moloney, 2009; Baines & Viney, 2010; Deng et al., 2010). These studies focus on how public affairs functions as a communication specialisation for the professional communication practice of managing public policy and political issues and relationships with community partners.

Communication practitioners specialise in public affairs either as commercial lobbyists or for industry associations, activist and community groups, NGOs, corporations, and government agencies (see, for a political context, Blumler, 2001). Heath and Ni (2010) noted that public affairs staff work with senior management to shape, define, and guide an organisation to 'manage itself in troubled waters, including engagement with key stakeholders and stakeseekers' (p. 564). Heath and Ni (2010) argued that this activity 'needs to be responsive and reflective, considering not only [an organisation's] interests but how others' interests are important to organisational and societal success' (p. 564). This involves managing a complex interface with government and non-government stakeholders to make sense of how external relationships impinge on organisational autonomy, and make sure decision-makers clearly hear and understand organisational interests (Harris & Moss, 2001). In this way, public affairs is a functional descriptor for issues management.

In their discussion of organisations and social contracts, Meznar and Nigh (1993, p. 31) argued that public affairs ensures an organisation's legitimacy by

influencing legislation affecting corporate activities;

influencing society by attempting to change the shared understanding between business and society, or to change society's perception of the organisation's behaviour;

influencing the organisation to comply with social contract items codified in law; and

scanning the environment to identify actual and potential gaps between society's expectations and corporate actions, and promoting changes in behaviour to comply with social norms.

Public affairs activities, sometimes also described as political strategy or communication (see, for example, Blumler, 2001; Deng et al., 2010), make newsworthy copy for journalists. For example, the resolution of debates about revisions to taxation codes, the imposition of new regulations, or the adverse impact of industrial development on the natural environment, ultimately impact on how an organisation goes about its business and provide scope for journalists' inquiring minds.

Differentiating tactical and strategic communication

This view of external organisational environments is key to understanding the role of strategic communication, and to differentiating between tactical and strategic communication—a view strengthened by Bach and Allen's (2010) comment that in order to shape their non-market environments, organisations need to be participants in the debates that play out in that space. Bach (2007) noted in this context that

> [n]on-market matters, such as reputation, the ability to work with NGOs, the capability to foresee relevant government actions and even to shape policy—these are all having an immense impact at a time when most companies are not even thinking about nonmarket strategy.
>
> *(Bach, 2007, Interview in Management-Issues online)*

Bach and Allen (2010) argued that most corporations take their non-market environments as a given, but that the 'next frontier' in strategic management was deliberately to shape the non-market environment, and create new market opportunities and lasting competitive advantage through a carefully crafted non-market strategy. This argument has direct implications for making a formal link between strategic business plans and communication strategy.

Brønn and Brønn (2002) described revisions to how an organisation views itself, its relationships, and its place in the external environment as an enormous challenge. Cornelissen (2005) argued that recommendations by strategic communicators on organisational responses to political issues, reputation protection, crises, and long-range positioning, are about advancing top-level strategic goals and objectives, rather than about implementing tactics. Gregory (2000) and Ströh (2006, 2007) have similarly argued for a differentiation between tactical practice and strategic considerations. In Grunig's (2009) view, communication practitioners working in the symbolic, interpretive paradigm of marketing communication generally believe publics can be persuaded by messages that change their cognitive representations, an approach that devotes excessive attention to the tactical role of communication in negotiating meaning by emphasising messages, publicity, media relations, and media effects. A contrasting strategic management, behavioural paradigm builds relationships with stakeholders. This paradigm facilitates two-way communication and dialogue and includes a framework of research and listening, as a result of which messages reflect the information needs of publics as well as the advocacy needs of organisations.

Issues management as strategic practice

Identifying current and emerging issues about which an organisation needs to be concerned is the primary step in decision-making about strategic communication directions. Argenti, Howell, and Beck (2005) argued that decisions about strategic communication are driven by issues related to regulatory imperatives, organisational complexities, and the need to increase credibility. This reflects the summary of scholars' definitions of issues analysis reported by Bigelow et al. (1993), who noted that issues analysis is prominent in discussions of organisational responses to environmental turbulence, corporate political strategy, and corporate social responsiveness. Management scholars (see, for example, Ghemawat, 2010; Bach & Allen, 2010) stress the need for important issues such as corporate reputation, values, and identity to be dealt with in a strategic way, as did Vasquez (1996) when he argued issue development public relations practitioners engaged in boundary spanning 'out of concern for an organisation's values, issues, images, and identity' (p. 73).

Scholarly discussion of issues identification, analysis, and management is usually confined to commercial business contexts, but they are also preoccupations of government agencies, non-government organisations, and in the not-for-profit sector. Bigelow et al. (1993) noted that issue discussions could occur in arenas other than governmental ones, such as bargaining with local communities or intersectoral collaborations. Dougall (2008) argued that contemporary issues management was 'much more than a defensive process useful to corporations' (p. 10) and that

> [t]he shared concerns of stakeholders and other interested publics—advocacy organisations, non-government organisations, government departments and agencies, the news media and opinion leaders—bring issues to life and keep them on the public agenda.
>
> *(Dougall, 2008, p. 10)*

For example, a business organisation might engage in issues management to deal with calls for greater workplace safety rules, a government agency to deal with reckless driving by young men, a charity about the need for funds to support medical research, or politicians to build support for party policies or government decisions.

Heath (2001) linked issues management, which he described as a partner to public relations, to strategic business planning and management. In this role, issues management 'understood' public policy

> and communicates to foster understanding, accuracy and satisfaction as well as to minimise conflict. ...It scans, identifies, tracks, monitors, and analyses issues to determine which strategic planning, ethical, and communication options meet the challenges facing the organisation.
>
> *(Heath, 2001, p. 36)*

Many scholars regard issues management as strategic rather than tactical (Bach & Allen, 2010; Ghemawat, 2010; Heath & Palenchar, 2009; Jaques, 2009a, 2009b; Tench, Verhoeven, & Zerfass, 2009; Dougall, 2008; Porter, 2008; van Riel & Frombrun, 2008; Ströh, 2006, 2007; Argenti & Forman, 2002, Gregory, 2000; Lauzen, 1997).

Jaques (2009a) argued that not every issue is strategic, but that all issues management should be strategic in its approach and implementation, and that the practice is a strategic, executive activity (Jaques, 2012).

Issues management, then, is a strategic process by which organisations identify, analyse, and deal with issues that are important to them to help plan and manage responses. In this formal process issues are identified and prioritised early so that organisational resources can be mobilised to 'develop and implement practical plans in order to achieve planned, positive outcomes' (Jaques, 2010, p. 436). Such plans include both strategic and tactical elements of issue responses (Jaques, 2007). The question is, however, whether practitioners actually operationalise issues management as a strategic activity. The research suggests they are struggling to do that.

Avoiding surprises

Van Riel and Frombrun (2008) listed marshalling resources to understand issues and prepare to address them as the second activity in issues management. By doing that, an organisation can make timely responses to issues so that it can 'dictate its own course rather than having its course dictated by events' (Guth & Marsh, 2006, p. 204). Similarly, Bigelow et al. (1993) noted that in the traditional view of issue life cycles, organisations lost considerable decision-making discretion if they waited to respond to an issue until legislation and regulations to deal with it are prepared. In their view, stakeholders, new facts about an issue, and mismanagement of an issue can 'catapult an issue to the forefront of the public agenda' (Bigelow et al., 1993, p. 22).

An objective of issues management is to reduce the possibility of 'strategic surprises' (Brønn & Brønn, 2002, p. 250). Wartick and Rude (1985) regarded issues management as an early warning system for potential environmental threats and opportunities that helps minimise surprises associated with social and political change. Thus, issues management could be applied to public policy, social, and strategic issues. It is this focus on issues management that makes it a political activity.

An issues management process that identifies emerging threats to organisational reputation can lead to changes in corporate behaviour, an ability to detect issues and develop responses while issues are emerging, enhanced organisational credibility, and can help organisations avoid serious mistakes (Wartick & Rude, 1985). However, Harrison (2011) warned that issues needed to be defined in terms of their impact on an organisation as this focussed attention on a real problem.

Issues management as multifunctional practice

In professional practice, issues management is most often led by a senior in-house strategic communicator in an environmental scanning role that identifies and analyses external and internal issues for senior management to understand the opportunities and threats they pose. This interpretation of issues from an organisation's external environment is often described as boundary spanning, which Lauzen (1997) regarded as a unique contribution to the issue-analysis.

However, while senior communication counsel lead issues identification, analysis, and management efforts, other organisational experts like lawyers, accountants, and production and planning managers, and sometimes external consultants, contribute. In this way, issues management is multidisciplinary. Thus, issues management is a multifunctional discipline that amalgamates

> organisational functions and responsive culture that blends strategic business planning, issue monitoring, best-practice standards of corporate responsibility, and dialogic communication needed to foster a supportive climate between each organisation and those people who can affect its success and which are affected by its operations.
>
> *(Heath & Palenchar, 2009, pp. 8–9)*

Moloney (2006), Dougall (2008), and Harrison (2011) also took a multifunctional view of issues management. Moloney (2006) described the practice as teamwork involving other organisational specialists like lawyers, engineers, planners, and marketers. The communicator's role in this team is 'external research of the operating environment' (Moloney, 2006, p. 37), the focus of issues management. Moloney (2006) also regarded the multidisciplinary approach to issues management as a dialogic practice and notes that this may be a result of the adoption of stakeholder involvement and corporate social responsibility practice in some business sectors.

Issues management requires research expertise, mindfulness, and a 'rich and current understanding' of the organisation's socio-political environment and the industry in which it operates (Dougall, 2008, p. 10). It also requires an ability to advocate with senior managers, and across organisational boundaries so it is, then, a complex discipline for which one person is unlikely to have all the required attributes (Dougall, 2008). Harrison (2011) argued that an issue rarely had a simple, single dimension and that therefore the definition of an issue needed to be agreed with a usually cross-functional management team.

While these points might be described as a normative view involving a dialogic approach to issues management, Moloney (2006) has argued that issues management could be against the public interest, especially when it involves a business, or an industry association, lobbying against a regulatory policy wanted by an elected government. However, Moloney notes that this problem is diluted by a general public competition of ideas in which pressure groups counterargue the business case put, and so alert public opinion and government.

Roper and Toledano (2005) took a similar critical approach to issues management. They argue that the dominant view of issues management typically involves proactive identification, and subsequent 'defusing', of problems before they escalate, and that it is closely linked to the development of public policy. However, in their critical view from what they describe as 'the edge,' contemporary issues management should also be concerned with a wider range of stakeholders and issues than those involving economic matters; it should include considerations about the environmental and social sustainability of organisations (Roper & Toledano, 2005, p. 480).

Responding to issues

How organisations actually deal with issues involves decisions about appropriate response strategies. The key to doing this is to identify the issues that need attention early and work out how they can be used in an organisation's 'strategic guidance system' (Heath & Palenchar, 2009, p. 89).

Heugens et al. (2004, cited in van Riel & Frombrun, 2008) argued that such decisions depend on the degree of activism surrounding an issue and the time available to respond, and include an organisation's ability to advocate a position, engage in dialogue, remain silent, or engage in crisis communication if an issue has developed to that stage. Heugens et al. (2004) suggested, for example, that when public activism on an issue is high, and there is no urgency to communicate, organisations should engage in dialogue with activists. Bigelow et al. (1993) pursue a similar theme when they argued in the context of issue evolution that well-informed stakeholders may become involved in an issue before others become aware of it. In their thesis, stakeholders engage and disengage in issues at different stages and that the path of an issue may be affected by this.

In context of the discussion in this book, issues management is more than the delivery of messages to politicians or journalists: it is about understanding issues, building and developing them, and presenting them to support an organisation's contributions to public debate (Thomson & John, 2007). Issues management reflects strategic thinking, the key to successful organisational performance in 'turbulent' environments (Brønn & Brønn, 2002, p. 249). That leads to a consideration of the dynamic nature of issues.

Issues dynamics

While an organisation's immediate market-environment communication needs cannot be ignored, the decisions practitioners take about mid- to long-term strategy are, or should be, influenced by their analyses of issues beyond the tactical day-to-day requirements of marketing communication. This presents a professional practice challenge because issues are not static and evolve, sometimes slowly (Bigelow et al., 1993, see especially pp. 19–22) as an organisation responds, or as publics, the news media, and governments give them attention (Hallahan,

2001). Guth and Marsh (2006) located issues in the evolution of public opinion which they argue forms after a public debate leads to consensus and public policy. That is, public opinion begins to evolve when an issue is injected into public consensus and public and private debates over the issue ensue. Bigelow et al. (1993) described this as the 'path' of an issue that is affected as stakeholders engage and disengage in an issues debate (p. 22). Harrison (2011) described issues as dynamic. Heath and Palenchar (2009) argued that as those involved in a dialogue advocate opinions, facts, evaluation, and conclusions, issues 'take on content' (p. 117).

Issues dynamics are usually discussed in the context of issue life cycles that describe the way in which issues move, broadly, from public opinion formation, to policy formulation, to public policy implementation (see, for example, Harrison, 2011; Heath & Palenchar, 2009; Bigelow et al., 1993). Harrison (2011) noted that issue life cycles are more complex than simple diagrams showing how they work, but described four stages of a public issue life cycle in the context of an organisation's discretionary ability to influence discussion. As issues may evolve over weeks, or years, an organisation's ability to influence them as public concerns about an issue rise over time, declines. Harrison (2011) suggested that there are four stages in an issue's life cycle

- define the issue
- shape the debates
- limit/contain the issue
- shape regulations, standards, plans

In the first two stages as public expectation change, organisations' discretionary ability to define and shape issues is high; that ability declines in the last two stages as an issue is politicised and 'the opportunity to take the initiative is removed...as formal government actions now control the outcome' (Harrison, 2011, p. 786).

Heath and Palenchar (2009) pointed out that issues identification is difficult because of the complexities of issues and organisations and that variables affect both the emergence and growth of an issue. That means analysis becomes more demanding when

- positions are ambiguous and complex
- many issues are being addressed and many participants are promoting their views
- an issue has not been well defined

So, as issues are dynamic, the ways in which they are framed, and the impact they have on organisations, alter in the context of debates about them. Heath and Palenchar (2009) noted that issues dynamics were not simply those that occurred when an organisation and an activist group engaged in debate but also occurred in industries, between activist groups, and between government agencies. In this

> array of players, issues managers are wise to be concerned about understanding the dynamics of the various publics and the dynamics that motivate them.
>
> *(Heath and Palenchar, 2009, p. 120)*

Hallahan (2001) also argued that issues are complex and dynamic and involve more than merely a dispute between two parties, and that to effectively deal with an issue, organisations and their managers need to develop an understanding of claims made and the context in which a particular issue evolves. Brønn and Brønn (2002) noted that the complexity of an organisation's strategic orientation results from the interaction of many factors characterised by 'uncertainty, causal ambiguity and the presence of multiple stakeholders' (pp. 247–248).

In their critical analysis of the linearity inherent in traditional issue life cycles, Bigelow et al. (1993) dealt with issues dynamics by arguing that issues may be at different stages of evolution depending on the perspectives and activities of each stakeholder. They argue that an issue's evolution begins before stakeholders have established positions and that public issues may be resolved in arenas other than governmental ones. Thus, the resolution of public policy issues is more complex than that for other strategic issues (in their example, seeking a limited number of stakeholders' support for a strategic decision to introduce a new product; see Bigelow et al., 1993, p. 21). In their typology of issues evolution, Bigelow et al. (1993) suggested that not all issues move sequentially through all the stages implicit in a traditional issue life cycle. This is because issues 'may be buffeted by a number of forces outside the control of any one organisation or stakeholder' (p. 21), causing deviations from the traditional issue life cycle model's linear, sequential path. These dynamic forces can be caused by facts, stakeholders, other issues, and an inability to resolve an issue. They argue,

> new facts and other issues may create a need for stakeholders to reinterpret issues and subsequently redefine their positions. The inflexibility of some stakeholder positions may stymie attempts to achieve resolution.
>
> *(Bigelow et al., 1993, p. 23)*

Bigelow et al.'s (1993) typology of issues evolution suggests that some issues follow a recursive path 'cycling back and forth through the stages' of the traditional issues cycle, and may never be resolved (p. 24). The evolution of other issues skips stages, or is interrupted by new facts, stakeholder actions, or other issues attracting attention. Their typology also proposes that some issues are enduring because of an added complexity that makes resolution elusive. For a recursive issue, such complexity may reflect stakeholder diversity, the cost of solutions, or the range of values about ethical dimensions of the issue. Bigelow et al. (1993) argued their typology challenged traditional life cycle models that suggest all issues follow similar paths. They contend that issues reflect distinct dynamics that are more complex than issue life cycle models suggest. This approach is reflected in Heath's and Palenchar's (2009) view that no organisation can dominate the course that an issue takes, and that issue resolution becomes dialogic (in Heath's terms, this is rhetoric as he regards communication as rhetorical practice; see Heath, 2001, pp. 31–50). When different people in an organisation's non-market environment have different levels of knowledge about an issue, the organisation is obliged to assert its point of view and offer reasons for why it holds that view (Heath & Palenchar, 2009).

Lauzen (1997) argued that the knowledge of the worldviews and values of internal and external organisational constituencies that communication counsellors develop as a result of their environmental scanning, make a unique contribution to issues analysis and management. In other words, understanding issues and their importance to an organisation contributes to how the organisation is managed. Defining issues management as a strategic practice in which organisations attempt to influence public policy (Gillions, 2009) reinforces the notion of organisations as social and political actors.

So, the foregoing discussion enables a hypothesis that the dynamic nature of issues impacts on an organisation's decision-making about strategic communication responses to non-market issues debates. In this hypothesis, issues are independent variables on strategic communication planning decisions, an example of contingency theory.

Contingency theory and dynamic issues

Contingency theory, an aspect of general systems theory, holds that 'one thing depends on something else' (Hodge, Anthony, & Gales, 2003, p. 17). This concept is the source of the metaphorical butterflies from Brazil. In a management context, however, contingency theory is used to argue that organisational structure depends on the context the organisation faces.

Applied to professional communication, contingency theory suggests that practitioners select positions and strategies to react to internal and external factors that apply to an organisation (Kang & Cheng, 2008). In their discussion of contingency theory, Cameron, Cropp, and Reber (2001) argued that an organisation's stance on an issue may change according to the dynamics of a situation. This is the core of their argument that contingency theory qualifies the excellence theory of public relations because an organisation's stance on an issue constantly moves from complete advocacy of a position to accommodation of a public demand. Mitrook, Parish, and Seltzer (2008) described this as a logical extension of the excellence theory of public relations. Pang, Jin, and Cameron (2010) argued that contingency theory liberates communication strategists to think outside the box and engage in strategic analysis.

Contingency theory is not an uncontested lens through which to view either management or communication decision-making (see, for example, Donaldson, 2006, for a detailed discussion of arguments for and against using contingency theory in management and Macnamara, 2012, especially at pp. 191–195, for a discussion in a public relations context). Nevertheless, some scholars have argued, in the context of applying contingency theory to communication practice, that independent external and internal variables do influence decision-making, which is a dependent variable (see, for example, Cancel et al., 1997; Murphy, 2000; Reber & Cameron, 2003; Shin et al., 2006; Pang, Yin, & Cameron, 2010).

Contingency theory is thus a useful tool for understanding how dynamic political, social, and economic issues debates impact on organisations' strategic communication decision-making.

Contingency theory and organisational structure

The use of contingency theory in management scholarship grew out of scholars' application of general systems theory to better understand organisational structures (Hatch & Cunliffe, 2006; Donaldson, 2006). In this view, organisations are complex systems involving dynamically interacting parts in which a change in one part can affect the behaviour of other parts (Beinhocker, 1999).

Hodge et al. (2003) argued that contingency theory helps to model how organisations' constituent parts and external factors interact to achieve organisational goals and that these complex systems are path dependent. Beinhocker (1999) held that random changes in complex systems produce unrelated outcomes. In this strategic systems model (Hodge et al., 2003) an organisation's structure is contingent on the contexts it faces. These complex systems are 'path dependent' (Beinhocker, 1999, p. 49), meaning that, like the mythical Brazilian butterfly, random changes produce unrelated outcomes. In this strategic systems model, an organisation's structure is contingent on the contexts it faces. Mackey (2009, p. 60) noted that many complex contexts support, enable, change, and threaten a system, or organisation.

Management scholars use contingency theory to explain how contexts, or internal and external variables, impact on organisation structures and behaviour. In one view, contingency theory is the essence of organisation theory (Donaldson, cited in Hatch & Cunliffe, 2006). Contingency theory's primary contribution to organisation theory is to illustrate there are many ways to successfully organise and enumerate the possibilities and their consequences (Hatch & Cunliffe, 2006).

Contingency theory and professional communication

The argument that complex systems such as organisational structures are affected by internal and external variables led scholars to apply contingency theory to communication practice. Kang and Cheng (2008) argued that contingency theory helped explain the influence of variables on how practitioners select a stance and communication strategy that is best for an organisation. Their research found, for example, that legal and regulatory factors were contingent variables affecting issues management. Other public relations scholars have used contingency theory to argue the limitations of the two-way symmetrical model of public relations theorised by J.E. Grunig et al. (2001), and to describe how practice moves along a continuum of pure advocacy to accommodation. They use contingency theory to understand the internal and external dynamics that could affect the stance an organisation takes on a particular issue (Pang, Yin, & Cameron, 2010). Cancel et al. (1997) argued that strategic communication was practised on a continuum from pure advocacy to pure accommodation depending on the circumstances, or contingent variables, the organisation faced. Research grounded in contingency theory found that 87 internal and external variables impact on practitioners' abilities to do their jobs (see, for example, Pang, Yin, & Cameron, 2010).

Brønn and Brønn (2002) hinted at another aspect of issues as contingent factors in decision-making: issues management, they argued, was a 'fundamental revision' (p. 252) of how organisations view themselves, their relationships with stakeholders, and their places in their external environments.

However, these discussions of contingency theory have focussed on the tactical level not the strategic level of communication practice, despite the continual inclusion of the term 'strategic' in most scholarly works. A longer term strategic view would take stronger account of the dynamics of issues debates over the mid- and long-terms, including the potential for other issues to emerge and how they might affect professional communication planning decisions.

To advance from the tactical, contingency theory can be used to help understand how social, political, and economic issues act as independent variables that influence organisational decisions on strategic communication directions. That is, while communicators must deal with an organisation's day-to-day needs, the decisions they take about mid- to long-term strategy are influenced by their analyses of the dynamics of issues beyond a tactical, current market environment approach.

Issue categories and communication decisions

To determine which issue categories could impact on strategic communication decisions, the research that informed the discussion in this book included a two-step qualitative content analysis of selected communication and business literature. This analysis identified a list of independent contingent variables.

The first step in the analysis identified a list of external variables that influence communication, and the definitions of them, via a content analysis of the works of Shin et al. (2006), Argenti et al. (2005), Ghemawatt (2010), Bach and Allen (2010), Reber and Cameron (2003), and Porter (2008). Porter's (2008) analysis of the forces that shape industry competition was included because those forces apply specifically in the market environment (Bach & Allen, 2010) and thus have communication implications. These six works were chosen because they represent both communication and management literature dealing with aspects of contingency theory and communication. The external variables were

- political/cultural/social environment which includes political social support for business
- an industry's environment, including competition, resources, and whether the industry was changing or static
- external threats like government regulation; potential for litigation and damaging publicity; a scarred reputation; activist causes
- the power of publics which includes past media coverage of that public, its willingness to dilute its cause, community perception of the public
- regulatory imperatives, including new regulation
- organisational complexity which means size and culture, its moral convictions, the urgency of situations a business faces; more markets, customers, products, services, employees, suppliers, investors, and involvement in global markets
- need to increase credibility
- identity and reputation, meaning clear, well-understood values, respect for diversity, strong leadership, or low business reputation and perception of executives
- composition of an organisation's non-market environment: for example, its regulatory environment, multiple political, cultural, and socio-economic stakeholder interests, activism
- actors and the issues they advance

Porter's five competitive forces: bargaining power of suppliers, threat of new entrants to the industry, rivalry among competitors, bargaining power of buyers, the threat of substitute products or services.

A content analysis of the authors' descriptions of the characteristics of these variables identified nine keywords that identified the broad socio-economic and political issues scholars are most likely to argue influence strategic decision-making. These were: advocacy, competition, complexity (of an organisation), credibility, socio-economic/cultural; political; regulatory environment; relationships; values.

None of these issue categories can be dealt with successfully in the short term; all require consistent long-term communication efforts to position organisational attitudes towards them. That is, the imperative is for strategic, not tactical, communication that recognises organisational non-market environments as the external space in which dynamic issues debates occur, and that organisations are social and political actors when they advocate positions on issues.

5

DECISION-MAKING AND COMMUNICATION STRATEGY

Decisions on professional communication strategic directions are influenced by internal discursive debates about the implications of external public policy issues on an organisation's performance. By adopting concepts from management and sociological research, scholars can explain how external dynamic issues debates in a non-market environment, and internal discourses, influence continuing organisational participation in those debates.

Scholars often call for professional communication researchers to engage with the theory and practice of other disciplines, especially management, broader communication theory, and social theory. The use of Hendry's (2002) concept of strategic management decision-making as a highly politicised, discursive social practice in this book is an example of theory from another discipline being applied to professional communication. This work provides a framework for understanding decisions about communication strategy directions. Another is sociological theory, used here to explain the influence of dynamic issues debates on communication strategy directions. That is possible by explaining dynamic issues debates through the spectrum of Giddens' (1986) structuration theory, which holds that 'structure' is influenced by the 'actions' of 'agents' and, in turn, influences them. Applying that theory to professional communication decision-making enables a construct that views formal decision-making occurring within organisations (social structures) and involving agents (senior practitioners and dominant coalitions); these structures influence decisions and are themselves influenced by the dynamics of issues debates.

With the exception of a growing number of critical scholars, especially in New Zealand and Europe, much of the research and teaching of professional communication practice has been grounded in what might called the North American School based on a dominant paradigm (Brown, 2010) situated in J.E. Grunig and colleagues' (1992) Excellence Study, and J.E. Grunig and Hunt's

DOI: 10.4324/9781003177340-5

(1984) four models of public relations (see for example, J.E. Grunig's discussion in Heath, 2001).

That paradigm holds that so-called excellent public relations is symmetrical. That is, excellent public relations engages in a two-way dialogue that involves mutual interaction between organisations and their stakeholders that involves understanding and respect. In this way, organisations can build relationships with stakeholders, improve understanding, and change organisational behaviour. Excellence theory regards public relations as managerial (J.E. Grunig & White, 1992). This worldview contrasts with the other three models: press agentry, public information, and two-way asymmetrical public relations, each of which is regarded as practice designed to change the behaviour of publics, but not that of the organisation. Press agentry describes a practice that seeks media publicity in 'almost any way possible' (J.E. Grunig & White, 1992, p. 39). The public information model is an approach that disseminates only positive information about an organisation. Two-way asymmetrical communication means using research to develop messages designed to persuade target publics to behave as the organisation wants. Mackey (2003) described the paradigm as the 'touchstone of much public relations theoretical work' (p. 1) and Brown (2010) noted it had become a watershed for public relations scholarship and for how the profession viewed the practice.

However, while the paradigm may still be the normative approach in public relations scholarship and teaching, it is not unchallenged, especially its implied assertion that symmetrical communication is some kind of utopian state in which all participants in communication always have equal power in the resolution of issues. For example, Hallahan (2010) argued that while excellence theory assumes public relations is ideally practised as two-way symmetrical communication, the ability of social media in particular to empower publics makes symmetry 'increasingly improbable' and that 'calls for symmetry might be irrelevant' (p. 639). That is because two-way symmetrical communication assumes organisations and their publics communicate on equal knowledge and power terms, while excellence theory 'essentially argues that organisations should cede any power advantage to publics' (Hallahan, 2010, p. 638). In Hallahan's (2010) view, social media enhances the power of publics to the extent that it might exceed that of organisations. Other scholars (for example, Cancel et al., 1997; Shin et al., 2006; Reber & Cameron, 2003) have used contingency theory to argue the limitations of two-way symmetrical communication by demonstrating the impact of factors beyond symmetry on the ability of organisations to communicate with stakeholders.

Critics view the paradigm as positivist because it seeks to 'discover universal laws of cause and effect which apply across different times and contexts' (Daymon & Holloway, 2002, p. 7). This reflects the view that the paradigm focusses too much on what practitioners do (Gower, 2006). Critical scholars argue that this positivist stance, based on the 'laws' of symmetrical communication and excellence theory, ignores a demand for organisations to reflect environmental and social responsibilities, meaning professional communication is still linked to notions of power (Roper & Toledano, 2005). Critical scholars also argue that symmetry's insensitivity to power differentials between organisations and stakeholders sets the public relations ethical bar too low (Brown, 2010, p. 284). Writing in a special issue of *Public Relations Review* dealing with applying sociology to public relations scholarship and practice, Bentele and Wehmeier (2007) argued the need to 'confront the empiricist and positivist tradition' (p. 294) in public relations research and argued that the discipline could be regarded as a 'functional social system' (p. 299).

Critical and interpretivist scholarship has been concerned with researching, understanding, and explaining the social, ethical, and political implications of professional communication (see, for example, Daymon & Holloway, 2002; Durham, 2005; Falkheimer, 2007; Gower, 2006; Moloney, 2006; Motion & Leitch, 2007; Roper & Toledano, 2005; L'Etang, 2005; Sandhu, 2009; Ihlen, et al., 2009; Brown, 2010; and Sison, 2010).

One aspect of this critical and interpretivist approach involves calls from scholars like Gower (2006), Sandhu (2009), and Frandsen and Johansen (2010) for public relations scholarship to utilise the latest thinking reported in management literature to inform its research, especially in relation to strategy. Public relations scholars have, of course, used theoretical paradigms from other disciplines, such as sociology, psychology, and management, and contingency theory from the physical and behavioural sciences, to help describe and explain professional practice.

Gower (2006), for example, argued that a focus on what practitioners do, rather than on the business drivers for practice, meant professional communication scholars had not kept pace with the evolution in the management literature's thinking about strategy. Gower (2006) argued that communication scholars and professionals should use management literature to update what they do, and how they do it. Frandsen and Johansen (2010) reflected that view by urging communication scholars and practitioners to engage with other disciplines to enhance their abilities to work with management leaders in a strategic way. Sandhu (2009) used institutional theory as an example of how communication scholars can use management approaches to research communication management and free their work 'from the iron cage of the excellence study' (p. 87). Those views are supported by Jaques' (2009a) argument that issues management, a communication practice that evolved as a business discipline to enable organisations to participate in, and respond to, discussions about public policy issues that affect them, ought to be better aligned with business strategic planning to enable them to work together. Others have argued that Giddens' (1986) structuration theory can be used to understand and explain how professional communication works and can be evaluated (see for example, Olufowote, 2003; Durham, 2005; Falkheimer, 2007 and 2009).

Critical scholars situate professional communication in the context of social theory (see, for example, Ihlen & Verhoeven, 2009). They are concerned about notions of power and communication. In particular, they seek to understand how professional communication works, and how it influences society and is in turn influenced by society (see, for example, the discussion in Ihlen & van Ruler, 2009, esp. pp. 1–11). Moloney (2006) described public relations campaigns as 'professionally self-indulgent' (p. 131) and the practice as 'weak propaganda' (p. 165) because it involved a one-sided presentation of data and relied too much on press agentry and asymmetrical communication. For L'Etang (2005), critical scholarship involved critiquing not only policy but professional practice, especially when challenging and debating strategies of domination that are implicit in social, economic, and political structures. Communication strategy clearly works in such structures especially when it is used to advance organisational views on public policy issues in non-market environments.

These critical approaches to examining professional communication suggest another research dimension: investigating how and why decisions are made about strategic professional communication directions, especially those related to issues management, and what influences them. An important step in doing this is to use interpretive literature, freed from the strictures of symmetry and excellence theory, conceptualise strategic issues communication planning and implementation as discursive social practices, and explore decision-making in that context.

Issues communication planning as discursive social practice

The traditional academic approach to strategic management views a strategy as something an organisation has, and that is developed by senior managers in one-off decisions at specific times (Frandsen & Johansen, 2010). In that tradition, strategy is something people do. However, more recent scholarship has focussed on 'strategy as practice' by researching the complex micro processes and practices involved in daily organisational life (Frandsen & Johansen, 2010, p. 301).

Researching and writing a communication strategy is a social practice, an approach inspired by pragmatist philosophy and the work of Mintzberg and Giddens (Marchiori & Bulgacov, 2012; Frandsen & Johansen, 2010). In this approach,

> [s]trategy making is not a rational, analytic, disembodied, and asocial activity but an interactive and contextually situated type of behaviour.
>
> *(Frandsen & Johansen, 2010, p. 301)*

King (2010) gave this view an extra dimension by arguing that strategies are not static and 'may emerge in the interaction between reader/hearer response, situated context, and discursive patterns' (p. 23). Marchiori and Bulgacov (2012) made a similar point when they argued that strategy is communicational practice and that the dynamic between communication and strategy is recursive. That is, there are internal organisational debates about strategic directions and that once a strategy is determined, it in turn influences ongoing discussions about future directions.

J.E. Grunig (2009) moved towards this view when he held that the symbolic, interpretive paradigm of marketing communication generally devoted excessive attention to tactics by emphasising messages, publicity, media relations, and media effects, whereas a contrasting strategic management, behavioural paradigm builds relationships, and facilitates dialogue. These arguments about relationships and dialogue suggest discursive social practice and intentional decision-making.

Motion and Leitch (2009, 2007) used the work of Michel Foucault to suggest ways of problematising the role of professional communication as discourse that influenced the concepts and systems of thought that shaped how people thought about things. L'Etang (2005) noted the nature of public relations as a social practice; Berger's (2005) work suggested discursive social practice via his examination of how power relations in dominant coalitions affect practice.

Strategic decision-making is a form of social practice in which discourse is a central feature (Hendry, 2000). This contextualises strategic decisions as an aspect of the organisational discourses through which strategic thinking is linked to action (Hendry, 2000). That link is reflected in the definition of strategic communication advanced by Hallahan and colleagues (2007), who argued that it involved organisations acting as social actors who used persuasive, discursive, and relational communication.

Bach's and Allen's (2010) view that organisations need to carefully manage key social, political, and environmental issues, and relationships with the actors (stakeholders) who care about them, in their non-market environment, is a reflection of organisations engaging in discursive social practice when they research, write, and implement communication strategies. In a strategic sense, this practice is about mid- to long-term concerns because non-market issues and relationships play out beyond an immediate focus on customers, competitors, and suppliers, but nevertheless impact on the market environment (Bach & Allen, 2010). Helin, Jensen, and Sandström (2013) reflect the argument of organisations as social actors when they argue that corporations are political institutions like any other social entity. That is, they are purposeful actors engaged in rational and deliberate decision-making about strategic issues. J.E. Grunig's (2006) notion of strategic communication as a bridge between organisations and their stakeholders suggests the importance of its role in providing organisational responses to business needs and concerns as Argenti et al. (2005), Cornelissen (2005), Sandhu (2009), Zerfass and Huck (2007), and Zerfass (2009) also argue.

Heath (2001, 2009) viewed professional communication practice as an essentially rhetorical action, or as he describes it, suasive discourse. In that construct, a rhetorical perspective of communication acknowledges a two-way discourse and that rhetoric, which he describes as strategic, is the ultimate social process. This social process involves the expression of opinions, preferences, and behaviours that create and maintain community.

The notion of strategic communication as a discursive social practice is reinforced by the view that communication practice is strategic because of its procedural and interactive nature. Thus,

[s]trategies are essentially processes of interaction and construction of meaning whose expressiveness comes from communication and language. As a process, communication has a movement itself, and once it becomes a continuous process it cannot have a defined beginning, middle or end.

(Marchiori and Bulgacov, 2012, p. 203)

Raupp and Hoffjann (2012) reflect this view of interaction and building meaning when they argue that communication strategies are processes that help organisations to structure and lend meaning to their perceived environments.

Management theory holds that decision-making involves internal discourses over strategic directions. That view applies equally to strategic communication decision-making about advocacy and responses to issues debates in an organisation's non-market environment.

Strategic communication and decision-making

Hackley (2000) posited that organisations are instruments of control and order in which systems ensure that business goals are met by selecting skills, controlling conflict, and managing how people work and the conditions under which they do so. Tsetsura's (2010) view was that by their very existence institutions strive to control human conduct by setting preferred patterns of conduct.

Bower and David (2007) noted that strategy is iterative and 'crafted step by step, as managers at all levels…commit resources to, policies, programs, people, and facilities' (p. 74). Strategic communication decisions are taken in this context: that is, they are designed to support an organisation to meet its business goals and objectives, and they are made in a controlled and orderly fashion in accordance with management processes, or preferred patterns of conduct. The decision-making process normally involves discussions about directions with managers outside the formal communication team, including approving the strategy and allocating resources to implement it.

In their discussion of public relations and management decision-making, White and Dozier (1992) argued that strategic management decisions affected organisational survival and growth, involved significant changes in direction, and needed to be based on 'adequate perceptions' of the organisation's environment. High-level strategic decisions required abstract thinking by senior managers and set a challenge for communicators to

understand and respect the qualitative differences between concrete operational decisions they routinely make as technicians and abstract strategic decisions they must make as managers.

(White and Dozier, 1992, p. 98)

Strategic communication decisions thus involved many senior people in an organisation and required substantial communication between them, negotiation and bargaining just to define and understand problems.

Raupp and Hoffjann (2012) noted that because communication decisions take account of the rationalities of communication management and the organisation, every communication decision has a strategic character. In their view, communication decisions are not objective but depend on, and are influenced by, organisational and societal cultures. Strategy making means taking conscious decisions that involve calculated choices in which goals are linked to possibilities of action. Initially there is no difference between strategies and decisions and

> [e]very decision is not only connected to previous decisions, but is oriented to specific rationalities and thus reproduces the organisation and its structures...At the same time every decision is the basis—in a structuration-theory perspective a 'resource'...for subsequent decisions.
>
> *(Raupp and Hoffjann, 2012, p. 150)*

Berger's (2005) critical, and seminal, work on public relations and power outlined the complexities that impact on the decision-making abilities of communication managers once they interact with dominant coalitions as the central decision-making groups in organisations. Berger (2005) saw several dominant coalitions in organisations and suggested that decision-making about communication strategy is less than organised, and that communication decision-making is often chaotic and constrained and influenced by internal power relationships. This interaction hints at the dynamic process advanced by Giddens (1986) in which 'structure' is influenced by the 'actions' of 'agents' and, in turn, influences them.

Hendry (2002) also argued that strategic decision-making in organisations, while purposive and structured, is often highly politicised and senior managers invoke strategic decisions to influence the actions of colleagues. Hatch and Cunliffe (2006) viewed decision-making through a political frame in which organisational power takes account of the interests of the subcultures, factions, and discourses in organisations. That means that where differences occur over goals and tactics, power and politics influence decisions. This is what Burkart (2009) described as practical discourse in which the object is to justify interests and decisions and value judgements are discussed. This practical discourse is echoed in the warning that Bower and David (2007) gave that organisational decision-making has vital consequences for strategy because decisions by managers at all levels of an organisation critically affect how strategy evolves, as do external forces like customers and capital markets. This reflects the professional communication tasks of environmental scanning and interpretive boundary spanning in which senior practitioners should engage in to inform the analyses of external issues, and their potential impacts on organisations, they present at the strategy decision-making table.

Hendry's (2002) concept of strategic decision-making is proposed in a management context, but his arguments can be applied to strategic communication decision-making. First, he sees decision-making as part of an organisational discourse using language-based communication. Second, he regards strategy as a form of social practice. Third, he links strategic thinking to action. Thus, a decision takes its meaning from the social practice and discourse in which it is located, and

> [i]n pursuit of their aims, strategists do all the things that feature in the traditional definitions: they evolve shared perspectives, create plans and enact ploys. Intentionally or otherwise they participate in the social creation of patterns and the positioning of their organisation's product-market offerings, and they observe such patterns and positions in other organisations.
>
> *(Hendry, 2002, p. 970)*

This argument also reflects the strategic communication planning process of environmental scanning, research, situation analysis, and the program design and implementation decisions that follow. That is, a communication strategy is developed through organisational social practice in which senior practitioners and dominant coalitions engage in discourses about the strategic implications of issues and how they should be addressed; this strategic thinking leads to decisions about the actions for which the strategy provides direction.

The point Bradley et al. (2013) made in a management context about the need to get agreement on required essential decisions, and the criteria on which those decisions will be made, before a strategy is created, is also vital for developing a communication strategy. Equally important in creating a communication strategy is the argument that strategists need to be sure that an organisation is willing to act on a strategy. Bradley et al. (2013) argued that creating a strategy is not a 'rigid, box-checking exercise' but an 'inherently messy' journey that 'embodies the spirit of debate and engagement' (p. 37). This view reflects Heath and Palenchar's (2009) point that debates about issues are routine in business management and communication practice when they argue that

> [s]haping keen insights into good strategies requires deep interpersonal engagement and debate from senior executives, as well as the ability to deal with ambiguity in charged and often stressful circumstances. When would-be strategists overlook these dynamics, they cover the essentials in name only…[and]…miss opportunities and threats, or create great paper strategies that remain unfinished in practice.
>
> *(Bradley et al., 2013, p. 37)*

In the sense that these approaches require discussion and debate about the criteria for decisions and agreement on whether the organisation will act on a strategy, they are an illustration of discursive social practice in decision-making. They also reflect Hendry's (2000) triadic conceptualisation of strategic decision-making: first that it is part of organisational discourse, second that strategy is social practice, and third that strategic thinking is linked to action.

This is a discursive social practice in which strategic communication practitioners identify (or should identify) and analyse external and internal factors that have the potential to impact on their organisations in the mid to long terms, and options for addressing them are discussed. It is also inherently political and often a reactive practice that follows the results of ongoing issues identification and analysis—Jaques' (2009a, b) point about issues management being strategic.

Communication decisions and stakeholders

The communication and management disciplines both draw on stakeholder theory to explore how relationships with the people who are important to an organisation should be managed. Stakeholder theory holds that organisational decisions and actions affect others, and that organisations must bear responsibility for such decisions and actions (Fassin, 2012). The theory suggests organisations must act ethically and transparently, have consideration and respect for, and fairly treat, all stakeholders—employees, customers, stockholders, regulators, activists, pressure groups, and the news media (Fassin, 2012). Ackermann and Eden (2011) described managing relationships with stakeholders, a process that often involves competing demands, as one of the most important tasks of strategy making. Tullberg (2013) argued that managers needed to recognise stakeholder needs and wants because the basic practical idea of stakeholder theory was that success depended on smooth cooperation with stakeholders.

Heath's (2001, 2009) argument that professional communication is essentially rhetorical practice is included in Smudde's and Courtright's (2011) view of stakeholder management as holistic, inherently rhetorical and three dimensional: creating stakeholders, maintaining relationships with them, and improving relationships. Each is dealt with daily, inspires cooperation between an organisation and its stakeholders, and, in a dialogic sense, means organisations adjusting to stakeholder concerns. This means that '[n]ever taking stakeholders for granted is a given' (p. 143).

Normative descriptions of the high-level functions of senior communication managers include the view that strategic decisions follow the identification and analysis of problems facing an organisation and consideration of how communicators can create meanings about these with stakeholders. Defining problems involves senior practitioners engaging in environmental scanning by researching both market and non-market environments for issues that concern, or should concern, an organisation. Doing this means identifying not only immediate issues but those likely to occur in the mid and long terms. In a boundary-spanning role, senior practitioners interpret what issues mean for the organisation and coordinate externally directed (sometimes also internal) communication responses. Each step in these processes involves decision-making: what issues do we face? Which are important now—and will be in the future? What impact do, or would, they have on the organisation? What is the probability of them occurring? What do they mean?

Inherent in environmental scanning and boundary spanning is the need to identify organisational stakeholders and explain their roles in issue activation and participation in ongoing issues debates to an organisation's senior management. Steyn and Niemann (2010) described this as a mirror function in which communication strategists acquired information about societal issues and stakeholders, considered the consequences of them for the organisation's stakeholders and strategies, and fed this into the organisation's strategy development processes. Ackermann and Eden (2011) based their research into strategic stakeholder management on three themes: identifying who stakeholders are in a specific situation; exploring the impact of stakeholder dynamics; and

> determining how and when it is appropriate to intervene to alter or to develop the basis of an individual stakeholder's significance, which...is determined through in-depth consideration of [a] stakeholder's power to... influence the organisation's direction.
>
> *(Ackermann and Eden, 2011, p. 180)*

In this role, strategic communicators are the objective outsider (sometimes called an organisation's devil's advocate) advising senior management on risks to organisational reputation, consequences for strategies, and the need to align goals and strategies to societal and stakeholder values and norms (Steyn & Niemann, 2010).

Issues evolve, sometimes slowly (Bigelow et al., 1993), as an organisation itself raises them or responds to them, and as publics, the news media, and governments give them attention (Hallahan, 2001). The result is that public opinion often changes when an issue arises, meaning public and private debates about it are likely to occur. This path alters as organisational stakeholders engage and disengage in an issues debate (Bigelow et al., 1993) by advocating opinions, facts, evaluations, and conclusions (Heath & Palenchar, 2009). Schwarzkopf (2006) also dealt with this dynamic path and the need for equally dynamic decision-making by noting that

> as word of new issues spreads through the [stakeholder] network, the sense of risk concerning management's decisions may increase, requiring management to change the nature of its communications.
>
> *(Schwarzkopf, 2006, p. 337)*

Communication decisions, issues dynamics, and stakeholders

Building and sustaining relationships between an organisation and its stakeholders is the essence of Ledingham's (2003) general theory of public relations. This view of communication as a strategic tool that builds and maintains transactional, dynamic, and goal-oriented organisation and public relationships driven by the perceived needs and wants of interacting organisations and publics, requires adept decision-making that reflects the dynamic nature of issues debates. The first step in that decision-making is understanding what stakeholders want from the organisation, their interest base, how they are likely to work towards achieving it, and their power base (Ackermann & Eden, 2011). Reporting the results of his research on stakeholder risk perceptions of managerial decisions, Schwarzkopf (2006) echoed this by noting that management should understand stakeholders' views in general and that there should be outreach to stakeholders about their concerns before sensitive decisions must be made.

Phillips (2003) argued for descriptive research on how managers actually make decisions involving stakeholders, including those he described as derivative—groups whose actions and claims have potential beneficial or harmful effects on the organisation, including the news media.

In professional communication practice, making decisions about how to deal with stakeholders is part of strategic planning and issues identification and analysis. Nevertheless, management literature about dealing with stakeholders provides a context for how a senior communication manager would take strategic decisions about an organisation participating as a social actor in issues debates. For example, Spitzeck and Hansen (2010), writing in the context of corporate governance, defined three aspects of stakeholder theory. They note that a normative view of stakeholder theory grants intrinsic value to stakeholder claims because of the moral rights of anyone affected by organisational decisions. Thus, stakeholder dialogue is not strategic but open and deliberative coming close to Habermas' ideal speech situation. On the other hand, a descriptive stakeholder approach identifies and classifies organisational stakeholders without assigning any value statements regarding the legitimacy of their claims, while an instrumental view gives powerful stakeholders a voice to help ensure the organisation's success. An instrumental perspective conceptualises dialogue with stakeholders as strategic and oriented around organisational needs, risk management, or realising opportunities. Decisions about how to communicate strategically involve applying all three of these views of stakeholder theory. For example:

- Using a normative approach, an ethical senior communication manager who supported the notion of open and transparent dialogue would recognise that stakeholders have a legitimate role in issues debates and seek to understand their points of view, a basic tenet of stakeholder theory.
- Using the descriptive approach, a manager would identify and classify stakeholders as an important first step in deciding how to engage in that dialogue.
- Applying the instrumental view of stakeholder theory, a manager would decide how to engage stakeholders on issues that could affect an organisation's ability to achieve its goals, and manage risks, all of which is the broad aim of strategic issues management.

Ackermann and Eden (2011), albeit writing in a management context, illustrated the importance of this kind of research and analysis as a precursor to strategic communication decisions when they note that it can provide clear indications about managing stakeholders. Further, they argue that analyses

> that pay attention to dynamics over time can allow managers to begin to piece together an unfolding 'game,' and this enhanced understanding can lead them to design a more robust and sophisticated strategy.
>
> *(Ackermann and Eden, 2011, p. 190)*

In a discussion that provides an example of the link between stakeholders and decision-making, and of this process as discursive social practice, Bradley et al. (2013) noted that getting executives to grapple with issues is messy and often involves necessary fights, but that

> [w]hen companies find ways to get executives grappling—throughout the strategy-development process—with the choices that matter, they make better, less biased decisions. They also improve the likelihood that the relevant stakeholders will be on board when the time comes to make and act on choices.
>
> *(Bradley et al., 2013, p. 44)*

Communication decisions and ethical practice

Ethical practice is a crucial element of both management and communication scholars' discussions of stakeholder theory. The importance of an ethical stance in dealing with stakeholders, including decision-making, is either directly stated, or implied in discussions of the theory and how it implements the notion of corporate social responsibility. In professional strategic issues communication, a demonstrated ethical approach to dialogues with stakeholders should be the hallmark of the approach both practitioners and dominant coalitions take. Organisations that adopt a less-than-ethical approach will soon be caught in the vortex of a new issue likely to damage their market-environment operations: a serious doubt about their integrity which would call into question their integrity, values, and credibility, and damage individual and corporate reputations.

A philosophical grounding for this approach can be found in Phillips et al.'s (2003) 'controlled burn' (p. 480) to clear away misinterpretations of stakeholder theory. One of Phillips' co-authors of this discussion about 'what stakeholder theory is not' is R.E. Freeman who first proposed the theory. Phillips et al. (2003) stressed that as a theory of organisational management and ethics, stakeholder theory explicitly deals with morals and values as a central feature of organisational management. This means that managers must pay attention to the interests and well-being of those who can help or hinder an organisation to achieve its objectives. While arguing that stakeholder theory does not provide an algorithm for day-to-day managerial decision-making, they note that it nevertheless provides a method by which stakeholder interests are derived, and serves as an admonition to managers that they should account for stakeholder interests in their decision-making. And Phillips et al. (2003) argued that managing for stakeholders includes managers communicating with stakeholders.

Harrington (1996) linked ethical practice directly to the analysis of public policy issues, especially regulatory policy, arguing that this required public conversations about relevant stakeholders and their legitimate interests. While that ethical analysis did not assure perfect vision, an approach that balanced the competing interests of all stakeholders encourages explicit instead of implicit choices on policy alternatives and consequences. Berman et al. (1999) argued for intrinsic stakeholder relationships based on normative, moral commitments to drive strategic decision-making. In their view, only strategically applying ethical principles when this was to an organisation's advantage was not acting ethically. And Ingley et al. (2011) posited stakeholder theory as the central paradigm of corporate social responsibility, arguing that in a governance sense this meant boards were trustees who balanced the interests of stakeholders for mutual benefit. In this view, boards had a boundary-spanning role at the apex of an open interacting system of relationships between internal and external actors. Boards, then, set the 'tone of sincerity and ethical behaviour in decision-making and accountability' (p. 583).

In their discussion of stakeholders and business ethics, Grace and Cohen (2013) noted that despite reservations about stakeholder theory, and the virtues of using the term in business ethics, awareness of, and reference to, stakeholders in decision-making is not an instant solution to moral problems. Nor does mapping stakeholders, a convenient starting point in decision-making, replace moral reasoning. Grace and Cohen (2013) argued that the

> virtue of the stakeholder concept is to remind managers, investors and others with a large vested interest in business organisations that a market economy is not an unrestricted one; that a free society makes demands on its citizens not only in a personal sense but also as members of social institutions.
>
> *(p. 65)*

Employees are among organisational stakeholders. Gast and Zanini (2012) argued that 'crowdsourcing' strategic decision-making by involving employees, who they note are often frozen out of strategic direction setting, injected diversity and expertise into the process, brought leaders closer to the implications of their decisions, and avoided small-group bias. This social strategy approach encouraged dissenting voices and had potential to enhance the quality of organisational dialogue and improve decision-making.

The role of a communication strategist is to assist an organisation to determine its values, manage its reputation, adopt sound governance, and fulfil social and environmental responsibilities. The obligation of decision-makers is to ensure organisations conduct themselves in a socially responsible way that will lead to an organisation being 'trusted by stakeholders' (Steyn & Niemann, 2010, p. 121). This view reflects the ethical aspect of symmetrical and dialogic communication in which organisations and their stakeholders are equals. In their exploration of dialogue in public relations practice and thinking, Theunissen and Wan Noordin (2012) argued that honest communication might lead to disagreement because it exposed differences. However, they viewed ethical communication with stakeholders from another perspective and argued that faced with unethical pressure from some stakeholders a more ethical communication decision might result in an organisation engaging in persuasion in order to change their views.

For Steyn and de Beer (2012), the quality of organisational decision-making processes would be improved when guided by efforts to gather, understand, and interpret the often-conflicting views of stakeholders. They argue that corporate communication assists decision-makers to realise the need for developing and communicating a value system that can provide a sound ethical basis for management strategies that are ecologically and socially sensitive. Rensburg and de Beer (2011) noted that stakeholder involvement in co-decision-making is one way of giving stakeholders a voice in organisations.

Grace (2013) contextualised ethical decision-making by arguing that ethics and communication were bound up with each other because ethics are formed communicatively. Ethical decisions about communication mean caring about how stakeholders receive messages, how messages impact on them, and the feedback they provide as this is basic competence in business communication.

Decision-making about strategic communication directions in the context of professional communication can, then, be conceptualised as a discursive social practice. Issues act as independent variables on organisations' initial decisions about what they needed to address with their communication strategies. But issues debates are dynamic and their changing directions impact on organisational decisions about continuing to participate in a debate. Thus, structuration theory provides a conceptual perspective from which to explain how initial decisions are taken and dynamic issues impact on further participation in issues debates.

Structuration theory and strategic communication decision-making

Structuration theory (Giddens, 1986) suggests an appropriate theoretical device for explaining how strategic communication decisions about organisational advocacy are first made, as well as how they are subsequently influenced by dynamic issues debates in non-market environments. Structuration theory has been described as a bold theoretical move that enables structure to be viewed as a process (Hatch and Cunliffe, 2006); Stones (2005) described it as distinctive and a 'hinge' between the interrelationships and interdependencies of structures and agents (p. 4).

Structuration theory has been used in a variety of management and sociological studies to investigate the relationship between agency and structure (see, for example, Olufowote, 2003; Stones, 2005; Tsetsura, 2010). Scholars have argued that structuration theory can be used to understand and explain how professional communication works and can be evaluated (see, for example, Olufowote, 2003; Durham, 2005; Falkheimer, 2007, 2009; Gregory & Halff, 2013). Putnam and Nicotera (2010) reflect the process of structuration when they defend the theory of Communicative Constitution of Organisation (CCO) by arguing that it helps to explain the idealised abstraction of an organisation by making allowances for processes involving individuals and corporate agents who act; become enacted in protocols, rules, and procedures; and endure across time and space.

Aspects of structuration theory influenced Hendry's (2000) views about strategic decision-making. Although they did not themselves link it to structuration, an example from Bradley et al.'s (2013) research findings showed the theory at work in internal debates about resolving an organisation's strategic directions. These researchers reported that the management team in one of their subject companies credited the sometimes-messy conversations and debates held during strategy framing as necessary to identify and resolve potential stumbling blocks. Gregory and Halff (2013) view structuration theory as helpful in understanding how organisations and their environments enable and reproduce each other through mediated and direct communication.

Communication and organisations

Scholars have explored the role of communication in not only enabling organisations but enacting organisation strategies. This focus began in the 1980s when organisational communication scholars began to investigate the 'force present within communication' that creates organisation (Bisel, 2010, p. 125). Reed (2010) described the assertion that communication is constitutive of organisation as 'bold' and 'ontologically audacious' (p. 151). This work reflects the principles of agency, action, structure, and duality of structuration theory (Reed, 2010). Bisel (2010) noted that structuration theory was an important chapter in the history of CCO theories and had influenced CCO theorists.

Kuhn (2008) theorised a communicative theory of the firm that regards the constitution of an organisation as the result of game playing by actors to marshal consent internally and with stakeholders. McPhee and Zaug (2000) argued that organisations are constituted in four different communication flows: how individual members influence their roles, statuses, and relations; how organisational leaders design and implement decision and control mechanisms; member engagement in interdependent work or deviation from collaborative engagement; and how the organisation works with other organisations.

Strategy, too, emerges from communicative action within organisations. King (2010), for example, noted the traditional understanding of strategy as planned action, but draws on Mintzberg to argue that strategies also emerge from communicative action regardless of what an organisation intends or plans for. That is,

> strategies may emerge in the interaction between reader/hearer response, situated context, and discursive patterns.
>
> *(King, 2010, p. 23)*

Marchiori and Bulgacov (2012) made a similar point in their proposition that strategy is communication practice and that the dynamic between communication and strategy is recursive.

Jarzabkowski (2008) argued that structuration theory provided an interpretive framework for explaining managerial strategising behaviour. From her research, Jarzabkowski (2008) found that managerial actors may be constrained by structuration patterns and argued this finding might inform research into how actors and actions shape institutions. Jarzabkowski (2008) found that managerial strategising behaviour changed over the course of shaping strategies.

Giddens' structuration theory

Structuration is the process of production and reproduction of social systems via the application of generative rules and resources (Giddens, 1986). In this process, 'structures' (which are composed of rules and resources) result from the 'actions' of 'agents,' or actors, who engage in social practices that are regular day-to-day processes or acts that occur in specific contexts in time and space. Thus, human beings are purposive agents with reasons for their activities about which they could elaborate discursively if asked. The consequences of their intentional or unintentional actions are events which would not have happened if that actor had behaved differently. In this view, in a given routine social actors know what they are doing, and they successfully communicate their knowledge to others. Actors also reflexively monitor their own activities, expect others to do the same for their own, and routinely monitor aspects, social and physical, of the contexts in which they move.

Giddens (1986) described agency as the capability people have to do things and argues that it concerns events perpetrated by people

> in the sense that the individual could, at any phase in a given sequence of conduct, have acted differently. Whatever happened would not have happened if that individual had not intervened.
>
> *(Giddens, 1986, p. 9)*

Structuration theory holds that structure both enables and constrains how individuals interact at the same time as those interactions set the structure that enables and limits them. One of the main propositions of the theory is that the production and reproduction of social action draws on the same rules and resources that were the means for system reproduction. That is, actors' agency, or a pattern to their routine actions, are conditioned by existing structures but also create and recreate those structures. Giddens (1986) called this a duality in social systems. The effect of duality is that organisations are 'reflexive participants' in the contexts they would otherwise govern (Durham, 2005, p. 34). Hay (2002), among critics of structuration theory, argued that it may compound the issue of dualism of structure and agency rather than solve it.

Giddens (1986) argued that the ability of social actors to influence a social system depended on

- the means of access actors have to knowledge in virtue of their social location
- the modes of articulation of knowledge
- circumstances relating to the validity of the belief-claims taken as 'knowledge'
- factors to do with the means of disseminating available knowledge

The context in which interaction takes place, including the involvement of co-actors, how communication occurs, and how these phenomena are used reflexively to influence or control interactions, is also an important aspect of structuration theory. So, too, is power, regarded by Giddens as 'the means of getting things done' (p. 283).

Giddens (1986) also applied structuration theory to decision-making by organisations and social movements—activists in the lexicon of Bach and Allen's (2010) non-market environment. In making decisions, organisations and social movements use authoritative and allocative resources within discursively mobilised forms of information flow. This is an important point in the context of examining how organisations strategically manage dynamic issues debates which are discursive by nature, just as the decision-making processes that lead to organisational action are discursive. Giddens (1986) described social movements as 'invariably oppositional' and situated in the same field as the organisations they confront (p. 204).

Original decision-making and subsequent choices about what information and argument to inject into, or withdraw from, the ensuing issues debates on the basis of what the other party proposes, is an example of structuration theory in practice, especially duality. Such examples of duality can be found in myriad public policy debates in all sectors of the economy. The duality of structuration is frequently observed in politics as governments, oppositions, activists, commentators, and organisations engage in, and react to, the arguments of, and posturing by, other social actors in public policy issues debates. For example, a local activist group would be regarded as oppositional when it campaigned against a widget manufacturing company's proposal to build a new distribution centre on vacant parkland in a regional city on environmental grounds. How the widget manufacturer decided to strategically manage the environmental land use issues associated with the project and raised by the community group would involve making decisions about what kinds of professional communication actions it would implement and the resources it would allocate to these tasks. The community group would make similar decisions about its resource allocations and communicative action.

Stones (2005), a defender of structuration theory who proposed changes to make it stronger, argued that it can

> focus on any set of surface appearances and make our understanding of them richer and more meaningful by elaborating upon the structures and agents involved and placing them in relevant networks of social and historical relations.
>
> *(Stones, 2005, p. 192)*

It is this notion of the potential of structuration theory (Stones, 2005) that enables it to be used to explain how dynamic issues affect strategic communication decision-making.

Professional communication and structuration theory

Critical scholars have embraced structuration theory as a way of examining and explaining professional communication, especially public relations, beyond what Sandhu (2009) described as the iron cage of excellence theory.

In Durham's (2005) view, structuration theory provides a way of understanding public relations practitioners as potentially powerful social actors, in which the corporate workplace and its actions are 'connected to the world beyond the company walls' (p. 33). That is, practitioners, other social actors, and institutions are implicated in the process of structuration in potential and active ways. Structuration theory enables a proposition that dialogues of change and conflict are valid contexts of social reproduction. Thus, a communication strategy grounded in the principles of structuration theory would enable a more interpretist approach that recognised actions result in unintended and recursive consequences instead of expecting strategies and tactics to involve static actions and equally static reactions. If they understood the dialogic process of structuration, practitioners would more effectively understand, and act on, the continually changing nature of their institution's place in society (Durham, 2005).

Durham's (2005) views, including his suggestion that a structurationist view of professional communication practice might lead to more conscious and effective engagement in the meaningful contexts within which practitioners work, reflect what the role of strategic communication decision-makers, including dominant coalitions, should be as they identify and analyse issues playing out in the argumentative context of their non-market environments, and reflexively react to dynamic issue life-cycles. This is the unfolding game described by Ackermann and Eden (2011). Their argument that different stakeholder interests can 'reveal multiple and subtly interwoven consequences which both influence, and are influenced by, other stakeholders' (p. 190), is a practical illustration of duality applied to strategic issues management.

Just as Falkheimer (2007) proposed structuration theory as a 'third way perspective' (p. 292) for describing the role of public relations, so, too, does it provide a way of explaining the role of organisational structures when decisions about strategic communication directions are taken. Falkheimer (2007) viewed public relations as a communicative structuration force and argued that the theory could be used to develop dynamic and process-oriented communication strategies. When viewed from a structuration perspective, core public relations means communication processes are dynamic, ideological, temporal, and spatial, are performed by all members of an organisation, and need to be analysed as an ideological communication force. Falkheimer (2007) argued that because structuration theory describes organisations as dynamic and transforming, it helps to explain the role of strategic communication. There are, however, two disadvantages in doing this. First, structuration theory lacks empirical grounding; second, the dynamic and eclectic character of the theory means it is 'so wide that it may be used in all fields of social and cultural science in several ways' (Falkheimer, 2007, p. 116). Nevertheless, Durham's (2005) and Falkheimer's (2007, 2009) arguments reflect the role of organisations and strategic communicators as social actors when they advocate positions on issues playing out in their non-market environments.

Structuration theory can be used to illustrate how a strategic discourse of decisions can act at the agency level of intentional communication and thus 'provide a common foundation for the competing rational, action based and interpretive views of strategic decision making' (Hendry, 2000, p. 971). For Hendry (2002), structuration theory allowed a 'rich, composite but internally consistent picture of strategic decision making' (p. 971).

Sison (2010) also regarded practitioners as agents and argued they should adopt 'the agency of critical conscience' (pp. 332–333) rather than of compliance and control that her research suggested was normative. In many ways, professional high-level, issues management practice requires a significant element of what Sison (2010) described as the agency of critical conscience. While not dealing with structuration, Brønn and Brønn's (2002) view that organisations must provide a framework for effective issues management mirrors this dynamic, and hints at the role of structure in strategic communication.

Olufowote (2003) proposed a framework for using the four central elements of structuration theory in professional communication. This included examining situated routine social practices, the depth and stability of structures (because structures partly explain why routines sustain themselves), the ways in which agents interact with structures, and the interplay between actors and institutions. This framework provides a way of viewing the social discursive practice that decides strategic issues communication directions as a structure influenced by interactions between internal and external agents/actors that may produce unintended as well as intended actions. Olufowote's (2003) argument that interactions between actors and institutions 'may reproduce, contort or radically transform structural influences' and that these interactions 'produce structures which shape later interactions' (p. 16) is central to the contention that dynamic issues debates impact on, and change, communication strategy. In this way, initial routine strategic communication decision-making, and that which occurs as an issues debate takes place, enacts the central themes of structuration theory.

Communication strategy and structuration

Machiavelli's (1532) treatise, The Prince, was a challenge to the Florentine Lorenzo de Medici to rule in a strategic way. Machiavelli's view that a successful prince understands that the times in which he rules is a metaphor for strategic issues management and communication. Understanding how dynamic public policy issues impact on organisations, and deciding how to deal with them, involves a challenge to think beyond day-to-day tactics and view strategic communication for what it is: mid- to long-term action.

Researching, writing, and implementing a communication strategy is a dynamic, iterative process, affected by internal and external discourses and decisions about issues, that requires senior practitioners and other executives to understand their times. Their times are not only the immediate concerns of the market environment, but the ebb and flow of issues as they are raised by other social actors in the non-market arena. Structuration theory can help explain how those dynamics influence decisions about the direction of strategic issues communication.

Structuration and strategic communication decision-making

Strategic issues communication can be investigated and explained using concepts from other disciplines. Concepts from management and sociological scholarship can inform how senior practitioners and dominant coalitions are agents, or social actors, when they engage in discursive social practice, make decisions about strategic communication directions, and respond to other social actors' arguments about those issues. Giddens (1986) structuration theory helps explain how this occurs, especially in Hendry's (2000) conceptualisation of decision-making.

The discussion so far leads to a consideration of the dualities inherent in strategic issues communication. Those dualities occur first as practitioners and dominant coalitions engage in, through formal organisational structures, discussions about the directions of strategic communication plans to address external issues, and second as they react to the dynamics of external issues debates. An example of duality is when communication strategies are shaped as

> public figures, organisational communicators, journalists, and other seasoned veterans of public debate are responsive to differences in the public

audience for debate on an issue at various points in the evolution of the issue.

(Van Leuven and Slater, 1991, p.177)

In another example of duality, McGrath et al. (2010) used the boundary-spanning role of public affairs to argue that its 'window out/window in' (p. 337) function

> seeks to both influence public policy in the organisation's favour and to ensure that issues of importance to the wider world are reflected within the organisation's internal thinking.
>
> *(McGrath et al., 2010, p. 337)*

Hendry (2002) explored the relationships between organisational strategic decision-making, thinking, and action, to argue that, by examining how decisions are invoked, reasonable inferences can be drawn about the relationships between strategic actions, decision processes, and ideas. That enables investigations of organisations' decision processes and their rationalisation of strategic behaviour in the form of decisions. Jarzabkowski (2008) argued that structuration theory can be used to explain how managers strategise.

The inherent dynamics of issues debates and the decisions, or actions, that senior practitioners and dominant coalitions, or agents, take to address them, is part of the relationship between thinking and action described by Hendry (2002). While contingency theory provides a way of identifying how public policy factors act as independent variables to influence initial strategic communication decisions, once an organisation has joined an issues debate, structuration theory can usefully explain how communication strategies change as dynamic issues debates influence decisions.

Major organisational decisions are made through formal structures. Those structures are the decision-making processes organisations use to set directions, manage resources, plan new projects, decide on communication strategies, and review corporate progress against objectives and plans. Scholars have applied structuration theory to understand and explain how these organisational structures work, who and what influences them, and how they change.

The process of structuration is enacted when the social structure that makes decisions about strategic communication directions is influenced, or changes, as agents (practitioners and senior managers) take initial action (decisions) based on internal discourses about issues management, for example, discussions about issue impacts. Additionally, the directions of communication strategies change as other social actors in a non-market environment engage in an issues debate, by advancing an alternative point of view. In this, senior communication practitioners and dominant coalitions are social actors when they advocate their views about public policy. The process is reflexive participation because it involves analysis of the impact of issues on the organisation. In this concept, duality occurs in two ways. First, there is a duality inherent in internal discussions about the importance of external issues, and the tactics an organisation will use to deal with them, as senior practitioners and dominant coalitions debate decisions about a communication strategy's direction. A second duality occurs when other social actors in an organisation's non-market environment, such as regulators, politicians, community groups, activists, and the news media, discuss and debate the same issues. These interventions influence how issues are subsequently framed and re-framed, and this influences the future course and content of the organisation's subsequent participation in the debates as practitioners and dominant coalitions react to them.

Sommerfeldt (2012) dealt with duality in the evolution of issues when applying structuration theory to an analysis of how activist communication practitioners conceptualise and communicate with their publics. Sommerfeldt (2012) noted that issues evolve with time and context and argued that the interactions between activist groups and their publics are structuring activities that shape the issue and the structures of future discussions. That is

> the structures of an issue debate generate the need and dictate the course of the interactions of actors, which reshape the structures of the issue and future interactions. As issues evolve, rules and resources available to actors change, and different activist group publics become (ir)relevant within the contemporaneous structures (domination, signification, and legitimation) that govern issues.
>
> *(Sommerfeldt, 2012, p. 283)*

Activist organisations participate as social actors in issues debates in organisations' non-market environments. Just as structuration theory can help to explain how interactions between activist groups and their publics change the shape of an issues debate, so, too, can it help to explain how strategic communicators react to changing circumstances brought about by other participants in public policy issues debates.

Communication strategies should be developed in a process that begins with an analysis of the potential impact that current and potential external socio-economic and political issues in an organisation's non-market environment may have on its ability to achieve its business goals and objectives. This issues management process is a discursive social practice involving internal discourses about the potential impact of issues and the probability they will occur. Yet the structures in which decisions about communication strategies are made are continually affected by the dynamic public issues debates they address. In other words, organisational responses to issues generate kinetic reactions from publics that result in issues evolving, a dynamic that affects how an organisation further contributes to an issues debate. The same thing happens when organisations respond to issues initially raised by external publics. This duality suggests that, together, Giddens' (1986) structuration theory and Hendry's (2002) conceptualisation of strategic decision-making construct a useful frame for examining and explaining strategic communication decision-making.

This hypothesis helps to further explain the concept of strategic communication as professional practice beyond the day-to-day requirements of integrated marketing communication. That is an important concept if professional strategic communication practice is to advance so that it is more highly valued by clients and senior managers. The point is: strategic communicators who understand their times, and the dualities inherent in issues management, will plan accordingly. Those who do not, like Machiavelli's prince, risk their own kind of prosperity: successful strategic issues management.

6

LINKING STRATEGIC COMMUNICATION AND THEORETICAL CONCEPTS

The essential problem that afflicts professional communication practice is that what is usually described as 'strategic' too often fails the test of reflecting the reality of what being strategic really means. Professional communicators are so busily engaged in the day-to-tasks of tactical and technical integrated marketing communication, that they are unable to pursue strategic communication that deals with emerging mid- and long-term issues. In reality, integrated marketing communication actually means using tools of the professional disciplines to concentrate on selling products. In this approach, 'strategy' has become a misused term to describe plans for using day-to-day news media relations and social media applications to boost sales efforts or provide instant responses to current issues. This has made it difficult and frustrating for those practitioners who do understand strategy to convince dominant coalitions and clients of the importance of the strategic communication imperative, and long-term issues management, as a value-added and high-order strategic function. And it reinforces the tactical focus that dominant coalitions appear to demand as they seek the glitter of a fancy Facebook page, a daily dozen tweets, and publicity on the nightly television news. Viewing this as a professional practice shortcoming, and as a gap in academic approaches, may be a heretical move, but advancing this view, and proposing a model for improvement, is necessary if scholars are to better understand and define strategic communication, and professional practice is to improve its organisational standing.

Strategic communication should be understood and applied as a higher-order, value-added corporate function that involves analytical research and provides effective ways of dealing with important external public policy issues. Organisations attempt to implement strategic communication campaigns while 'struggling to even define the concept of strategic communication and its value to the organisation' (Plowman, 2013, p. 556). Better implementation will only

DOI: 10.4324/9781003177340-6

happen through meaningful cross-disciplinary connections, a tighter definition of strategic communication, and by conceptualising a way in which the practice can be effectively and directly integrated with business planning. As a high-level corporate function this strategic imperative provides a compass for all other communicative activity. It is the omission of this concept that leads to a dysfunction between what is (and what should be) in the strategic communication literature and professional practice beyond the daily response to immediate market environment issues.

This chapter is a kind of Carrick bend, a knot used for joining nautical ropes, that links the nature of strategic communication, issues management, stakeholder relationships, organisations as social actors, decision-making as social practice, and structuration theory.

The long-term essence of strategic communication

In a professional communication context, strategy should require a long-term view of non-market environmental factors so that organisations can be proactive in their communicative efforts by considering potential difficulties and conflicts (Gregory, 2009b). Scholars argue that strategic communication operates at a level beyond functional, tactical approaches, embraces all organisational communicative interactions with stakeholders, and requires an alignment of communication with an organisation's overall strategy to enhance strategic positioning (Argenti et al., 2005; Cornelissen, 2005).

Strategic communication is a high-level, planned function that should be accepted by managers as the compass for addressing social, political, cultural, economic, and regulatory issues in debates that occur in an organisation's non-market environment. It has the same importance for organisations as corporate finance, legal affairs, human resources and operations. That is, dominant coalitions should recognise the strategic communication imperative as a high-level, organisational function. This requires a long game, not a short-term focus on immediate day-to-day tactical activities that prioritise product marketing, sales, and news media publicity. The importance of a focus on the long-term strategic communication imperative is that the resolution of issues occurring in non-market environments impacts on the ability of an organisation to successfully conduct business, whether it is a commercial entity, government agency, or not-for-profit.

Organisations that engage in issues debates through their representatives (or agents) are social actors advocating a position on those issues. Social actors are people or groups who participate in debates about public issues and attempt to remedy them by influencing other actors (Deephouse & Heugens, 2009)—organisations, governments, consumers, workers, and NGOs (Martin & Osberg, 2007). As social actors, private, public, and not-for-profit sector organisations must engage with their social and political environment in order to shape and influence debates about laws and regulations, and reduce the risks to the social and political conditions in which they operate (Deephouse & Heugens, 2009;

Bach & Allen, 2010). Engaging in social and political environments is not always defensive, nor necessarily positive, and can sometimes be controversial. Writing about this aspect of corporate engagement, and concerned about organisations' legitimacy in the context of Corporate Social Action, Yim (2021) noted that a corporation's explicit support for a controversial socio-political position could potentially alienate some stakeholders but also attract support from other activist groups (Yim, 2021). This meant an organisation's stand-taking

> may sometimes diverge dramatically from current mainstream societal values, but still maintain its legitimacy because that divergence is timely and is recognised as moving in the right direction by at least some of its stakeholders.
>
> *(p. 71)*

The notion that an organisation should engage as a social actor in public debates about issues that affect it differentiates strategic communication from other professional communication disciplines, including public affairs, which is normatively defined as a specialisation that deals with government affairs and lobbying, community relations, and corporate social responsibility (Harris & Moss, 2001). At its core, strategic communication is the channel through which organisations deal with mid- and long-term issues, especially those involving reputation, values, and long-term stakeholder relationships. None of this can be achieved in the short-term time frame in which tactical day-to-day aspects of professional communication are applied to sell products, promote events, lobby, deal with the mass news media, release information, or, in a political communication sense, get the publicity for political masters.

This view reflects Hallahan et al.'s (2007) argument that communicating purposefully to advance an organisation's mission is the essence of strategic communication. This is a substantial conceptual shift that goes beyond the application of functional tactics and means delivering multidisciplinary, purposeful, rational, and intentional communication based on deliberate decision-making. This presents a problem for scholars. Despite their academic research publications, conference papers, and seminars, professional practitioners still appear to be at least immune from the real meaning of strategy, or simply ignore it, just as they seem to ignore the importance of understanding how research, and theory, can inform their practice.

A consistent theme in the literature about the role of professional communication is that it must be aligned to business objectives to deal with significant issues that affect organisational success. These significant economic, social, and political issues are not resolved in a tactical time frame; they require careful identification, analysis, and planned communicative action over the mid to long term to support business strategy and directions. However, there is a perceived gap in this definitional dialectic: the omission of an explicit explanation of how significant mid- to long-term issues impact on the creation and implementation of communication strategies. With the possible exception of Argenti et al. (2005) and Bach and Allen

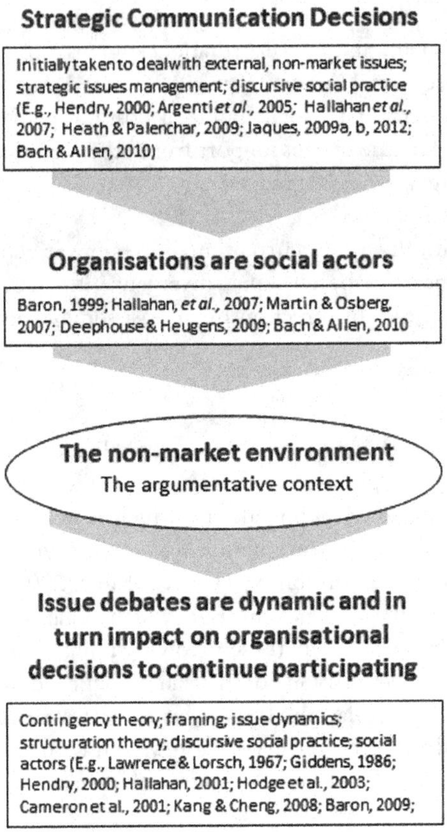

Strategic Communication Decisions

Initially taken to deal with external, non-market issues; strategic issues management; discursive social practice (E.g., Hendry, 2000; Argenti *et al.*, 2005; Hallahan *et al.*, 2007; Heath & Palenchar, 2009; Jaques, 2009a, b, 2012; Bach & Allen, 2010)

Organisations are social actors

Baron, 1999; Hallahan, *et al.*, 2007; Martin & Osberg, 2007; Deephouse & Heugens, 2009; Bach & Allen, 2010

The non-market environment
The argumentative context

Issue debates are dynamic and in turn impact on organisational decisions to continue participating

Contingency theory; framing; issue dynamics; structuration theory; discursive social practice; social actors (E.g., Lawrence & Lorsch, 1967; Giddens, 1986; Hendry, 2000; Hallahan, 2001; Hodge et al., 2003; Cameron et al., 2001; Kang & Cheng, 2008; Baron, 2009;

DIAGRAM 6.1:   The strategic communication process Diagram 6.1 summarises the strategic communication process in the context of the book, with references to scholars whose arguments have been used.

(2010), when they deal with why strategic communication is an organisational imperative, and why managers need to be social actors in issues debates, the literature tends to rely on a traditional realist or positivist assertion. That is, while the literature argues public relations, for example, has a strategic role it does not link that role explicitly with the need for organisations to participate as social actors in mid- to long-term issues debates. Diagram 6.1 illustrates the strategic communication process advanced in this book.

Issues and strategic communication in the non-market environment

Strategic issues management communication can be approached through a specific lens provided by Bach and Allen's (2010) explanation of the two distinct external environments in which organisations work and interact with stakehold-ers for specific reasons. The first, their 'market environment' defined by their relationships with suppliers, competitors, and customers, is where they do busi-ness. The second is the 'non-market environment' in which relationships with governments, regulators, NGOs, activists, and the mass news media about public policy issues unfold. This is the arena in which debates about mid- to long-term public policy issues occur, and in which organisations are social actors when they advocate a position. The outcomes of these mid- to long-term issues debates eventually affect an organisation's ability to achieve its goals.

The important distinction between these two environments is the definition of the non-market as a space for serious, perhaps extended, debate about, and resolution of, issues. The focus of definitions of strategic communication should take account of this external mid- to long-term environment. The point at which strategic communication can be differentiated from other, tactical, com-munication practice is the requirement that it should consider, and plan to deal with, mid- to long-term socio-economic and political issues that occur in non-market environments. Identifying these early, and planning to deal with them in a strategic time frame, prevents issues acting like the metaphoric butterflies from Brazil and impacting on market performance. That is, just as Jaques (2009a, b) argued that issues management must be strategic, so, too, must the professional communication that deals with issues.

While professional communicators must deal with an organisation's imme-diate needs, the initial and subsequent decisions they take with dominant coa-litions about mid- to long-term strategy should be influenced by analyses of issues occurring beyond a tactical day-to-day time frame. This is the point about organisations using communication techniques in their non-market environ-ments—the argumentative context—to legitimately advocate their views about issues where these can potentially impact on their ability to achieve business goals and objectives (Hallahan et al., 2007). To do this, organisations must be social and political actors whether managers 'like it or not' (Bach & Allen, 2010, p. 48). Such participation is an important strategic opportunity because politi-cians, regulators, non-government organisations, and activists won't hesitate to impose new rules on an industry, unless organisations present their views about those issues as active participants in the process.

The need for senior managers and practitioners to understand that socio-eco-nomic and political issues dynamics play out in an organisation's non-market envi-ronment, not in its market environment, is crucial for planning strategic responses to them in line with overall business strategy. Such dynamics include not only the ebb and flow of a debate that occurs when an organisation and activist group engage with an issue, but also those that occur within industries, between activ-ist groups, and between government agencies (Heath & Palenchar, 2009). The essence of the non-market environment construct is that issues unresolved here can impact on organisational markets. It is thus a requirement that they be dealt with in this space in a strategic way. That is the strategic communication imperative.

At one level, the impact of public policy issues debates on organisational planning for communication strategies can in part be explained by contingency theory. In this application of contingency theory (see Diagram 6.2), dynamic issues are independent variables, and strategic communication decisions are dependent variables. That is, strategic communication decisions depend on the issues identified by environmental scanning and boundary spanning as being important enough for an organisation to deal with. Consequent decisions about strategic engagement on issues in turn depend on how issues debates evolve, or are resolved.

Communication scholars have used contingency theory to investigate public relations practice in the guise of strategic communication. Much of their work, especially that grounded in excellence theory and symmetry, describes tactical choices and does not deal adequately with the factors that influence decisions about mid- to long-term strategic communication directions. Understanding the interplay between issues dynamics and communication decisions requires

DIAGRAM 6.2: Issues as independent variables affecting strategic communication decisions Diagram 6.2 illustrates how contingency theory can assist in explaining the influence of issues as independent variables on strategic communication decisions (dependent variables).

a new analytical frame. Structuration theory and its notion of duality provide such an analytical frame. Suggesting structuration theory as a frame for analysing strategic communication decision-making requires a discussion about adapting concepts from other disciplines to professional communication scholarship.

How other disciplines' concepts help understand strategic communication

Professional communication scholarship has traditionally taken a view of practice that has been grounded in J.E. Grunig and colleagues' (1992) Excellence Study and J.E. Grunig and Hunt's (1984) four models of public relations. While professional communication scholars have used theoretical concepts from sociology, psychology, management, and behavioural sciences to critique the 'excellence' approach, and research and explain other aspects of professional communication, this does not go far enough, especially for explaining the strategic aspects of professional communication.

Critical scholars situate professional communication in the context of social theory (see, for example, L'Etang, 2005; Ihlen & Verhoeven, 2009) when they seek to understand how professional communication works, and how it influences society and is in turn influenced by society (see, for example, Ihlen & van Ruler, 2009). These scholars have freed research about how professional communication works from what Sandhu (2009) described as the iron cage of excellence theory which has for so long been the dominant frame for such research. Critical approaches to examining professional communication suggest another dimension to strategy development: how are strategic decisions made and what influences them? Thus, the concepts of discursive social practice, organisations as social actors, issue framing and management, stakeholder relationships, decision-making, and strategic planning from other disciplines, help to explain strategic communication decision-making.

Other scholars (for example, Olufowote, 2003, Durham, 2005, Falkheimer, 2007, 2009) have urged the use of structuration theory as a device to better understand and explain how professional communication works and can be evaluated. That view includes how the notion of the duality of structure can explain the impact of dynamic issues debates on strategic communication decisions.

Another aspect of the critical and interpretivist approach to understanding professional communication as a theoretical concept and as practice has been an argument that scholarship in this area should be better informed in its research, especially in relation to strategy, by the latest thinking in management scholarship. For example, Frandsen and Johansen (2010) urged communication scholars and practitioners to engage with other disciplines to enhance their abilities to work with management leaders in a strategic way. That view is consistent with Jaques' (2009a) argument that because issues management evolved as a business discipline the practice ought to be aligned better with business strategic planning.

Strategic communication decision-making

Managers and senior communicators engage in discursive social practice when issues analyses are discussed in decision-making structures to determine how the organisation should deal with them, and subsequently when organisations advocate positions in public issues debates. Hendry (2002) extended this view by arguing that strategy itself is a form of social practice in which debate about decision-making is a central feature and he linked strategic thinking to action.

Decisions about the initial directions of communication strategies, and how subsequent decisions are taken, are reactions to the dynamics of issues debates. First, decision-making is part of an organisational debate. Second, strategy is a form of social practice. Third, strategic thinking is linked to action. In short,

> [i]n pursuit of their aims, strategists do all the things that feature in the tra-
> ditional definitions: they evolve shared perspectives, create plans and enact
> ploys. Intentionally or otherwise they participate in the social creation of
> patterns and the positioning of their organisation's product-market offer-
> ings, and they observe such patterns and positions in other organisations.
>
> *(Hendry, 2000, p. 970)*

This is analogous to the processes of planning communication in a strategic way after external research informs initial and subsequent decisions about strategy directions. This is a discursive social practice because communication planners discuss external and internal factors that can potentially impact on their organisations and recommendations for action with dominant coalitions in formal management structures.

The ethical dimension to strategic communication decisions that affect relationships with organisational stakeholders is important because, as Steyn and de Beer (2012) argued, the quality of organisational decision-making is improved when the often-conflicting views of stakeholders are included in decision-making. Considering stakeholder views, including those of activists, in decisions about strategic communication, is key because a primary concern of this professional practice is building, maintaining, and enhancing organisation relations and reputation, both of which are about stakeholders. Neither can be achieved in a short-term, tactical approach to communication.

Arguments advanced in the literature make the point that internal debates between senior practitioners and senior organisational managers, or dominant coalitions, about external public policy issues, and decisions about responses to them, involve discursive social practice. Those decisions are based on issues identification and analysis, and the actions that follow them are designed to influence public debates about issues. Those debates are never static, just as Heraclitus pronounced that everything changes and nothing stands still.

Because the changing nature and framing of issues in public debate impacts on how organisations deal with them, structuration theory is a useful construct for investigating and explaining the dynamics of communication decision-making.

This enables those dynamics to be viewed in the context of structuration theory's process of production and reproduction of social systems via the application of generative rules and resources as a result of the 'actions' of 'agents.' Additionally, the theory explains through the concept of duality how individuals interact in issues debates, but also constrains how they do this.

Scholars suggest that structuration theory enables communication practitioners to be viewed as potentially powerful social actors, and as a construct to develop dynamic and process-oriented communication strategies (Durham, 2005; Falkheimer, 2007). For example, Falkheimer (2007) argued that from a structuration perspective, core communication processes were dynamic, ideological, temporal, and spatial, and were performed by all members of an organisation, and that because of this the theory helps to explain the role of strategic communication. Structuration theory also provides a foundation for understanding competing rational, action-based, and interpretive views of strategic decision-making, which can be described as a discursive social practice (Hendry, 2000).

Structuration theory, used in the context of Olufowote's (2003) proposition, suggests a theoretical frame for explaining how dynamic issues impact on the formal structures that organisations use to make strategic communication decisions. This framework, based on the four central elements of structuration theory, includes examining situated routine social practices, the depth and stability of structures, the ways in which agents interact with structures, and the interplay between actors and institutions. Diagram 6.3 illustrates the duality involved in making decisions about strategic communication directions and how other scholarship explains the dynamic nature of issues debates.

Theorising a paradigm shift to a new planning model

Communication, management, and sociological literature suggests a special context for strategic communication as a mechanism to assist organisations to deal with mid- to long-term issues. Scholars regard strategic communication as a unifying framework in which purposeful influence is the fundamental goal of communication, and as intentional communication that requires purposeful actors, and rational and deliberate decision-making.

In this process, there is an explicit involvement of senior managers, or dominant coalitions, in decisions about strategic communication directions. That provides a conceptual key to overcoming the inability of communication strategists to convince dominant coalitions of the importance of mid- to long-term issues management as a vital element of strategic communication's role as a value-added and high-order organisational function. That is, senior managers understand business strategy, recognise the need to plan for their businesses' (used in its broad definition) sustainability and growth beyond their immediate competitive environment, and are also involved in strategic communication decisions. So, as the nexus between communication strategy and practice is often dysfunctional, the way forward is to identify a mechanism to more effectively align and integrate

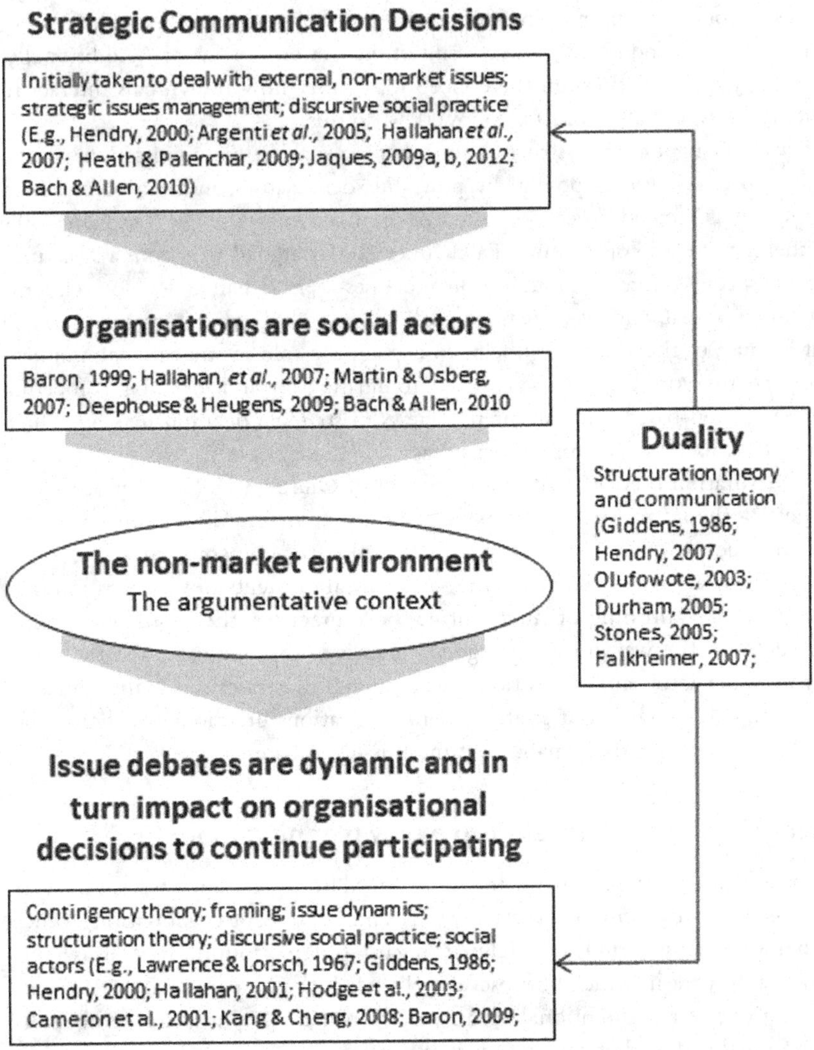

Strategic Communication Decisions

Initially taken to deal with external, non-market issues; strategic issues management; discursive social practice (E.g., Hendry, 2000; Argenti *et al.*, 2005; Hallahan *et al.*, 2007; Heath & Palenchar, 2009; Jaques, 2009a, b, 2012; Bach & Allen, 2010)

Organisations are social actors

Baron, 1999; Hallahan, *et al.*, 2007; Martin & Osberg, 2007; Deephouse & Heugens, 2009; Bach & Allen, 2010

The non-market environment
The argumentative context

Duality

Structuration theory and communication (Giddens, 1986; Hendry, 2007, Olufowote, 2003; Durham, 2005; Stones, 2005; Falkheimer, 2007;

Issue debates are dynamic and in turn impact on organisational decisions to continue participating

Contingency theory; framing; issue dynamics; structuration theory; discursive social practice; social actors (E.g., Lawrence & Lorsch, 1967; Giddens, 1986; Hendry, 2000; Hallahan, 2001; Hodge et al., 2003; Cameron et al., 2001; Kang & Cheng, 2008; Baron, 2009;

DIAGRAM 6.3: The impact of duality on communication strategy decision structures Diagram 6.3 shows how the concept of duality in Giddens' (1986) structuration theory can explain the influence issues have both on the process in which decisions about strategic communication directions are made and the dynamics of issues debates.

communication strategy-making with business planning. If that alignment and integration can be made, dominant coalitions are more likely to understand the value-added role of the strategic communication imperative in achieving mid- to long-term organisational goals, especially if the link is expressed in terms senior managers already understand.

TABLE 6.1 Baghai et al.'s (2000) three planning horizons for business growth

	Horizon 1	Horizon 2	Horizon 3
Focus	Executing to defend, extend, and increase profitability of existing businesses	Resourcing initiatives to build new businesses	Uncovering options for future opportunities and placing bets on selected options
Outputs	Annual operating plan: tactical plans, resourcing decisions, budgets	Business building strategies: investment budget, detailed business plans for new ventures	Decisions to explore: initial project plan, project milestones

From Baghai et al. (2000), p. 130.

Table 6.1 illustrates the specific focus of each of the three time horizons Baghai et al. (2000) posited that businesses should use to plan for growth, and also shows the outputs from those horizons.

The concept of dealing with commercial business growth in the three planning 'horizons' explained by Baghai et al. (2000; see Table 6.1) is a logical base from which to do this.

This concept can be adapted to issues management and strategic communication practice to propose a model for the way in which it should be planned and practised.

Towards a better understanding of strategic communication

While the Carrick bend of this chapter joins concepts about the nature of strategic communication, issues management, and organisational and communication decision-making, it also enables a scaffold that will support a greater understanding of this professional communication practice. That is, strategic communication is not normatively defined *specifically* as a professional practice that deals with managing mid- to long-term social, political, cultural, and economic issues, which can potentially affect how organisations achieve their goals.

With few exceptions (for example, Heath & Palenchar, 2009), the professional communication literature and professional practice do not directly focus on dealing with non-market issues in a strategic way, nor are organisations explicitly regarded as social actors when they engage in public policy issues debates. Making decisions about communication strategy directions is a discursive social practice, a point also not covered explicitly in the literature about strategic communication. Including this concept in a definition of strategic communication would help build a better understanding of the practice among scholars and practitioners. There is also a gap in the literature about how issues debates in organisational, non-market environments impact on the process in which initial communication strategy decisions are made, and on how communication strategies are revised as a result of issues dynamics. Conceptualising this process as the enactment of structuration, especially the concept of duality, helps to explain strategic communication as a high-order, value-added professional practice beyond day-to-day tactical and technical applications of professional communication.

Despite calls for greater engagement with theoretical concepts from other disciplines, professional communication researchers have not yet explained how the dynamics of issues debates affect decisions about strategy directions and implementation through frameworks provided by other scholarly disciplines.

7

A STRATEGIC COMMUNICATION PLANNING MODEL

Senior communication practitioners have professional agency in decision-making about how an organisation should manage an issues debate. The notion that issues are best addressed in a planned and strategic way is strongly supported by senior practitioners according the research in Australia, Europe, and the Asia-Pacific region. However, a constructivist interpretation of that research suggests a paradox: that communication practitioners' commitment to strategy is often trumped by acquiescence to demands from senior management and clients for tactical solutions to immediate issues, especially in government agencies and private sector consultancies. This happens because senior communication practitioners are unable to effectively exercise their agency when decisions about managing issues communication are made. That is, in the internal discursive social practice that results in decisions about strategic communication directions, practitioners often lose out to other agents who are able to direct decisions because of their organisational seniority, political position, or who simply pay the bills and therefore want a particular output.

An immediate response to an issue may be all dominant coalitions and external clients want, but that kind of communication, directed at current issues, occurs in market environments and implements a tactical, rather than a strategic, approach. Communication action in this space ignores the strategic imperative that requires meaningful, long-term engagement with stakeholders about socio-economic and political issues in non-market environments. A tactical approach may include responding to issues, but it does not guarantee they will be resolved. A strategic approach means issues would be identified and analysed for their impact on an organisation, and communicative action designed, well before they emerge in a market context. Strategic engagement leads to outcomes: the resolution of issues, especially those related to organisational reputation and long-term stakeholder relationships before they impact on an organisation's

DOI: 10.4324/9781003177340-7

day-to-day business. To be effective, practitioners and senior managers who take decisions about communication strategy directions should understand not only the external non-market environment in which issues debates occur, but also recognise that debates with stakeholders about reputation and values are dynamic and rarely resolved in short time frames. This does not avoid the need to address immediate concerns in market environments, but it does require strategic issues management communication to be aligned with organisational business planning. Is there a way of overcoming managerial demand for instant, technical approaches that would help practitioners and that managerial dominant coalitions will recognise as a value-adding activity? I contend the model proposed here, based on a management approach to business planning, is one way of doing that.

Understanding practitioners' views about communication strategy

The unique sample of senior practitioners who provided their direct insights into the factors that influence their decisions about communication strategies for my research comprised a professional demographic that has not previously been studied on the topic of strategic communication and long-term issues management. These senior people are responsible for advising on, and making decisions about, 'strategic' communication in the private sector, government agencies, commerce, and public relations consultancies. They held titles such as Chief Executive or Director. The research cohort had demonstrated professional seniority: slightly more than half had practised for at least 15 years; one third had practised for more than 20 years. The largest single group were those who described themselves as communication consultants. Gender distribution was almost equal: females (51%) and males (49%). Despite variations in responses between practitioners in different sectors, and some gender differences, the data generated by the research were generally consistent, suggesting that the sample's attitudes towards the factors they consider in taking strategic communication decisions may be typical of those held by senior people in the wider profession. Their responses confirm the concept that strategic communication should focus on mid- to long-term practice to deal with issues in the non-market environment.

Strategic communication, values, reputation, and stakeholder relationships

Identifying and managing issues related to organisational values and reputation and building and maintaining stakeholder relationships are, for this sample, the two most significant factors that influence communication decisions. While there are differences in the priorities given to these categories across sectors, dealing with issues about reputation and stakeholder relationships are immediate concerns for all respondents, but they are not always factored into longer range planning. This reflects discussions about the importance of managing stakeholder relations in the management literature dealing with strategic business planning.

Issues drive strategic communication

A consistent theme in the research findings is that strategic communication is concerned about advancing an organisation's interests by advocating its positions on external issues that affect its ability to achieve its goals. This applied across all sectors. Most said they engage in analysis of potential and emerging issues as ongoing practice. All were concerned about how issues impact on current business activities; most also engage in issues identification for the medium term; less than half attempt long-term issues analysis. This supports the argument that strategic communication is about organisations as social actors engaging with stakeholders in the non-market environment. This in turn advances understandings of strategic communication by giving the practice a significant rationale in a specific context, thus contributing to a more complete definition of what it really is, or should be.

Issues as risks

A majority of respondents described their issues analysis practice as 'risk analysis' because their organisations are concerned with identifying the impact of potential risk on broader business operations. Respondents view potential damage to an organisation's reputation as a primary risk factor. One public sector communicator noted that potential risks required management plans that rated the risk, provided a 'treatment' for it, and a report at least quarterly on progress with the plan. In this way the agency did not wait for a risk to become a crisis. Other practitioners gave examples of issues being listed in corporate risk registers. A consultant noted that assessing risk for clients was about mapping out not just a particular issue but how that issue then links in with other threats.

While this theme does not specifically advance understandings of strategic communication, it does provide a possible key for practitioners to use to convince senior management of the importance of long-term issues management. That is, dominant coalitions understand risk, so presenting mid- to long-term issues in that context may help practitioners to convince senior management of the need for mid- to long-term stakeholder communication about such issues. This would link communication practice more closely with business management principles.

Engaging with opponents

Respondents were willing to recommend dialogues with opponents about issues, but their decisions to do this depend on the situation they are addressing. In an example of 'situation,' most respondents say a threat of litigation against their organisation would constrain their decision to enter a dialogue, but they would recommend engaging with organisational critics even if this would result in negative publicity, especially when the organisation's reputation is threatened. Respondents believe senior managers should engage with critics. The extent to which a stakeholder group is covered by the mass news media is not a significant variable that practitioners take into account when they consider whether to engage with a group in their non-market environment. This contributes to an understanding of the factors that influence senior practitioners in making decisions. Dialogue with stakeholders is important to them, but they are nuanced about the circumstances in which it could occur. The view that mass news media coverage of a stakeholder would not influence a decision about engaging with them reinforces the findings about stakeholder relationships and practitioners' views about the importance of dialogic strategic communication.

A tendency to tactical practice

Despite their strong support for strategic communication planning and practice, many respondents are required to take tactical approaches as a result of client or employee demands. This applies across all sectors, but is especially the case for practitioners working in state and federal government agencies when demands from ministers' offices often divert their attention from strategy to day-to-day political issues. Respondents noted that senior managers and clients sought better strategic issues identification and analysis and communication practice after crises, especially those about reputational issues.

Here, then, is what might be described as the concept of the 'conflicted strategist'—senior communicators who acknowledge the need for strategies but too often struggle to implement them because of tactical demands. As one government communicator working for a large, politically sensitive, federal agency, discussing the ability of communicators to prepare strategic plans, noted:

> I think we know how to do it, and we're probably good at it actually...I wouldn't pretend that there's actually nobody looking strategically [but] certainly my experience has been the lack of opportunity to sing that song.

and

> The day-to-day thing takes over. It and the size of the operation is a reflection of the daily tasks if you like. They're huge and they're substantial, and...all of them are absolutely in a short-term government framework. It really is...the government's today, issues today, program today policy that we're working on.

A senior private sector consultant described this as society's 'short termism' that 'runs riot throughout every business, with very few exceptions, and certainly in government.' The consultant argued that managing directors and politicians were infected by short termism because they were focused on whether they would still have jobs in three years' time. However, 'the politicians are worse—they only look at the next election. So, it's short termism all the way.' However, in a pragmatic view, one state government agency practitioner noted that the political importance of aspects of their work could not be denied, even on relatively low-level issues, and this meant they would generally be in contact with the minister's office 'very early in the process.' The practitioner argued that the political dimension 'actually forms the…response, or the sort of communications [sic] we would initiate.'

In an illustration of the importance of tactical communication in some sectors, an industry association practitioner noted that issues analysis was normally done in the context of an election cycle, especially when there was an expectation of a change of government. However, working in the 'daily political climate…you just know when to act and when to leave and when to respond.' This meant,

> we have to be fairly clever in how we do things…we spend very little time in putting together strategic plans, if you like, because our daily work very rarely conforms to a plan that looks to the 12 months ahead, but we'll know broadly what we're going to be doing, but we don't have a point one, two, three, four will be achieved by the third week of the second quarter and all of this sort of stuff, we can't operate that way.

This notion is important because it highlights one of the realities of professional communication practice: the conflict between best practice and client demand. A short-term appearance in the daily mass news media may deliver an output but it does not produce effective issue outcomes that consistent stakeholder relationships build by generating understanding about organisational positions on public policy issues. Thus, tactical practice (beyond that required by crisis communication) in an issues management context is indeed 'short-termism' and has implications for practice in all sectors, including political communication. It is worth noting in this context, however, that Kanihan et al. (2013) found that communication managers who were formally in dominant coalitions were more likely to actively participate with senior management on communication issues, and were trusted, understood, and could influence that group as well as be involved in wider business strategic decision-making. They argued that a direct reporting line to the chief executive made it more likely that a communication manager's recommendations would be implemented.

Attempting a strategic approach

Quantitative and qualitative data from my research support the arguments of Argenti et al. (2005) and Hallahan et al. (2007), that strategic communication is concerned with long-term considerations of how organisations should participate as social actors by advocating their views in debates about public policy issues. Respondents overwhelmingly (64.1%) believe that a communication strategy is critically important to their organisations or clients, compared with 30.8% who say it is important. The remaining respondents regarded a communication strategy as either totally unimportant (1.3%), or simply unimportant (1.3%). Surprisingly, 2.6% simply did not have any view on the importance of a communication strategy to their organisations or clients.

Senior practitioners also strongly support the role of communication strategies in advancing corporate goals and objectives in the mid and long terms. Most believe communication strategy should be aligned with corporate business plans, and focus on organisational values and reputations, and maintaining relationships with stakeholders. They agree that emerging political issues, and the need for senior executives to build relationships with government, are matters that involve strategic communication. Most respondents do not regard their roles as being focussed only on generating financial returns.

The research findings that senior practitioners attempt to take a strategic approach and say they are willing to recommend communicating with stakeholders in a wide range of circumstances, suggest they accept dialogic communication as a method for engaging with stakeholders on issues (Schwarzkopf, 2006; Spitzeck & Hansen, 2010; Ackermann & Eden, 2011; Ingley et al., 2011; Bradley et al., 2013).

On one level, these findings support the traditional strategic communication definitional dialectic. That is, most respondents believe that strategic communication advances corporate goals and objectives in the mid to long terms, its role should be to advocate organisational positions on issues, and aligning it with corporate business plans enhances an organisation's strategic positioning. This reflects definitions that strategic communication is purposive and intentional (Sanhu, 2009), responds to business needs and concerns (Argenti et al., 2005; Cornelissen, 2005), involves organisations as social actors in issues debates (Hallahan et al., 2007; Bach & Allen, 2010), and is focussed on the long term (Zerfass & Huck, 2007).

Yet, on another level, it seems a more complete, perhaps more nuanced, definition is needed. That definition would differentiate strategic communication from what is essentially normative tactical practice by including a time horizon. It would explicitly link the notion of what is 'strategic' to long-term stakeholder engagement, the creation and protection of reputation, and active organisational participation as social actors in issues debates in non-market environments. That is, the traditional understanding of what strategic communication is supposed to do should be enhanced by recognising stakeholder engagement and organisational reputation as primary influences on decisions about the directions of communication strategies.

Similarly, practitioners' willingness to recommend engagement with stakeholders on issues in a wide range of contexts, including in the long term, also suggests the need for a more complete definition. For example, almost all respondents agreed strongly that stakeholder engagement is important for creating a positive reputation, and a significant majority rejected a statement that it would be a waste of time for managers to engage over the long term with organisational critics. The stakeholder relationship variables that respondents consider include the circumstances in which they would build and maintain relationships with stakeholders, including engaging in dialogue with those who oppose their organisation's views, or threaten its reputation. The strength of respondents' views on five variables related to stakeholder engagement is illustrated by the finding that 95% reject the statement that open dialogue with stakeholders is 'not important,' and 97% support the view that stakeholder engagement is important in creating a positive organisational reputation. A majority (87%) do not agree that long-term dialogue with their organisation's critics is a 'waste of senior managers' time.' Additionally, the idea of engaging in dialogue with a stakeholder who is threatening an organisation's reputation is strongly supported (61%), but 46% of practitioners would not recommend that senior managers engage with a perceived radical group.

Engineering a strategic approach is not easy for senior practitioners. They generally support the desirability of a strategic approach, yet face barriers imposed by clients or employers to actually implement a long-term approach. One industry association practitioner illustrated the difficulty of convincing senior management to engage in a strategic approach to communication with the rather cynical comment,

> When sufficiently motivated (i.e. concerned) communications strategies are seen as critically important and there is widespread interest and buy-in to the message development process, but little thought is given to communications at a strategic level on lower order issues.

That comment is reflected in the finding that while respondents say they routinely engage in issues identification and analysis as ongoing practice, most primarily deal with issues that impact on the current business activities of their employers or clients. Overall, respondents were less likely to think about the mid term, and most did not consider the likely probability or impact of potential long term issues. However, senior practitioners working in the private sector for a business, as lobbyists, consultants, or in industry associations, were more likely to believe a communication strategy was important, or critical, and to focus on identifying issues expected to impact in the mid term, than were their colleagues in the public, university, and not-for-profit sectors.

Despite often being required to practice in a short-term, tactical way, most practitioners do not believe communication should only focus on advancing their organisation's financial performance. Coupled with their views about stakeholder relationships and the issues that are important to their decisions, this suggests respondents do differentiate between the roles of marketing and strategic communication. An example of this is that practitioners working in private sector businesses nominated 'emerging Australian political issues' as the primary influence on strategic communication decisions. This requires a mid- to long-term focus rather than day-to-day tactical communication.

Female practitioners are more likely to regard strategic communication as important than males. Female practitioners also say they engage in identifying and analysing issues likely to occur in the longer term more than do male practitioners. However, with few exceptions, most respondents were concerned that they were often required to engage in short-term tactical practice that diverted them from strategic approaches, especially those who work for communication consultancies or public sector agencies. Public sector practitioners believe that the demand they experience for tactical communication reflects the political reality and context of what they do. This suggests public sector practitioners, who are responsible for on-going information programs about citizens' rights and responsibilities (for example, you need to be vaccinated, or now's the time to pay your annual income tax), may be diverted to more politically motivated activity that promotes a current government's good works. This becomes a sensitive public issue during election periods (in Australia at least) because it involves spending millions of dollars from public funds for what are claimed to be political purposes.

The concept of duality in Giddens' (1986) structuration theory may help explain why respondents reported a tendency to tactical practice. Giddens (1986) proposed duality as a major element of structuration theory. Duality rests on the notion that the production and reproduction of social action draws on the same rules and resources that are the means for system reproduction. In this context, it may be that the practitioners in my study found themselves continually asked to take tactical approaches because by constantly doing this they inhibit their ability to work strategically. That is, their tactical role becomes self-reinforcing. Additionally, they may not have the managerial skills and competencies that would enable them to convince senior management of the need for a strategic approach to issues communication.

This research supports the view of Bach and Allen (2010) that organisations need to engage in socio-economic and political issues debates in their non-market environments whether managers like it or not. How these issues are resolved impacts on organisations' market environments—that is, how they are able to successfully conduct their business. It is then a strategic imperative for organisations to identify and analyse potential emerging mid- to long-term issues and plan communication initiatives accordingly. That is, in the parlance of the old-fashioned movie hall westerns, head these issues off at the pass.

Significant issues

Significant socio-economic and political issues with which senior practitioners are concerned when, with dominant coalitions, they make decisions about communication strategy directions, were identified in the research. Practitioners prioritised those that influence strategic communication directions. Ranked first priority in this list were issues that related to an organisation's reputation, values, and credibility. Relationships with stakeholders, and current Australian political issues, were ranked equally as the second priority influences in decision-making about strategy. Other issues that influenced decision-making, in priority order, were regulatory issues that affect the industry, the state of the economy, emerging Australian political issues, the organisation's competitive business environment, social and cultural issues that impact on how the organisation competes. It was curious that despite the survey being conducted at a time when world and Australian politics were consumed by vigorous debates about climate change and, in Australia, carbon and mineral 'resource rent' taxes, issues related to the natural environment that might impact on organisations were rated as the lowest priority by practitioners in all sectors. This may be a result of participants also being asked to prioritise current Australian political issues, leading some to include environmental issues in this category.

Senior female practitioners appear to be more strategically focussed than their male counterparts given the priority they assign to stakeholder relationships for which there was a statistically significant difference between genders (two-tailed t test, $p \leq .05$, t = 0.041). While practitioners of both genders rated issues about organisational reputation, values, and credibility as their highest priority, females gave stakeholder relationships their second priority. Males rated current Australian political issues as their second priority—and stakeholder relationships as their fifth priority. At interview, most of the practitioners who participated were not surprised by these differences in approaches between genders. However, the strength of female practitioners' responses to taking a long-term view of issues analysis and management, including building and maintaining stakeholder relationships, may have implications for professional practice given the tendency of males to short-term, tactical delivery.

To a large extent these findings confirm those of scholars who have previously investigated the 'drivers' of strategic communication decisions from a contingency theory perspective, including the role of issues as independent variables, and on which some of my research questions were based (for example, Cancel et al., 1997; Murphy, 2000; Reber & Cameron, 2003; Argenti et al., 2005; Shin et al., 2006; Pang, Yin, & Cameron, 2010). However, I contend that the findings enable a more fine-grained understanding of how and why Australian practitioners make strategic communication decisions because the research had a strategic practice focus beyond previous studies' examinations of the variables that affect the way in which practitioners do their jobs.

Reputation, values, and credibility

Practitioners overwhelmingly regard strategic communication as a tool for creating, and protecting, a positive reputation for their organisation and promoting its values. They believe that aligning communication to an overall business or corporate plan helps to enhance its strategic positioning. Issues related to reputation, values, and organisational credibility comprised the single most important issue category that concerned the study's participants and they rated it as the primary priority in the current, mid, and long terms. Engaging with stakeholders to address these issues is not a short-term professional approach related only to generating bottom-line profit. It requires an approach to communication that involves a consistent effort in a long-term time frame. Ghemawat (2010) illustrated the point in the context of CEOs needing to manage relationships with government by arguing that 'the insistence that the marketplace should completely dictate outcomes is unlikely to win friends and influence people' (p. 60). The views of other scholars about the imperative of viewing strategic communication as a long-term enterprise support this (see, for example, McCarthy & Hatcher, 2004; Argenti et al., 2005; Cornelissen, 2005; Bach & Allen, 2010; Rensburg & de Beer, 2011).

Senior Australian practitioners' attitudes towards the importance of reputation, values, and credibility in their decision-making reinforce the argument that they attempt to be strategic in their approach to communication because building, sustaining, and enhancing organisational reputations and credibility, and promoting values, requires continuing long-term efforts. Here, too, is an important point of differentiation between the tactical functions of other professional communication disciplines which work in market environments to enhance financial performance through tactical product promotion often utilising the mass news and social media. Strategic communication embraces all organisational communicative interactions with stakeholders in non-market environments (Argenti et al., 2005; Cornelissen, 2005; Hallahan et al., 2007; Bach & Allen, 2010). In this sense, a strategic communication plan should set overall directions for all other communication activity and, because it should be primarily concerned with issues debates in non-market environments, focus on establishing and maintaining an organisation's reputation, values, and credibility.

This is perhaps a heretical departure from the approach that views professional communication as an element of integrated marketing communication directed at seeking news media coverage for products or events. There is more to professional communication practice than a focus on day-to-day support for marketing efforts, especially if that communication is to be labelled as 'strategic.' That suggests that a more complete definition of strategic communication is needed to extend current explanations of what it actually is, especially as most seem to concentrate on its abstract role, not its actual, potential, and imperative role in the professional communication canon.

Stakeholder relationships and management

The data relating to building and managing stakeholder relationships suggest this communication function should be regarded as long-term practice and included as an element of any definition of strategic communication. Linking strategic communication to stakeholder relationships reflects the importance of issues management in that context, and contributes significantly to a better understanding of the nature of strategic communication.

The importance of this is demonstrated by the finding that respondents overall consistently rated stakeholder relationships as their second most important issue priority. As already noted, senior female practitioners give stakeholder relationships a higher priority than do male practitioners. Significantly, the strategic importance of stakeholder relationships is indicated by a willingness to engage in dialogue with stakeholders, even when faced with negative publicity, although fewer (61%) would do so with a stakeholder who threatened their organisation's reputation. Similarly, respondents believe senior executives need to build and maintain relationships with governments and factor emerging political issues into business planning. Senior Australian communicators generally do not believe that top-level managers would waste time by engaging in these dialogues. However, they are less likely to recommend engagement with stakeholders with whom their organisation had previously had negative experiences.

Senior Australian practitioners overwhelmingly support engagement with stakeholders in most circumstances and time frames. This supports Jaques' (2009a, b) argument that issues should be managed in a strategic way. When data on respondents' agreement with the importance of stakeholder communication is cross-tabulated with data that reports the time contexts in which they deal with issues, 75% agree that stakeholder communication is important in the current term. However, 78% say this activity is important in the mid term; and 78% say it is important in the long term. This is reinforced by a rejection of a statement that stakeholder dialogues are not important in any time horizon. Slightly more reject this statement for the mid and long terms (81% for both horizons) than reject it for the current horizon (79%). That suggests a recognition that, because issues are raised and debated in non-market environments, engagement with issues definers and other stakeholders requires a consistent long-term dialogue to work through issues even though that might at times irritate the relationship. For example, fewer senior Australian practitioners in the sample appear to be concerned about the prospect of litigation preventing interactions with stakeholders than are their US counterparts (see, for example, Reber & Cameron, 2003; Shin et al., 2006).

While 36.6% of respondents in my study would not engage with stakeholders when litigation was threatened, almost half (47.9%) had no view about this. This supports the finding that respondents are prepared to engage with stakeholders who oppose them, or with whom their organisations have had past negative experiences, and reinforces the strategic nature of issues management communication.

These are activities that can realistically only be effectively managed with a mid- to long-term approach. This is, as one federal government practitioner noted, 'what strategic communication really encapsulates.' Taking decisions about how to build and maintain stakeholder relationships involves strategic thinking that goes beyond immediate day-to-day tactical practice. And that, in turn, requires organisations to engage as social actors with stakeholders about important issues that concern them both in non-market environments. This ought to be reflected in the definition of strategic communication. In addition, mid- to long-term management of stakeholder relationships needs to be more precisely reflected in the ways practitioners plan issue responses.

Long-term issues management

With the exception of lobbyists, respondents to the online survey questionnaire say that they engage in issues analysis as 'ongoing practice.' However, practitioners who work in private sector businesses (100%), universities, industry associations (100%), or as consultants, are more likely to engage in ongoing issues identification and analysis than colleagues in state and federal government agencies, or not-for-profit organisations. This finding reflects the critical importance that respondents working in private sector business-related contexts place on strategic communication and their mid-term issues management practice, and, because it provides a differential between sectors, contributes to scholarly understanding of strategic communication.

Professional lobbyists viewed communication strategy as critically important and said they are concerned about mid- and long-term issues. While only three lobbyists were represented, it was nevertheless interesting that given their business is about dealing with client issues in a political environment, it was odd that only one lobbyist said they engage in issues analysis as ongoing practice. It is tempting to ignore this data in the context of the information generated by respondents from other sectors. However, the finding presents an intriguing topic for future research: an exploration of the nature of professional lobbying in Australia. For example, it may be that this finding can be explained by the circumstances in which lobbyists are employed. It could be that lobbyists are required to focus on immediate political and regulatory market environment issues that concern their clients rather than identify potential emerging issues irrespective of an individual practitioner's acceptance of the importance of taking a longer term view. That is, despite their support for strategic approaches and nod towards mid- and long-term issues management, do they actually engage in this practice?

Senior practitioners said managing issues in the current term was either critically important or important (100%) reflecting the point that despite the strategic imperative to engage in a strategic approach to professional organisational communication, practitioners must also deal with immediate matters. This is perhaps also reflected in their attitude that it is critical to manage issues in the mid term (96% say this; 68% say it is important) than in the long term (47% say this horizon is critical; 43% that it is important).

Practitioners cannot avoid responding to current issues (Argenti et al., 2005; Cornelissen, 2005), especially as they are often required to deal with urgent demands to respond to mass news media enquiries about, for example, how the latest government announcement, natural disaster, potential industrial strike, or misbehaviour by a director, will impact on their organisation. It is axiomatic that day-to-day issues of this kind, and responses to them, impact on an organisation's reputation, values, and credibility. This is an example of the duality (Giddens, 1986) of issues debates on the decisions practitioners take, and the advice they give to senior management, on communication directions. While they may not use the term 'duality,' senior practitioners need to recognise the impact of market environment issues dynamics in their environmental scanning as a prelude for issues analysis and management. It is the early identification and analysis of issues that might occur in the mid- and long-terms that provide a mechanism by which communication practitioners can work in a strategic and dialogic way. Doing this avoids having to later deal with issues in a tactical context because of a crisis and the demands of the media news cycle. At the very least, mid- and long-term analysis provides time to develop arguments to manage an issue in the current term.

It may be that internal and external demands on communication practitioners to respond in the context of the daily news cycle is the reason respondents place far less importance on the medium- and long-term contexts for issues analysis and communication. That is, they may not have the resources to do anything other than deal with tactical requirements, especially those in small organisations. Nor might they have sufficient agency to persuade other internal actors to address the long-term in the discursive social practice that leads to decisions about strategic communication directions. More importantly, a lack of practitioner agency may reflect a misunderstanding by senior management that professional communication is only about generating mentions in the various platforms of the mass news and social media. This suggests relationships between senior practitioners and dominant coalitions are fraught with hierarchical issues involving senior management's lack of understanding about effective long-term communication. Some respondents hinted that this is the case, especially those working in state and federal government agencies. It appears that political imperatives dominate what and when is communicated and override any ongoing communication strategy agencies have to support their role in providing services. It may also be the reason so many agencies revert to traditional advertising approaches to promote citizens' rights and responsibilities, and the services available to them.

While practitioners must engage in tactical approaches, they do highly rate the importance of communication strategy, and issues management, especially issues related to stakeholder engagement, and organisational reputation, values, and credibility. All these rely on long-term communicative action. Practitioners are likely to be diverted from strategic approaches and this suggests senior managements do not prioritise, nor properly understand, the role of professional communication beyond the tactical use of the mass news and social media. A government communicator with extensive private practice experience noted that many senior managers generally understood the place of communication but often tried to do it themselves and 'often don't recognise the role that professionals can play in that area.' This point was echoed by another government practitioner who said that 'everybody thinks they can communicate.' A consultant observed that many chief executive officers did not understand that communication 'is their job' and

> that's why you don't see public relations people on boards, because they don't recognise the value, they don't understand the importance of it.

Finding a way for practitioners to demonstrate the importance of strategic approaches to communication to dominant coalitions is, then, vital. It would enhance their agency in discursive debates about strategic directions. Data from the European Communication Monitor (2020–2021) suggest that practitioners' agency is less than effective: almost a third of respondents believe linking business strategy and communication is the fourth most important 'strategic' issue they face. Additionally, a quarter of the respondents to the Asia-Pacific Communication Monitor (2020–2021) rated this as their seventh most important 'strategic' issue. Additionally, a mechanism for practitioners to convince dominant coalitions of the strategic imperative would have significant implications for professional practice given the view of 'strategic communication' as a long-term, planned, purposive activity (for example, Argenti et al., 2005; Cornelissen, 2005; Hallahan et al., 2007; Zerfass & Huck, 2007; Sandhu, 2009; Bach & Allen, 2010). In that context, there is a question about whether senior Australian practitioners work as strategically as they say they do if a majority does not attempt to identify issues that might impact on their organisations in the longer term, which is at least five years in the future. Addressing significant issues related to organisational reputations, values, and credibility, and managing stakeholder relationships, requires a planned, consistent, long-term, and focused approach based on environmental scanning and analysis that extends beyond five years.

One practitioner contextualised this by arguing that the proposal for a mineral resource rent tax in Australia during the first term of an Australian Labor Party Federal Government (2007–2010) should not have surprised that industry. The respondent argued that the mining industry

> should have been into this a long time ago, and they should have been talking to the Ministers and the decision-makers long ago…they should have had things in place long ago. My guess is they didn't.

This practitioner also argued that colleagues would be more successful in longer term issues communication if they could convince senior managers to focus 'two and three and four years out, and say doing this now will give you a better chance of succeeding out there' (SC079, interview transcript). That includes advocating an organisation's views, and recognising those of stakeholders and other social actors, in issues debates in non-market environments and recognising that issues debate dynamics impact on organisational positions. In this way, strategic communication can be more accurately conceptualised as an intentional, planned, long-term practice in which social actors interpret the organisation to its stakeholders, and stakeholder views to the organisation (Montgomery, 2012; Raupp & Hoffjann, 2012; Hallahan et al., 2007; Sandhu, 2009).

Adopting that approach would require professional communicators to plan more strategic stakeholder dialogues to build perceptions of their organisations by engaging with, and helping to shape, their social and political environments. Strategic communicators should do this in a way that balances organisations' rights to contribute and shape public issues debates with the interests of stakeholders—a Habermasian view that social actors' motivations should conform to the needs of the overall system (Holtzhausen, 2010; Calhoun, 1992).

Sectoral differences

Practitioners in the public, private, and not-for-profit sectors do consider different issues, or primary divers, when they plan strategic communication directions. Identifying this is important for explaining the contexts in which 'strategic' communication is pursued. These sectoral differences are in many ways axiomatic because they relate to the specific contexts in which respondents work. Practitioners working for not-for-profit organisations rated stakeholder relationships as their most important communication driver because these relationships determine the success of fund-raising efforts; industry association practitioners prioritise regulatory issues because these are a major reason such organisations exist; and universities rely on their reputations, values, and credibility to attract students and research funding. Practitioners working for commercial businesses regard emerging Australian political issues as their primary communication driver, a not surprising result given the impact dynamics of these issues have on market environments. Nor is it surprising that communication consultants are primarily concerned with stakeholder relationships as these involve not only their clients but also the target publics they engage in their professional work. Government agencies regard current political issues as their primary communication driver, reflecting their close working relationships with ministers and their staffs, and the need to keep aware of the impact of the current political environment on policy-making.

A senior practitioner working for a health-related, not-for-profit organisation explained the importance of building and maintaining stakeholder relationships in this way, 'How and what we communicate to these groups is critical to their learning and understanding of the issues and also to their future health and wellbeing.'

Knowing that there are sectoral differences in priority issue categories that drive communication strategies is not only interesting for its own sake, but it also enables a more textured understanding of this practice and thus how it is explained in the scholarly literature. At their most basic level these findings demonstrate that current discussions of strategic communication do not deal with the nuances of practitioner understandings of 'strategy,' nor the contexts in which they work. For example, the focus of state and federal government practitioners is quite definitely on the current term because they are driven to take this approach by ministers or ministers' staff, principally media advisers. The literature should reflect this in explorations of why the political apparatus appears to regard short-term communication more importantly than that in the mid- to long-terms. It may be that political media advisers are too narrowly focused on the 24-hour media cycle and, with political party secretariats, do not understand how the principles of strategic communication, applied to politics, would assist in building mid- to long-term stakeholder (that is, voter) support for policies. That senior communicators in higher education regard reputation, values, and credibility as the major issue category that informs their decisions, while those in government agencies view current Australian political issues as the major factor, illustrates the specific contexts in which they work. Similarly, practitioners in industry associations are primarily concerned about regulatory issues that affect their industry, while those in not-for-profits rate stakeholder relationship as the major category.

Identifying these differences adds to understandings of strategic communication because it demonstrates the diversity of the practice, and helps to explain the reasons why some practitioners, especially in government agencies and industry associations, are so focussed on tactical communication. This theme also suggests two topics for future research: first, how industry associations promote their views on issues, and second, an exploration of the relationships between government agency communication staff and ministerial media advisers. Findings from such research would add to a deeper understanding of how organisations view strategy and how they go about their communication decision-making.

A definition of strategic communication

The definitional dialectic initiated with Hallahan et al.'s (2007) proposition that strategic communication involved more than the traditional positivist approach to professional communication, has focussed on how organisations communicate across organisational endeavours. The emphasis has certainly been on the strategic application of communication, and how organisations function as social actors to advance their missions through purposeful, informational, persuasive, discursive, and relational communication. Yet, while extant definitions regard strategic communication as a unifying framework that recognises that purposeful influence is the fundamental goal of communication by organisations (Hallahan et al., 2007), they do not locate the practice in a specific time frame or environment. Nor do Falkheimer and Heide (2018) when, in the context of their discussion of strategic communication as practice, they referred to it as 'a fundamental part of an organisation's management function' (p. 73). Accepting that strategic communication helps organisations to reach set goals, practitioners propose a range of functional tasks set in a frame of the practice being 'about doing the right things' and which includes all forms of internal, external, formal, and informal communicative action which occurs at all levels of an organisation (p. 74). This view includes the example of a communication director working on communication strategy. Yet there is no sense in this work that strategic communication is about the mid- and long-terms, nor about identifying and planning to resolve potential issues well before they occur in current market environments, nor that it is actually, or should be, a specialised practice in a dimension beyond the daily grind of tactical action. This is not to deny the essential need for people at all levels of an organisation to be consistent in how they communicate internally and externally in line with corporate goals. But it is to advance a view that, after more than a decade of a research and publishing focus, scholars and practitioners should have found a way of defining strategic communication for what it actually is. That is, it is my view that a change to the principles that govern extant definitions of strategic communication is needed to more precisely explicate what it actually involves. Making that change means accepting that strategic communication is not an element of marketing communication, but practice that sets the important directions for the tactical, technical processes normatively used in professional communicative action. This approach would elevate strategic communication to a professional practice more effectively aligned with the way management approaches strategic planning, and that essentially deals with mid- to long-term issues management.

To do that, a refined definition of strategic communication would likely more accurately conceptualise it as professional practice that deals with organisational reputation, values, credibility, and relationships with stakeholders. Respondents to my research overwhelmingly rated these issue categories as their first and second most important priorities for strategic communication. These issues were also highly rated drivers of strategic communication in international research studies (for example, Cancel et al., 1997; Murphy, 2000; Reber & Cameron, 2003; Argenti et al., 2005; Shin et al., 2006; Pang, Yin, & Cameron, 2010). In my research, practitioners consistently held these factors were priorities for communication activity across the current, mid, and long terms. Issues related to reputation, values, and credibility were rated significantly higher than other issue categories. Because practitioners overwhelmingly believe communication strategy is critically important to their organisations and clients, a refined definition would give them an enhanced reason for understanding what it actually involves. That, in turn, would be a useful argument to convince dominant coalitions to understand the value-added benefits that strategic communication brings to their business.

Research consistently finds that practitioners categorically support the role of communication strategies in advancing corporate goals and objectives. Most believe communication strategies should be aligned with corporate business plans, and focus on organisational values and reputations, and maintaining relationships with stakeholders about issues that are important to the organisation. In my Australian research, respondents include emerging political issues, and the need for senior executives to build relationships with the government as matters that involve strategic communication. Most respondents do not regard their roles as being focussed only on bottom-line results, despite often being required to work tactically.

These findings reflect scholarly arguments that communication strategies should be aligned with overall business strategies (for example, Argenti et al., 2005; Bach & Allen, 2010). Asked for their reaction to a statement that aligning communication and business strategies would not enhance their organisation's strategic position, about three-quarters of respondents strongly disagreed (73.6%). While 20.8% simply disagreed with the statement, none agreed in any way with the statement that business and communication strategies should not be linked, although four had no opinion. This reflects the view of a majority of practitioners who agreed (50.7%) or agreed strongly (42.3%) that strategic communication involves advancing corporate goals and objectives in the mid to long terms.

It is in these findings that there is scope for proposing a refined definition of strategic communication. Thus, a more complete definition that reflects the realities of what that professional practice should be, and delivers a more precise context for it, is that strategic communication can be conceptualised as

> [p]lanned and purposeful mid- to long-term communication in which organisations as social actors discursively manage reputation, values, and credibility by maintaining effective relationships with stakeholders about dynamic non-market environment policy issues.

Existing definitions do not locate strategic communication specifically in the non-market environment, nor do they define 'strategic' by contextualising a time frame, and they do not suggest a specific purpose that reflects practitioner concerns. This refined definition does these things: it proposes a specific strategic time frame, and posits organisations as social actors who contribute to public debates about issues related to stakeholder engagement in a specific external arena—their non-market environments. In doing this, the proposed definition explicitly differentiates strategic communication from general tactical practice in a market, or bottom line, environment. The proposed specific primary aim of maintaining stakeholder relationships to build and protect organisational reputations, values, and credibility reflects the concerns of senior practitioners as well as the arguments of management and communication scholars about the importance of these.

Organisations' reputations and credibility are, of course, built from external stakeholders' attitudes towards an organisation. How those attitudes are built—earned—and maintained in external organisational environments is one of the primary tasks of a communication strategy (see the discussion in Frandsen & Johansen, 2014, especially at pp. 183–185; Wood, 2014). Values are the beliefs and ideals an organisation holds, and which inform the way in which it goes about its business. In this sense, values are determined internally meaning that stakeholders may not be aware of them. However, as Wood (2014) pointed out, while corporate values inform the way an organisation operates, and influence strategy and communication with stakeholders, they are also in some way included in the tactics designed for external publics that implement communication strategies. It is for this reason that values are included in the proposed definition of strategic communication.

The proposed definition explicitly locates public policy issues debates in the non-market environment in recognition of this as the arena in which these debates occur. This brings the argument of Bach and Allen (2010) that management needs to recognise the importance of addressing non-market issues directly into discussions about the nature of strategic communication. Finally, the definition recognises that issues debates are discursive and dynamic and that how they play out impacts on organisational decisions to engage with them—a recognition of the notion of duality.

The strategic imperative paradigm shift

Informed by a refined definition, it is possible to hypothesise a paradigm shift that more effectively links strategic communication to mid- and long-term, organisational strategic business planning. That hypothesis is appropriate because communicative action to promote, build, and maintain positive organisational reputations, values, credibility, and relationships with stakeholders is a long-term strategic action that reflects, and supports, long-term business planning.

The next sections discuss this hypothesis, first by reviewing how decisions about strategic communication directions can be interpreted.

Interpreting decisions about strategic communication

Organisations are social actors when they raise or respond to public policy issues in their non-market environments, and their continuing engagement with those issues requires dynamic decision-making (Hallahan et al., 2007; Bach & Allen, 2010). In this view, the process of making decisions about communication strategy directions is conceptualised as a highly politicised and discursive social practice aimed at generating action that interprets an organisation to its stakeholders (Hendry, 2002; Raupp & Hoffjann, 2012). This philosophical perspective assumes that those who make communication strategy decisions understand the external environment in which issues debates occur, identify and analyse issues that impact on their organisations, and recognise the motivations of those who respond to issues raised by the organisation, or advocate their own issues.

In this perspective, strategic communication is a sense-making activity that advocates an organisation's views on important public policy issues to external stakeholders (Raupp & Hoffjann, 2012). When stakeholders engage with these views by also participating as social actors in an issues debate, the organisation's environment, which was factored into the original sense-making, is in turn transformed (Raupp & Hoffjann, 2012). Viewed from this perspective, strategic communication reflects the concepts embodied in Giddens' (1986) structuration theory.

Influences on communication strategy decisions

A central argument I have advanced is that decisions about the directions of a communication strategy are influenced first by public issues debates in an organisation's non-market environment, and second by subsequent decisions about managing advocacy of the organisation's positions as those issues evolve. In this argument, the action of deciding the directions of a communication strategy involves a discursive social practice that is continually affected by the dynamics of debates about the issues with which the strategy was first designed to deal. In other words, organisational responses to issues generate kinetic reactions from other social actors that result in issues evolving, thus affecting how an organisation further contributes. Marchiori and Bulgacov (2012) viewed this as a continuous and interactive process that does not have a defined beginning, middle, or end.

The argument here draws on Hendry's (2000) concept of strategic decision-making as a form of social practice in which discourse is a central feature. The proposition is that the act of discussing strategic issues communication directions reflects Hendry's (2000) view of decision-making as a social practice. Communication decision-making is often chaotic and constrained and influenced by power relationships inside organisations, often highly politicised, and involves taking account of the interests of the subcultures, factions, and discourses in organisations (Hendry, 2000; Berger, 2005; Hatch & Cunliffe, 2006). Among the factors that make decision-making chaotic and politicised are the often-uncertain conditions in which decisions must be taken, and whose values are represented in the process (Deetz, 2003). That means that where differences occur over goals and tactics, power and politics influence decision-making (Hatch & Cunliffe, 2006). This is what Burkart (2009) described as practical discourse in which the object is to justify interests and decisions and value judgements. Thus, the development of communication strategies is dynamic because it involves iterative issues analysis and decision-making. Primary and subsequent decisions about an organisation's strategic communication directions, and issue advocacy, are affected by internal and external debates about issues that occur in an organisation's non-market environment.

Contingency theory and communication decisions

One way of explaining the process of making decisions about the direction of a communication strategy is to use the principles of contingency theory. Using contingency theory means that issues can be regarded as independent variables that influence a strategy, or a dependent variable. That is, the direction of a communication strategy is determined by decisions based on an analysis of issues likely to emerge in the mid- and long-terms during an internal debate about how to manage them. When an organisation implements its communication strategy to advocate its positions on issues, non-market environmental debates alter as other social actors contribute, or raise new issues to which the organisation needs to respond. Issues evolve depending on the perspectives and activities of each stakeholder (Bigelow et al., 1993). Thus, the evolution of an issue is influenced by the kinetic energy of dynamic forces (independent variables) outside the control of the organisation. This creates a need to reinterpret issues and subsequently redefine positions (Bigelow et al., 1993). That some issues follow a recursive path 'cycling back and forth through the stages' (Bigelow et al., 1993, p. 24) of the traditional issues cycle, and may never be resolved, reflects the effect that independent variables have on the dependent variable, a communication strategy.

This is how contingency theory has been used as a traditional mechanism through which to explain influences on professional communication practice (Cancel et al., 1997; Reber & Cameron, 2003; Shin et al., 2006). However, contingency theory implies a positivist approach to explaining the process in which dynamic issues affect decisions about communication strategy directions. Nevertheless, it is an important theoretical lens, and, for that reason, a brief return to the earlier discussion of contingency theory and issues management is important in this chapter.

While contingency theory can explain what happens, it does not explain why and how decisions about communication strategy directions are made. A constructivist realism social ontology that informed my research suggests that understanding how strategic communication decisions are made needs a more textured, perhaps more complex, approach than traditional positivist descriptions of what it is, how it is used, and what variables affect it. These factors need to be contextualised so that the practice can be understood in its own terms (Hay, 2002). Giddens' (1986) structuration theory provides a way of doing that because, as Durham (2005) argued, it enables a more interpretivist approach that recognises actions result in unintended and recursive consequences.

This has important implications for strategic communication practice. As structuration theory recognises that organisations are dynamic and transforming, it helps to explain the role of strategic communication (Falkheimer, 2007). In addition, if practitioners understand the dialogic process of structuration, they would better understand and act on the continually changing nature of their institution's place in society and thus more consciously and effectively engage in the meaningful contexts within which they are working (Durham, 2005).

A structurationist interpretation of strategic communication decisions

The process of structuration is enacted when the process, including the rules by which communication strategy decisions are made (a 'structure'), is influenced by 'agents' (practitioners, senior managers), or changes as these 'agents' take 'action' based on internal discourses about issues management (for example, discussions about issue impacts). In this process, senior communication practitioners and dominant coalitions are social actors when they engage in internal discussions about potential issue impacts, priorities, and communication strategy directions, as they are when they advocate organisational views in external non-market environments. In this view, decisions are influenced not only by initial assessments of issue impacts, but by organisational structures that Olufowote (2003) argued 'coordinate actors' in ways influenced by both social systems and interaction partners (p. 12) as well as by ongoing analysis of dynamic issues debates as other social actors advance their views in the organisation's non-market environment (see Figure 7.1).

In this conceptualisation, generative rules and resources are the established norms (formal and informal processes senior managers and communication practitioners follow to debate, consult, and decide about issues and strategic directions), language, and power. They are exercised in the discursive social practice that involves organisational actors making decisions about the directions of communication strategies. These processes include environmental scanning of an organisation's non-market environment and boundary spanning by communication practitioners to interpret issues for senior management. These are the day-to-day routine, or regularised, acts Giddens (1986) regarded as social practices.

Thus, a practitioner's analysis and planning decisions about how to deal with issues, taken with other senior managers, should determine the directions of a communication strategy. A duality occurs when external social actors enter an

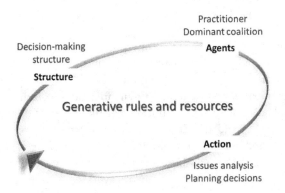

FIGURE 7.1 Communication strategy decision-making in a structuration perspective

Figure 7.1 conceptualises strategic communication decision-making as an example of structuration when the internal process of making strategy decisions is regarded as structure, practitioners and dominant coalitions are agents, and decisions about issues analysis and planning are defined as actions. This becomes a more complex construct when the actions of external social actors on issues dynamics are also considered.

issues debate in an organisation's non-market environment and interact with the organisation by pursuing their own positions on an issue, or by raising new issues. This interplay changes the parameters of an issues debate, forcing organisations to modify their strategic advocacy positions, or even to withdraw from a debate. For example, one senior government communicator noted that current political issues could draw practitioners away from strategic approaches to influence day-to-day activities and 'change the path of them so quickly.' A senior private sector consultant noted at interview that, especially in government, the ability to communicate strategically 'gets swallowed up in the imperative of the day-to-day media cycle.'

The concept of issue life cycles illustrates how structuration theory, especially duality, can explain strategic issue communication decisions. Scholars argue that issues are dynamic and complex and that how they evolve, and are resolved, depends on a range of variables, including the perspectives of stakeholders. Heath and Palenchar (2009) contextualised this when they argued that even identifying issues is difficult because of their complexities and the effect of variables on the emergence and growth of an issue. Issues dynamics involve how they are framed, how they impact on organisations, and the contexts in which they are addressed (Harrison, 2011). This includes not only debates between organisations and activists, but also within industries, between activist groups, and between government agencies (Heath & Palenchar, 2009).

The evolution of issues depends on the perspectives and activities of stakeholders and begins before stakeholders decide their attitudes towards them (Bigelow et al., 1993). Thus, not all issues move sequentially through all the stages implicit in a traditional issue life cycle because they may be buffeted by forces outside the control of any one organisation or stakeholder (Bigelow et al., 1993). This is the essence of Sommerfeldt's (2012) view that issues evolve with time and context and that interactions between social actors shape issues and the structures of future discussions. In Olufowote's (2003) terms, the 'interplay between actors and institutions produce[s] intended and unintended outcomes, which are to enter into the constitution of subsequent interactions' (p. 16). Thus, issues dynamics and the consequent discursive practice involved in making decisions about them by an organisation's communication strategists and dominant coalition illustrate how structuration theory, and the concept of duality, is appropriate for understanding the process of deciding how strategic communication should deal with issues in a non-market environment.

Olufowote (2003) argued that structuration theory can be applied in communication scholarship in part because research should examine 'the relationship between virtual outcomes of interaction processes and their influence on subsequent interactions' (p. 21). Olufowote (2003) proposed a framework that includes examining routine social practices, the structures themselves (because structures partly explain why routines sustain themselves), the ways in which agents interact with structures, and the interplay between actors and institutions. The framework is an appropriate way of examining the interactions between the dynamics of issues debates and organisational decisions to communicate (see Figure 7.2).

The discussion so far regards strategic communication decision-making as a routine organisational discursive social practice, conceptualises a decision-making process as a structure, and argues the interaction between social actors and organisations, and the resulting dynamic influences of public policy issues debates, are dualities that impact on a communication strategy. Olufowote's (2003) framework demonstrates how structuration theory can help to explain how decisions about communication strategies are made.

This leads to a conceptualisation of the processes involved in making decisions about strategic communication directions from a structuration perspective (see Figure 7.3). This concept recognises that the process of making decisions about dealing with issues is dynamic and affected by the actions of internal agents when communication strategies are initially prepared, and by external agents, or social actors, as public policy issues are debated in the non-market environment.

Explaining strategic communication decisions with structuration theory

Research cited earlier provides examples of how structuration theory, using Olufowote's (2003) framework, can explain decisions about the directions of communication strategies.

As we have seen, practitioners overwhelmingly identified organisational reputation, values, and credibility as the single most important issue category that drove their communication activities, both in their day-to-day activities and over the mid and long terms. When the data were cross-tabulated by sector, this issue category emerged as the special focus of practitioners in higher education. This was not a surprising finding because universities depend on their reputations, values, and credibility to attract research funding and students. All respondents support engaging in long-term dialogue with stakeholders who criticise their organisations and would do so when reputation is threatened (a majority said they usually did this). An illustration of a structurationist interpretation of how these two findings might interact is set out in the following higher education example.

A higher education institution's communication strategy (structure) would be based on decisions to build and maintain the university's reputation as a credible research and teaching organisation by promoting its values to selected stakeholders, perhaps more narrowly defined as specific target publics, through a series of goals, objectives, message delivery strategies, and tactics. The issues analysis on which the strategy is based would list damage to reputation as a risk. To achieve its reputational goals and objectives, and contain the risk, the university (a social actor, or agent) would engage in long-term dialogue (action or interplay) with stakeholders who have the ability to support or to threaten its reputation.

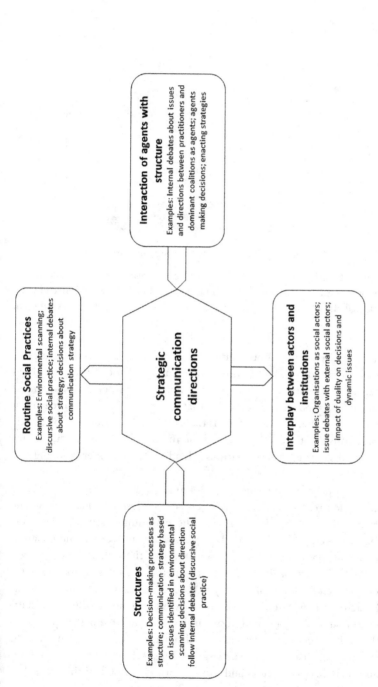

FIGURE 7.2   Olufowote's structuration framework and decisions about strategic communication directions Adapted from Olufowote, 2003.

Figure 7.2 illustrates how Olufowote's (2003) framework applies to the argument that Giddens' (1986) structuration theory can be used to explain how decisions about strategic communication directions are made, including those that result from the duality that occurs when dynamic issues debates influence continuing organisational participation.

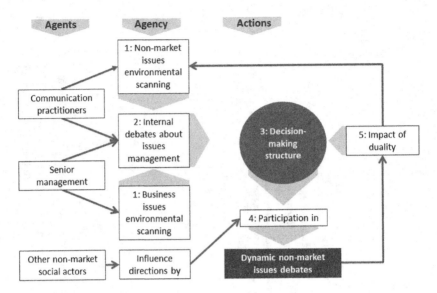

FIGURE 7.3 Impact of duality on communication strategy decision-making

Figure 7.3 conceptualises how structuration theory can explain how initial and subsequent decisions about the directions of a communication strategy are influenced by the actions of internal and external agents, or social actors. It illustrates the duality inherent in the process.

Decisions (actions by agents) about doing that would be made after an internal debate, which in Hendry's (2000) argument is a form of social practice, about the importance of reputation and a strategy to build and protect it. While most participants (Giddens' purposive actors) in that debate are likely to agree about the importance of reputation, the reality is that it would be influenced by political and power considerations as it balanced the interests of the subcultures, factions, and other discourses in organisations (Hendry, 2000; Berger, 2005; Hatch & Cunliffe, 2006).

This is an example of what Olufowote (2003) suggested happens when actors interact with structure. Debates (actions/interplays) with stakeholders about values and other issues that would flow from the communication strategy decision-making process (structure) would take place in the university's non-market environment. The positive or negative outcomes of these dialogues (actions/interplays) would impact on its ability to compete with other institutions for students and research funding, an activity that occurs in its market environment. Other social actors (agents), for example, disaffected students, disillusioned staff, activists, neighbours not consulted about university land management developments that affect them, regulators, or politicians, may engage in existing debates about the university, or raise new issues. This reflects Olufowote's (2003) notion of interplay between actors and institutions. As a result of this interplay, communicators (agents) would need to re-visit the issues analysis that informed the original approach and re-calibrate (actions) strategic directions to continue to protect the institution's reputation.

This process is both an example of Bigelow et al.'s (1993) point that the evolution of issues may be changed by dynamic forces outside the control of the organisation, creating a need to reinterpret issues and subsequently redefine positions, and of Giddens' (1986) duality of structure conceptualised in Figure 7.3.

Similarly, the finding from my research that communicators in government agencies are regularly diverted from implementing their planned strategies by pressure to deal with current political issues, can be explained by structuration theory. That is, ministerial staff, principally media advisers, are social actors who use their agency (power) to divert communicators' focus from strategy to daily tactics to deal with immediate political issues. This illustrates the internal interplay between actors (media advisors) and institutions that explains why senior government practitioners at both state and federal levels rate current political issues as the primary drivers of 'strategic' communication.

Giddens' (1986) structuration theory can also explain how regulatory issues are the main driver of industry associations' strategic communication. One of the main reasons for establishing an industry association is to enable a collective approach to public policy debates about regulation, as well as to present a united front in discussions with politicians and bureaucrats about wider industry issues. Industry associations keep a keen watch on official proposals to change, or introduce, new regulations and monitor debates instigated by politicians, bureaucrats, activists, and non-government organisations. In pursuing their goals and objectives, industry associations engage in routine internal and external social practices, in which agents (association members and officers) interact with structures (communication strategy decision-making structures), both of which are affected by the interplay between actors and institutions (Parliament, the bureaucracy, non-government organisations, activist groups).

These examples, and the discussion about using structuration theory to better understand strategic communication decision-making that preceded them, respond to the challenge that scholars further embrace theoretical approaches from other disciplines to more effectively explain the role of professional communication (for example, Gower, 2006; Sandu, 2009; Frandsen & Johansen, 2010). An attempt to do that is set out in the arguments in this work. In particular, suggesting Giddens' (1986) structuration theory can help to explain how dynamic issues debates influence decisions about strategic communication directions not only meets this academic challenge but suggests how practitioners might better understand the challenges they face in those debates.

Having accepted that challenge, another step is to propose that Baghai et al.'s (2000) concept that corporations should plan for growth in three time 'horizons' can be applied to issues identification and analysis to more effectively link business and communication strategies.

Linking business and strategic communication planning

The research findings and analysis reported here help to explain how issues influence 'strategic' communication decisions. They also suggest a need for communication to be closely, and more effectively, linked to business planning for two reasons. First, practitioners believe it should be, and scholars argue that it must be, if strategic communication is to successfully support organisational goals. Scholars have consistently argued the importance of linking strategic communication planning with corporate plans (for example, J.E. Grunig & Repper, 1992; Argenti et al., 2005, Cornelissen, 2005; Jones & Bartlett, 2009; Bach & Allen, 2010; Ghemawat, 2010). So successful have the arguments been that there is an assumption that it actually happens. So, it is, as has been argued here, not at all clear that strategic communication plans are in fact closely tied to corporate strategies, or that practitioners and dominant coalitions recognise what an effective strategic approach to communication involves. Second, if senior practitioners are to convince dominant coalitions to accept longer term, methodical approaches to issues identification, analysis, and communication, they need a model that demonstrates how that can be done. At the least, a model would give them the key to sit at that much desired, and elusive, C-suite table to make the case for strategic communication's undoubted value-added contribution that will protect their organisation from issues that should be addressed before they impact on the market environment. That approach takes strategic communication away from the notion that it is what Falkheimer and Heide (2018) described as a 'soft power discipline,' and supports their view that communication professionals must

> show communication impacts that convince management of its value.
>
> *(p. 83)*

Hypothesising a paradigm for making that formal link between corporate business planning and strategic communication operationalises the proposed definition of strategic communication set out above. The new paradigm will contribute to scholarly discussions about what strategic communication actually is, and where, and how, it differs from the tactical, technical elements of marketing communication. Senior practitioners will have their C-suite key and the ability to focus on mid- to long-term management of socio-economic and political issues. An illustration of the importance of this paradigm for professional practice is regularly reported in sequential editions of the European Communication Monitor that aligning communication strategies to business strategies is considered one of the most important strategic issues for practitioners.

The so-called drivers of strategic communication identified by Argenti et al. (2005)—regulation, organisational complexity, and the need to increase credibility—are all mid- to long-term considerations, as are the significant research findings about practitioner concerns to protect reputation, values, and credibility, and engage effectively with stakeholders. Those drivers provide a rationale for a paradigm that makes the business-communication strategic link far more effective. In doing that, mid- to long-term issues management communication would be elevated to a position as equally important as market-driven tactical communication, and, as the strategic communication imperative, arguably more important.

How might the link between business planning and the development of an effective issues management communication strategy be effectively made?

Gower (2006) noted that much of the public relations literature has particularly focussed on what practitioners do, rather than on the business drivers for practice, and argued public relations scholars have not kept pace with the evolution in the management literature's 'thinking about strategy' (p. 185). Gower (2006) argued that:

> If we are to be a management function, we need to bring that literature into ours and update what we do and how we do it.
>
> *(p. 185)*

That also tends to be the case with strategic communication literature. The paradigm shift theorised here brings the management literature into the communication arena in a direct way by suggesting an explicit alignment of strategic communication, as defined in this chapter, to the business planning model proposed by Baghai et al. (2000). That alignment would provide both management and senior practitioners with common ground on which they could accept the similarities in strategic business and communication planning and thus advance organisations' chances of effectively dealing with non-market environment issues. It would enable management and communicators to differentiate between strategic and tactical approaches to overcome some of the issues research has identified, especially in government agency communication. Government communicators are often required to chase media pressure and politically driven agendas rather than concentrate on strategic approaches. One government agency practitioner noted that State Governments struggled to commit to strategic communication and issues management beyond hourly, daily, or weekly media cycles, and other government practitioners argued this was often driven by ministerial media advisers. Yet there is no reason why government agency communication should not be regarded as strategic function, aligned with agency strategies, while ministerial media advisers deal with day-to-day issues.

So, how to make this paradigm shift?

Baghai et al. (2000) argued that business growth for corporations could be managed across 'three horizons' simultaneously in order to distinguish between the embryonic, emergent, and mature phases of a business' life cycle. The horizons they proposed are:

Horizon 1: extending and defending core business. This horizon encompasses the businesses that are at the heart of an organisation and with which customers and analysts most readily identify. Horizon 1 is critical to near-term performance as cash and skills generated in it provide resources for growth. One of the primary management challenges is to shore up competitive positions aided by, among other things, marketing.

Horizon 2: building emerging businesses. In this horizon, management is concerned with the emerging stars of the company, because they transform companies. Thus, Horizon 2 is about building new streams of revenue which may be extensions of current business or move in new directions.

Horizon 3: seeding options for future businesses. Horizon 3 businesses are options on future opportunities. Horizon 3, then, is the longer term future in which real activities, such as research projects, test market pilots, alliances, and so on, mark the first steps towards actual businesses which, if they prove successful, will be expected to reach the profitability of those in the Horizon 1 stage of growth.

In the context in which the term 'business' is used in this book, that is, the core activities of organisations, it is possible to adapt Baghai et al.'s (2000) concept to organisations not only in the private sector, but also to government agencies, industry associations, not-for-profit groups, and universities.

As an example, current business for an industry association means the issues it needs to deal with immediately, mid-term issues are the policy recommendations it needs to promote during the life of a legislature to ensure both sides of politics understand its position in detail, and the long term involves difficult, emerging issues related to, say, a free-trade agreement, community health, or education.

In this way, mid- to long-term strategic communication for non-market environments can conceptually be located explicitly in

Horizon 2: in which it would support organisational efforts to strategically enhance reputations, provide counsel on the public communication aspects of regulatory issues, and manage relationships with stakeholders in the context of business building strategies

Horizon 3: where its focus would be on long-term socio-economic and political issues identification and analysis, strategic counselling, and associated communication program planning

That leaves Horizon 1, the focus of which Baghai et al. (2000) explained is on extending and defending core business to increase profits. This focus consolidates the important tactical role of integrated marketing communication. Horizon 1 is the market environment in which the immediate tactical activities involved in issues and crisis communication, event management, product promotion, personal selling, advertising, and some of the corporate communication and public affairs functions (immediate day-to-day political lobbying, for example) of public relations, occur. These tactical activities are generally focussed on enhancing an organisation's bottom line. For business corporations, that means financial profits. For not-for-profit organisations, a market environment focus means fundraising, either through grants or donations, and building stakeholder relationships. For industry associations, universities, and communication consultants' clients, that means advancing views on current issues. For government agencies, the non-market environment is about providing citizens with information about their rights and responsibilities, a broad task that practitioners say is often diverted by demands for attention to current political issues. The communication focus of each horizon and associated outputs is illustrated in Table 7.1.

This conceptualisation does not imply that all issues debates in Horizon 1 are de facto non-strategic. Organisations do, and will, participate in some issues debates in Horizon 1 based on the tactical implementation of a strategic communication plan. As with the concept of a non-market environment, communication on the same issue must sometimes occur in each horizon. For example, tactical political lobbying in Horizon 1 about, say, taxation relief for working mothers by an organisation representing them will reflect the identification of this issue as a mid- to long-term concern for that group and the communication strategy designed to promote their views. It is for this reason that Table 7.1 lists day-to-day media relations, tactical lobbying, and crisis communication as communication outputs in Horizon 1.

Implications for future research and practice

The research presented here, the proposed definition of strategic communication and paradigm shift to more effectively link business and communication

TABLE 7.1 Horizons for strategic communication

Table 7.1 conceptualises how strategic communication planning can be aligned with business planning using Baghai et al.'s (2000) 'horizons for growth.' The table shows the specific professional communication outputs in this alignment

	Horizon 1 Now	Horizon 2 Mid term to 5 years	Horizon 3 Long term 5 years
Focus	Current business	Emerging business	Future business
Outputs	Environmental scanning	Issues identification though	Long-term issues identification
	Boundary spanning	environmental scanning	and analysis
	Day-to-day media relations	Building stakeholder	Strategic stakeholder
	Tactical lobbying	relationships	relationship management
	Crisis communication	Policy development and	Persistent government and
	Marketing communication	lobbying	community relations
		Specific project communication	Strategic planning

Adapted by the author from Baghai et al. (2000), p. 130.

planning, has implications for professional communication scholarship and practice. These implications are discussed in the following sections.

Implications for professional communication scholarship

This work demonstrates that embracing theoretical approaches from other disciplines, especially management and sociology, can help to more effectively explain the role of professional communication. That has been pursued specifically by demonstrating how management, sociological, and professional communication literature about the concept of strategy, decisions to be made, and stakeholder relationships, and by utilising Giddens' (1986) structuration theory, can better explain how strategic communication decision-making takes place, and its role in issues management in organisational non-market environments. That includes arguing that the non-market environment is the most appropriate context in which to locate public policy issues identification, analysis, management, and communication, especially in the context of pursuing stakeholder relationships and the protection of organisational reputations.

The latter point is significant because it provides a mechanism for operationalising Bach and Allen's (2010) advice that whether they like it or not, senior managers need to pay greater attention to issues that play out in their non-market environment because of the implications those issues have for market communication. De Figueiredo and de Figueiredo (2002) found from their experiment on non-market business strategy that managers could adapt and learn about their environments. It is in these contexts that Argenti et al. (2005) argued for senior managers to recognise the imperative of engaging in strategic, as distinct from tactical, communication. In addition, the use of Baghai et al.'s (2000) horizons approach to business planning creates a new domain for scholarly discourse about communication practice by proposing a different way of thinking about strategy.

By doing this, scholarly understanding of strategic communication is advanced through the lens of a refined, more complete definition, and the use of structuration theory to understand how dynamic issues debates impact on communication decision-making. This is operationalised by the proposed direct, explicit linking of strategic issues communication planning and implementation to strategic business planning.

Potential future research

This approach highlights the need for further research into the concept of strategic communication and how it is practised. The suggestion for a particular approach to defining, understanding, and implementing the practice outlined here should be tested. At the least, more knowledge is needed about why communication practitioners and their senior managers hold different views of what it actually means to communicate an organisation's views on important public policy issues in a strategic way. Further research to extend the findings reported here would provide scope for more contributions to the scholarly literature about strategic communication and potentially lead to an enhanced understanding of professional communication practice.

Additionally, in-depth research could also investigate the notion that a lack of practitioner agency in decisions about strategic practice may explicate in more detail the reasons senior managers appear to misunderstand the value of strategic approaches to professional communication to their organisations. This would include collecting data from senior managers in commercial businesses, not-for-profit groups, industry associations, and government agencies. The research cited here did not explore the differences between male and female senior management styles in detail, nor whether this impacts on practitioners' ability to exercise their professional agency in decisions about strategic communication practice. This finding emerged from the analysis of the quantitative demographic data but became a topic in the face-to-face interviews. This suggests an area for extended research as a project that would reflect the arguments of Lawrence and Lorsch (1967) about the importance of management practices to organisations.

An exploration of formal organisational structural relationships between senior communication practitioners and dominant coalitions, or whether practitioners reported directly to chief executives, was not part of the present work. However, it may be that, as Kanihan et al. (2013) found in their study of communication managers working for US corporations, that formal membership of a dominant coalition, and a direct reporting line to the chief executive, positively impacts on how decisions about issues analysis and communication strategy directions are taken. That suggests there is scope for future research to identify whether such relationships with senior management impact on the ability of business and government agency communication managers to work in a strategic way, and whether that helps to deliver positive outcomes for issues communication.

The finding that some respondents prioritise current Australian political issues suggests potential further research to identify the specific political issues with which they are concerned, especially with a cohort of practitioners working in private sector businesses, government agencies, communication consultancies, and industry associations. Understanding these issue categories in detail would inform scholarly discussion about how practitioners in different sectors work. That may also have implications for professional practice.

Other than to identify whether there were sectoral differences in the factors that practitioners use in making strategic decisions, the research was not designed to investigate in detail how they actually go about their strategic practice. Nevertheless, two potential research topics are suggested by the findings on sectoral differences: the nature of professional lobbying in Australia, especially given the limited responses from this communication specialisation to the research, and how industry associations promote their views on issues. Such research should attempt to more closely understand the roles of these closely related political communication specialisations in a democratic society.

While the finding that government communicators are often forced into tactical practice by other, perhaps more powerful, agents was not entirely unexpected, it does suggest an area for future research. The professional working relationships between government agency communication practitioners and ministerial media advisers and other staff, and how each understands the other's role, is one potential field for such future research. The results of this research would increase academic understanding of the processes of this aspect of government communication and enable informed scholarly discussion of the implications of the agency which ministerial offices exert over communicators in bureaucracies.

Implications for professional practice

The refined definition of strategic communication and concept of aligning planning directly with business planning in the three horizons advanced by Baghai et al. (2000) have two important potential consequences for professional practice.

First, they provide communication strategists with a framework to support their case with dominant coalitions for a more strategic approach to communication because it locates communication directly in a management planning construct. Managers understand management constructs. Linking communication planning to a management construct provides common ground for understanding how an organisation's chances of effectively dealing with non-market environment socio-economic and political issues can be planned. This concept would enable management and communicators to differentiate between strategic and tactical communication to overcome some of the issues identified by the research because this paradigm shift delivers a practical reality to the importance of dealing with non-market issues over the mid and long terms. These time periods are the essence of non-market issues debates.

Second, this concept provides practitioners with the rationale for a paradigm shift in the way in which they engage in strategic issues management and communication. Planning strategic communication in Baghai et al.'s (2000) horizons' model provides direction for the mid- and long-term environmental scanning needed for effective strategic communication planning. In addition, the proposed definition of strategic communication illustrates the long-term nature of building and maintaining effective, ethical stakeholder relationships around non-market issues about organisational reputation, values, and credibility. The need to address these issues and focus on stakeholder relationships were the two most highly rated drivers of strategic communication nominated by respondents to my research questionnaire.

The two professional practice implications outlined here reflect the argument of Huebner et al. (2008) that practitioners should have an in-depth understanding of the settings in which communication about decisions takes place, as well as be aware of who needs to be involved in facilitating strategies. That includes involving managers in communication processes as well as establishing communicating as an 'effective management process' (Huebner et al., 2008, p. 218).

Conclusion

This work has identified issues that senior Australian communication practitioners in the public, private, higher education, and not-for-profit sectors consider when they make decisions about strategic directions. It has also identified factors, like the agency of senior managers, and, in a government communication context, ministerial staff, that influence those decisions and are outside the control of practitioners. The work has also proposed a proposed new definition of strategic communication that more completely describes the practice, its contexts, and the time frames in which it should be implemented.

Researching and writing a communication strategy should primarily be driven by the need for organisations to contribute to, and thus influence, public discussions about socio-economic and political issues that affect relationships with their stakeholders, and thus their reputations. This book includes an argument that these debates occur, and are resolved, in an organisation's non-market environment, and that they impact on decisions about strategic communication directions. It argues that such issues are not static and the resolution of them ultimately affects an organisation's ability to meet its goals. There is a duality in this process: the parameters of public debates about issues constantly change and these dynamics in turn influence how organisations continue to advocate their views in those debates. To cope with these dynamics, I have theorised a paradigm shift that illustrates how communication strategies can be carefully aligned and integrated with business planning processes. This paradigm would mean that socio-economic and political issues that affect organisational reputations and stakeholder relationships can be more adequately identified, analysed, and managed in time frames that are appropriate to the ability to actually resolve them. That is, non-market issues cannot be resolved by tactical communication especially if they affect how stakeholder relationships are built and maintained. For this reason, strategic communication should be differentiated from other forms of professional communication to more precisely position it as mid- to long-term practice that applies in non-market environments. This differentiation would reposition strategic communication in a new dimension: a focus on issues that do not immediately occur in a bottom-line market context but one that is actually strategic in purpose and action.

In making these arguments, the book provides professional communication practice with a new planning model, fills gaps in the literature, and contributes to scholarly debate.

A REFLECTION ON AN UNENDING JOURNEY

This journey has not ended. At every waypoint it delivers another surprise. That is the nature of research. The process starts with assumptions about what you will discover. Along the way, countless narrow lanes divert you into chasing ideas, points of view, and outright assertions that will confirm the assumptions, challenge their validity, or lead to them being dumped. Hopefully the research process will also ignite some critical thinking about dominant paradigms and how they can be amended by applying the views of scholars you encounter along the way. At this waypoint on my journey, Argenti et al., Bach and Allen, Baghai et al., Giddens and Deetz entered the frame. What is almost certain, though, is that one narrow lane that takes you to scholars like these will guide you to a totally new direction that ends with different assumptions and findings you never expected. A eureka moment; the nature of research. This journey has not ended. Perhaps it never will because it has produced a new approach, the strategic communication imperative for mid- and long-term issues management. That is a new paradigm with scope for others to investigate, analyse, and critique.

And so, to Stanley Deetz, a critical US communication scholar. Deetz has argued for greater engagement by researchers in the worlds they study to enrich the 'everyday ways of talking and thinking about communication by scholars and other communities' (Deetz, 2008, p. 295). In Deetz's (2008) view, the interests of researchers do not always reflect those of students or other communities and that, in trying to 'get things right and unquestionable,' scholars were often not 'right about very interesting things and unclear as to how our abstracted claims connected back to outside problems and communities' (p. 290). In urging what he described as 'co-generative theorising' as a way of engaging with the world being studied, Deetz (2008) argued for a focus on mutual understanding of community or organisational life realities, and for scholars to generate new ways of thinking. Deetz had earlier argued that the point of research was not to

DOI: 10.4324/9781003177340-8

get it right but to 'challenge guiding assumptions, fixed meanings and relations' (Deetz, 2001, p. 37).

I have attempted to follow Deetz's (2001, 2008) maxims by engaging with a professional communication community that the research studied, and by challenging assumptions, including my own, about senior Australian communication practitioners' organisational work realities. That has led me to differ from the dominant fixed meanings about what strategic communication is. Too often, especially in professional practice and scholarship, those fixed meanings assume a 'strategic' label can be applied to what is in reality tactical and technical communication. Strategy is about future-oriented, long-term thinking. To be strategic, professional communication decisions should be informed by the identification and analysis of socio-economic and political issues that will potentially emerge months and years in the future. To be effective in this role, strategic communication should be planned and implemented in parallel with the mid- and long-term horizons used in strategic business planning.

In conceptualising this new paradigm for planning strategic communication based on a definitional re-positioning to account for the realities of issues dynamics, this work has challenged normative descriptions of strategic communication in practice and scholarship. That is, the findings provide data from respondents' direct, personal insights about what actually happens in the contexts of their daily work and that, in turn, is data that challenge assumptions. Even though the research results at times seem axiomatic, they are now at least confirmed and say something relevant about the reality of some aspects of professional communication practice.

Purposive sampling provided an 'elite' or 'key' cohort that delivered a deep professional knowledge about the factors that drive senior communicators' decision-making. This was a deliberate choice because participants did have specialist knowledge about the issues being investigated and had shared senior characteristics and experiences, and the ability to provide relevant detailed data. Yet, because this was by design a narrow sample of senior professionals with decision-making authority, it is not possible without further research to generalise the results to other populations and certainly not to lower levels of Australian practice. Greater representation of senior practitioners from not-for-profit organisations and professional lobbyists would have enriched the study. Research from broader international contexts does suggest that the Australians are not far from the experiences of their world-wide colleagues. This is why I have at times made a reasonable inference that the respondents' data also refer to practitioners more broadly. Take that how you will, but, if you have the time and inclination, explore the topics with practitioners in your own realms to prove the ideas either sound or otherwise.

Some questions in the online questionnaire could have been extended to enable richer data. For example, the formal reporting relationships between senior communicators and dominant coalitions were not tested, and the questions about the time frames in which issues identification and analysis occurs could have been more directly linked to the concept of market and non-market environments.

Finally, I came to this research project with an academic background preceded by lengthy professional practice as a senior issues analyst and 'strategic' communicator in a national industry association, federal government agencies, and higher education, following a prior career as a journalist in the daily news media. I thus brought assumptions from the realities of my working life in professional communication to the project, as well as from the paradigms that have informed my university teaching and research. I readily admit to at times being conflicted by how these experiences interact, especially as I explored scholarly literature about strategic communication. My understanding of what it is, and how it is practised and investigated, is perhaps another example of the duality Giddens (1986) included in his structuration theory. Among my assumptions were that professional communicators could implement their strategic plans, knew what being strategic actually means, and had the support of dominant coalitions. The research challenged those assumptions.

While the identities of those who participated in the research are anonymous, some of those invited to contribute were current and former professional colleagues. This presents a potential limitation to the study given the possibility that responses to survey questions and face-to-face discussions may have been inadvertently influenced by professional familiarity. In other words, while I attempted to avoid them doing so, did these respondents answer as they thought I would like them to answer? In this context, have I unwittingly allowed experience-based biases and orthodoxies to creep into the study design and questions (Gast & Zanini, 2012)?

Among the initial assumptions underlying the study was that senior communicators always engage in strategic practice, gender made no difference to how this was done, and dominant coalitions implicitly supported them, as this had been my personal experience. These professional practice assumptions were challenged by the project. So, too, were the academic paradigms, as I understand them, that inform communication research and teaching, particularly those that are grounded in the US literature, and what now appears to be a dominant European focus on strategic communication research. As examples of these challenges, the almost cynical way in which some consultants commented about what they do, and why they don't always produce strategies, led to a sense that commercial considerations were almost more important to them than actually doing a good job at professional communication. As for scholarship, I found myself closer to Deetz's (2008) view that the current frames that guide professional communication research and teaching (the so-called iron grip excellence theory, for example) often reflect something other than what actually happens in the profession. This presents a further question about my research analysis: did the social ontology of constructivist realism that informed my approach to this work enable me to be sufficiently objective in challenging assumptions? My view is that it did. Someone else might join this never-ending journey to test that assumption.

APPENDIX 1

Research approach and headline results tables

This appendix outlines the methods used to investigate how the senior Australian communication professionals who participated in this research project understand their organisations' external environments and what influences the communication decisions they take. It also presents some headline results, in tabular form, from my doctoral research that were used to support the arguments the book advances.

The research examined a significant professional practice problem: the inability of senior practitioners to convince dominant coalitions and clients of the need to identify and resolve external issues through mid- to long-term communicative action. This is a significant problem because dominant coalitions and clients need to accept that dealing strategically with non-market environment issues is a high-order, value-added organisational function that should be planned in the same way as strategic business plans because they potentially impact on performance.

For this investigation, the research used a sequential between-strategy approach that involved a purposively selected sample of senior Australian communication practitioners answering an online questionnaire of Likert scale-type questions. The survey instrument also provided opportunities for respondents to give additional open-ended qualitative comments. Invitations to participate were derived from publicly available lists and my personal knowledge.

Research approach

Most research in professional communication scholarship is informed by one of two worldviews: either from a realist, or positivist, perspective or by an nterpretist stance (Daymon and Holloway, 2002). A positivist approach is mostly associated with quantitative research, while an interpretist worldview normally applies to qualitative methodologies. Realist or positivist research emphasises objectivity, distances researchers from the data, and is 'not well suited to description' as investigators seek to discover 'universal laws of cause and effect' across different contexts and times (Daymon & Holloway, 2002, pp. 7–8). This approach disengages researchers from exploring participants' subjective perspectives that could help explain why things happen the way they do. On the other hand, interpretivist researchers 'explore people's intentions, motivations and subjective experiences' to understand how and why people act on the basis of the meanings they hold (Daymon & Holloway, 2002, p. 4). People attribute the meanings they develop to their own actions and to those of others (Daymon & Holloway, 2002).

A positivist worldview has tended to dominate academic and professional communication research as scholars seek to describe professional practice, and practitioners seek to identify, for example, demographic profiles of target publics, who are more precisely defined than the broader term, stakeholder. Questions asking why certain approaches are taken in practice by employing qualitative, interpretive methods are not often pursued.

The worldview that underpinned my research is that positivist and interpretist approaches can, and should, be integrated to produce a detailed, nuanced understanding of social phenomena, like public policy issues debates, and their impact on decision-making about communication strategy directions. My professional practice experience provides the context for this worldview. Knowing what strategic decisions are taken is not enough; knowing why they are taken, and understanding 'why' from senior practitioners' perspectives, delivers a richer contribution to academic and professional knowledge.

This project differs from many professional communication academic research studies because it integrates positivist, or quantitative, and interpretivist, or qualitative, worldviews to utilise all possible methods to answer the research questions—an approach Tashakkori and Teddlie (2009) described as flexible. Thus, the research collected quantitative data through an online questionnaire and sought to interpret that data by exploring participants' direct experiences in two ways. First, the online survey questionnaire included opportunities for participants to provide additional qualitative comments to explain or expand on their quantitative responses. Second, following the closure of the online survey, a number of semi-structured, face-to-face interviews explored the intentions, motivations, and experiences of senior practitioners as architects of strategic communication directions. This approach to data collection means the investigation employed a between-strategies data collection method in which quantitative and qualitative techniques are applied sequentially (Tashakkori & Teddlie, 2009).

The study design

A research study design provides a framework for collecting and analysing data. The framework reflects the priorities given to a range of dimensions of the process, including the importance given to understanding behaviour, and its meaning, in a specific social context, and appreciating the interconnections between social phenomena (Bryman, 2008). Bickman and Rog (2009) described this as the architectural blueprint that links the design, data collection, and analysis to the research questions. Crotty (1998) argued that the basic elements of a research design are the methods that will be used, the methodology that governed the choice of methods, the ontological perspective (although he is not certain that ontology is the best term for a theoretical approach) behind the methodology, and the epistemology that informs the theoretical perspective. That is, a research study design should carefully set out and explain the data collection techniques, the plan of action, the philosophical stance the researcher has adopted to contextualise the methodology, and the theory of knowledge embedded in the ontology (Crotty, 1998).

The study design was grounded in a social ontology of constructivist realism, a position that enabled organisations to be viewed as social actors when they contribute to debates about public policy issues that affect, or could affect, their ability to achieve their objectives. The epistemology, combined with an interpretist view of the research results, also informed the analysis of the data. The research questions were pursued using integrated quantitative and qualitative strategies to collect empirical data. In this design, the ontology, epistemology, and methodology have a logical, directional, and dependent relationship (Hay, 2002). The first relates to the nature of the social and political world (the social phenomena of participating in issues debates), the second to what can be known about it (what influences strategic communication decisions, and why), and the third to how knowledge about how issues influence strategic decision-making can be acquired (Hay, 2002).

Ontology

This study is informed by a social ontology that views 'the world as a world of meanings and interpretation' (Biesta, 2010, p 103). A social ontology differs from a mechanistic ontology in that the latter is concerned with identifying causes and effects, while the former seeks to understand the intentions of, and reasons for, social action (Biesta, 2010). However, a social ontological position does not reject the notion of causes and effects, but assumes,

> human action is *motivated* so that we need to look for intentions and reasons for action in order to provide an answer to the question of why people act as they act.
>
> *(Biesta, 2010, p. 103, emphasis in original)*

My ontological perspective is that debates about public policy issues are social phenomena that constantly change as a result of interventions by, and interactions between, social actors in an organisation's non-market environment (Bach

& Allen, 2010). These dynamic issues debates are influenced by, for example, the views of activists, regulators, politicians, non-government organisations, media commentators, as well as those of the organisation itself. From this perspective, I assumed senior communication practitioners not only attempt to identify current and emerging public policy issues in their organisations' non-market environments, and interpret what they mean for the organisation, but also decide how to respond to them. This is a recursive practice in that issues become dynamic when the course of debates is influenced, or changes, as different social actors, or advocates, participate in them. The dynamics of an issue debate may mean that communication practitioners need to decide on new responses, withdraw from the debate, or approach it from a new perspective. A constructivist realism worldview enables a researcher to view an issues debate as a reality, but also accept the need to interpret why it has become an issue for an organisation and understand its importance.

A constructivist ontology regards social phenomena and their meanings as being continually accomplished by social actors, that is, entities continually shape each other in the context of constantly changing social interactions (Bryman, 2008; Tashakkori & Teddlie, 2009). Crotty (1998) described this as people 'engaging with objects in the world and making sense of them' (p. 79). A constructivist ontology guides an exploration of the motivations of social actors to try to understand, or interpret, how and why people act as they do by utilising qualitative research techniques (Daymon & Holloway, 2002, p. 4). For this research, that meant interviewing senior communication practitioners about their strategic decision-making practice to understand why specific public policy issues are important and in what contexts.

Hay (2002) described constructivism as a 'broad church' that encompassed a diverse range of positions (p. 208). These constructivist positions range from privileging the constitutive role of ideas (Hay [2002] described this as 'thick' constructivism) to critical realism that tends to emphasise how the material world constrains discursive constructions (Hay, 2002, p. 208).

A realist ontology usually leads to quantitative research. It assumes that the real world exists independently of people's perceptions, theories, and constructions (Maxwell & Mittapalli, 2010). A researcher adopting a realist ontology seeks cause and effect across different contexts and times, and believes that researchers are separate from those they observe, and that research findings are true (Daymon & Holloway, 2002; Cupchik, 2001). Realist researchers believe that natural and social scientists should use the same kinds of data collection in their efforts to understand reality (Bryman, 2008). For this investigation, a realist stance means generating statistical data to identify the categories of issues that practitioners consider in their decision-making, and compare differences between sectors, and the contexts in which decisions are made.

A constructivist realism ontology provides a way of philosophically viewing these two research approaches as complementary because it builds bridges between the two research approaches to 'accommodate the best' of each (Cupchik, 2001, para. 33). That's because a researcher adopting this position utilises the similarities between, and the strengths of, the two stances, such as, for example, the way in which both deconstruct subjects of inquiry, and focus selectively on the object of the research, either by a detached experimenter or an engaged interviewer (Cupchik, 2001). A constructivist realism ontological stance enables a researcher to integrate quantitative and qualitative techniques to explore research questions (Cupchik, 2001). Thus, the two approaches offer complementary views of the social world because the richness of qualitative research can enhance the precision delivered by quantitative methods. Cupchik (2001) noted that constructivist realism is

> a position which acknowledges that social phenomena exist in communities quite independently of professional researchers...An emphatic approach would be one in which an attempt is made to understand these phenomena holistically and from the perspective of the participants.
>
> *(Cupchik, 2001, para. 30)*

A constructivist realism ontology thus provides a philosophical basis on which to answer research questions by collecting comparative data about the public policy issues that concern senior communication practitioners in their strategic decision-making, and explore why these issues are important from the perspective of senior Australian practitioners who participated in this research.

Epistemology

This investigation is based on my philosophical stance that organisations are social actors when they engage in debates designed to influence other actors about public policy issues. This theory of knowledge includes the view that issues debates play out in an organisation's non-market environment and decisions about organisational strategic directions for these debates involve discursive social practice. In order to investigate how this occurs, and build an understanding of why senior practitioners take their decisions, a survey research epistemology was adopted.

In Crotty's (1998, p. 9) view, an epistemology 'bears mightily on the way we go about our research.' This reflects Hay's (2002) argument that an epistemology relates to what can be known about a social or political world and informs the methodology for finding that knowledge. No one epistemology provided an appropriate theoretical approach for this study. However, the exploration of 14 participants' experiences of issues analysis and strategic decision-making through in-depth, face-to-face qualitative interviews enhanced the scope for hypothesising a paradigm shift in how strategic communication should be planned and used. This built on the traditional survey research approach to provide a nuanced interpretation of the data.

An interpretivist approach

To keep the investigation consistent with its underpinning philosophical view that organisations are social actors in issues debates, and its ontological stance, it needed to go beyond reporting how strategic communication decisions are made and explaining the reasons for them. This was especially so in the context of my claim that most strategic communication research is positivist. That imposes a requirement to ask how and why strategic communication decisions are made and attempt a conceptualisation of strategic communication as a specific construct. That, in turn, suggests a need to hypothesise how strategic communication might become a more effective professional practice. Elements of grounded theory, especially Charmaz's constructionist approach, provided a useful pathway for doing this. Adopting these elements enabled a reflexive and open research approach in which data collection and analysis, hypothesising a theoretical concept, and reviewing literature was cyclical (Daymon & Holloway, 2002).

Grounded theory, developed by the sociologists Glaser and Strauss, is informed by symbolic interactionism (Grbich, 2013; Daymon & Holloway, 2002). It seeks to understand

> how individuals interpret each other's behaviour and language, how people give meaning to their own actions and thoughts (by communicating) and reorganise them when interacting and negotiating with others.
> *(Daymon and Holloway, 2002, p. 119)*

Because researchers using an interpretist stance observe and try to understand participants' points of view about their worlds (Daymon & Holloway, 2002), utilising this approach enabled the exploration outlined in this Appendix. My approach tended to be hermeneutic, particularly once the survey had been completed, and utilised elements of Charmaz's constructivist version (Grbich, 2013). Grbich (2013) noted that Charmaz challenged the so-called objective nature of the original version of grounded theory to bring researchers and participants closer together in the collection of data and to re-focus on investigators' critical reflective role in recognising and managing their biases. While some scholars have criticised Charmaz's version (see, for example, Grbich's 2013 discussion at p. 88), its critical and reflective focus was important and helpful for interpreting my research. That is, my depth of strategic communication decision-making experience informed the project. While that experience impacted on the project's philosophical basis, its social ontological stance, and the epistemology, it also delivered prior knowledge that is difficult to ignore and which some might therefore regard as bias. This required that I critically reflect on interactions with participants during face-to-face interviews and how my personal knowledge may impact on how questions are framed.

This is an appropriate addition to the epistemology because there is little prior knowledge of why strategic communication decisions are taken in response to dynamic public policy issues debates. It enabled me to generate a theoretical construct for the practice (Grbich, 2013; Daymon & Holloway, 2002). It is also consistent with the project's ontological stance because it enables not only a description of the phenomenon of strategic communication decision-making in the context of dynamic issues debates, but also an interpretation of the research data by seeking relationships, patterns, and links to develop theoretical ideas about this practice (Daymon & Holloway, 2002).

Survey research

An online survey was the most effective way of reaching the senior decision-making practitioners who comprised the expert population of interest for this research.

Online surveys are regarded as an expedient way to collect data and they enable participants to respond in their own time frame (Hays & Swanson, 2012). However, response rates are often lower than hoped for, especially when no rewards for participation are offered (as was the case with this research). Hays and Swanson (2012) cited Sheehan's (2001) argument that a proliferation of online surveys results from a general increase in the use of technology generally. In this context, Bryman (2008) noted that completing an online survey may be more comfortable for respondents because of the long periods they spend online anyway. While response rates to invitations to participate in electronic surveys are sometimes not as high as those for paper-based surveys, Wellington and Szczerbinski (2007) argued that they are potentially more efficient. Bryman (2008) reflected these points in his lists of advantages and disadvantages of online surveying. Among Bryman's (2008) advantages are low cost, fewer unanswered questions, and better responses to open questions. Disadvantages include lower response rates, and a need for motivation that suggests 'solicitation to participate must be especially persuasive' (Bryman, 2008, p. 653).

These advantages and limitations of survey research in general, and online surveys in particular, were considered in planning this project. A decision to proceed with an online survey, as opposed to emailing a hard copy questionnaire, was based primarily on the argument that it would be expedient (Hays & Swanson, 2012) for the busy senior practitioners invited to participate in this way, and Bryman's (2008) view that there would be fewer unanswered questions and better responses to open questions. In addition, the choice of the SurveyMonkey software for the questionnaire delivered flexibility in a data collection format that is widely used and thus familiar to most respondents. This software also provided analysis capabilities, such as the ability to cross-tabulate responses, or filter the data for specific sectoral-only responses. In addition, survey research reflected the between-strategy data collection approach used for this project because it provided a convenient method for collecting quantitative and qualitative data from the population of interest (Lewis-Beck et al., null).

The second step involved one-on-one, face-to-face, semi-structured qualitative interviews with a second purposively selected sample of 14 respondents. One-on-one, semi-structured interviews deliver a powerful data collection strategy because the researcher–interviewee interaction they enable leads to richer and more extensive material than surveys (Tashakkori & Teddlie, 2009; Yin, 2009). Daymon and Holloway (2002) noted that interviews provide freedom to prompt more information if 'something interesting or novel emerges' and allow participants to explore their ideas deeply, and to exert control over an interview if they wish, because participants' ideas have priority (p. 167). Bryman (2008) reflects this view when he argued that interviews should have an emphasis on how the interviewee frames and understands issues and events, that is, exploring what the interviewee believes is important for explanations of forms of behaviour, patterns, and events. Open-ended interviews help researchers to seek explanations of vague answers, and sometimes generate considerable information, which may lead to a re-conceptualisation of the topic being studied (Tashakkori & Teddlie, 2009).

Sampling frames

A sampling frame defines a population of interest by describing a set of elements from which a sample of the target population can be selected (Currivan, 2004). For example, a sampling frame for a readily identifiable small population could simply be a list of relevant people (Henry, 1990). Sampling frames can be derived from lists such as school rolls, general practitioner patient lists, telephone directories, residential address lists, postcode address files, 'even just a street map' (Gomm, 2004, p. 78). Bryman (2008) cautioned that a list of respondents derived from a sampling frame cannot represent the population if the frame is not comprehensive or accurate. The sampling frames for my online survey and the face-to-face interviews defined the population of interest as senior private, public, and not-for-profit sector practitioners who are:

- engaged in a planning (strategic) role
- have leadership responsibilities
- have significant professional practice experience (that is, more than five years)

Sample selection

Not all professional communication practitioners are directly involved in making decisions about the directions of communication strategies in concert with dominant coalitions. This role is usually undertaken by the most senior organisational practitioners, so it was important that this study's research sample reflected that reality of professional practice.

Research sampling decisions are made to either compare groups or focus on specific people (Flick, 2005). Thus, Flick (2005) argued that research participants should be selected according to expected new insights into a developing theory—an important consideration for this research given the interpretivist element of the epistemology. Decisions about who should be included in a sample aim at obtaining material that provides the 'greatest insights, viewed in the light of the material already used and the knowledge drawn from it' (Flick, 2005, p. 64). In addition, a sample should be selected in ways that are relevant to the questions being asked.

Because the research was focused on discovering and understanding the factors that influence strategic communication decision-making, a sample of senior communication decision-makers, a specific population of interest, was required. It was therefore important that criteria for invitations to participate in the online questionnaire and face-to-face interviews be based on the sampling frame that defined practitioners' seniority, length of practice, organisational level, and decision-making role. A population of interest defined in this way can provide the best insights into how organisations deal with public policy issues management and the resulting strategic communication responses because these are the practitioners who can provide the rich, in-depth information that Daymon and Holloway (2002) noted guides sampling decisions. A purposive sampling approach enables a researcher to personally identify a population of interest who meet the criteria and can provide relevant insights into the research subject. Purposive sampling is typically associated with qualitative research and has been defined by Tashakkori and Teddlie (2009) as 'selecting a relatively small number of units because they can provide particularly valuable information related to the research questions under examination' (p. 25).

Purposive sampling (also described by Kalton [1983], cited in Burton [2000], as judgement sampling or expert choice) allows participants to be selected on the basis of shared characteristics, experiences, and their ability to provide detailed data important to the study's aims and relevant to the research questions (Bryman, 2008; Jupp, 2006; Daymon & Holloway, 2002). That is, participants' knowledge is relevant 'to understanding a social phenomenon' (Bryman, 2008, p. 415). Purposive sampling thus enables the selection of 'elite' or 'key' participants based on the researcher's view of the depth of information the sample will provide, or its unique perception of the phenomenon being investigated (Collins, 2010, p. 357).

This is a deliberate approach to sample selection that includes participants with particular characteristics appropriate to the needs of the research and emerging theory, who reflect the general characteristics of the population being studied, and provide an exemplary and revelatory target population with specialist knowledge of the research issue (Lewis-Beck et al., null; Wellington & Szczerbinski, 2007; Jupp, 2006). This produces a small, strategic, and theoretically interesting sample (Bryman, 2008; Gomm, 2004). Purposive sampling provides the most information about a particular phenomenon because it leads to a greater depth of data from a small, carefully selected sample (Tashakkori & Teddlie, 2009). A disadvantage of purposive sampling is that it rests on what Jupp (2006) described as the subjectivity of the researcher's decision-making, which could be a source of potential bias, thus challenging the validity of the research.

For my research, it was important that participants had specialist knowledge of the research topic because they are the in-house and consultant practitioners who take the professional decisions about managing issues and the directions of strategic communication. These practitioners fit Gomm's (2004) argument that sampling of this kind is appropriate when a researcher believes the people of interest are relevant to the research. In addition, purposive sampling is a logical outcome of a constructive realism ontology that seeks explanations for why strategic communication decisions are made from the people who actually make them. Additionally, purposive sampling was appropriate for my research epistemology. In Crotty's (1998) view, an epistemology 'bears mightily' on the way research is conducted, and, in Hay's (2002) terms, relates to what can be known about a social or political world and informs the methodology for finding that knowledge.

The survey questions

The questions in the online survey questionnaire and protocol for the semi-structured, face-to-face interviews were derived from a review of relevant scholarly literature on strategic communication planning and implementation.

The first four questions in the online survey asked for demographic details to assess the seniority of the sample by asking about their length of practice, actual jobs, and the sector in which they worked. A question about respondents' gender was included as a filter through which to assess whether gender was a variable in responses to the other questions. Data about the sector in which respondents worked provided a filter through which to cross-tabulate the findings to specifically answer Research Question 2.

The following five Likert-scale questions were designed to elicit data to answer the research questions. Respondents were asked about their organisation's attitudes towards communication strategies, how often they identified potential and emerging issues, and the business planning contexts in which they did this. A question asking respondents to give a priority ranking to a series of statements about potential issues was designed to provide specific data about the relative importance of issue categories to help to answer Research Question 1. Respondents were also asked to indicate their level of agreement (from strongly agree to strongly disagree) to a series of statements about the contexts in which they would communicate with stakeholders, their dominant coalitions' attitudes towards communication, and how communication strategies should be aligned with business planning. This question was designed to provide data to answer all research questions, and theorise how professional communication strategies might be more effectively linked to business planning.

Respondents were able to give detailed qualitative comments after each question, and as the sole focus of the final question. The protocol for the semi-structured, face-to-face interviews, based on the review of literature and findings from the online survey, was aimed at generating senior practitioners' direct and detailed qualitative insights into their experiences in strategic decision-making and of their external environments. These qualitative responses were to enable a richer interpretation of the online survey's findings.

Together, the quantitative and qualitative responses to the online questionnaire and qualitative analysis of the transcripts of the semi-structured, face-to-face interviews enabled a new definition of strategic communication to be conceptualised.

Face-to-face interview participation

Invitations to participate in the semi-structured, face-to-face interviews were e-mailed to a second purposive sample of senior practitioners with an information sheet about the project. Those who participated may not have completed the online survey questionnaire. The interview sample was, like those invited to participate in the online survey, relevant, senior, and able to discuss their direct, personal experiences in strategic communication decision-making. A total of 14 interviews were conducted face-to-face at participants' workplaces; one interview was conducted via telephone because a mutually agreeable date for a face-to-face session could not be arranged. Table A1.5 gives details for participants in the semi-structured, face-to-face interviews.

Sample selection

Respondents to the online survey were selected via purposive sampling: 186 senior communication practitioners in communication consultancies, private sector businesses, Federal, State, and Territory Government departments and agencies, professional lobbying firms, industry associations, universities, and not-for-profit groups were identified and invited to participate via a personal email. The purposive sample was selected from publicly available lists and the researcher's personal knowledge. Invitations to participate in the online survey and face-to-face interviews were based on the following characteristics. Participants needed to be senior private, public, higher education, or not-for-profit sector practitioners who are:

- engaged in a planning (strategic) role
- have leadership responsibilities
- have significant professional practice experience (that is, more than five years)

The sampling frame for this research outlined above was designed to identify this population of interest (Lewis-Beck et al., null). These practitioners formed a readily identifiable small population with direct personal experiences in the research topic.

The senior practitioners invited to participate in the research were identified from publicly available online databases, the investigator's personal knowledge from professional practice and experience as National Secretary of the Public Relations Institute of Australia, and via snowball sampling in which colleagues nominated possible participants.

Purposive sampling sought senior male and female practitioners from private commercial businesses, communication consultancies, State and Federal Government agencies, industry associations, higher education institutions, and professional lobbying firms based in the national capital as participants.

Data analysis

The study generated two data sets. The first comprised the results of the survey that utilised a SurveyMonkey online application that enabled the data to be sorted, cross-tabulated, and filtered by demographic and other response characteristics. The second, qualitative data set comprised the transcripts of face-to-face interviews.

The research process and analysis of the data was primarily deductive in that both were based on hypotheses about issues management and strategic communication practice identified from the theoretical literature. That is, the research and analysis sought to identify from the data what Hay (2002, p. 30) described as 'testable propositions' from established theory about professional practice. However, aspects of the analysis led to inductive inferences about senior practitioners' professional worlds, especially when the data seemed to contradict theoretical assumptions about issues identification and analysis and strategic communication practice. This inductive element reflected the interpretivist element of the project's epistemology and enabled the conceptualisation of strategic communication and how it might more effectively benefit organisations.

Analysis of the quantitative results

The data generated by the quantitative online survey provided descriptive statistics about the respondents, the sector of the economy in which they worked, how their jobs are classified, their professional issues management practice, views about the importance of strategic communication for the clients or organisations, the categories of issues they deal with, and the circumstances in which they are prepared to communicate with stakeholders.

Using the cross-tabulation function of the electronic database, responses of practitioners from different sectors to questions about their practice could be compared in what Tashakkori and Teddlie (2009) described as typology development in which,

> individuals are first classified into different types. These groups are then statistically compared with each other on *other* available quantitative...data.
> (Tashakkori and Teddlie, 2009, p. 305, emphasis in original)

The quantitative data were also analysed to identify the categories of issues senior practitioners are most concerned about. The SPSS statistical package was used to test for variance in gender responses and whether differences in these responses were significant. The results of these analyses informed the development of the protocol for the semi-structured, face-to-face qualitative interviews, thus enabling responses to the online survey to be more fully investigated. For example, analysis of quantitative data from State and Federal Government practitioners identified current and emerging political issues as the two most significant issue categories that determined their approaches to professional practice. State and Federal Government interviewees were therefore asked about the reasons for this focus. A similar approach was used with all interviewees when the quantitative data identified a statistically significant difference between genders on the importance of issue categories. In this case, interviewees were asked for their reactions to, and explanations for, the finding.

Analysis of qualitative interviews

Analysis of the qualitative data sought to understand participants' direct experiences of issues management and strategic communication decision-making.

Qualitative data analysis enables a researcher to discover and understand rich details about participants' experiences and how they make sense of them (Grbich, 2013). The research was investigating senior practitioners' first-person experiences and intentionality as social actors in issues debates. Exploring senior practitioners' experiences in this way enabled an understanding of the structures of their professional worlds and how they react to those structures (Grbich, 2013). This was an important aspect of the deductive and inductive observations of the researcher during both the interviews and data analysis as theoretical propositions about professional practice were tested and sometimes negated, and as a conceptualisation of strategic communication emerged.

The first step in analysing the qualitative data began by assuming that strategic communication decisions are based on issues analysis by applying Grbich's (2013) four steps for phenomenological reduction. This step revealed the positivist nature of strategic communication research from the literature. This in turn led to an underpinning assumption in the data collection and early stages of the qualitative data analysis that strategic communication is indeed strategic and all senior practitioners experience decision-making in this context. The fourth step in the analysis led to an inductive view that strategic communication decision-making is discursive special practice. In the context of the data generated by the quantitative survey, the question that needed to be answered in the qualitative analysis became how and why do practitioners make their strategic decisions? This analysis enabled the investigator to discover and understand participants' first-hand experiences, how they make sense of them, and their intentionality as social actors in issues debates and explore their understanding of the structures of their professional worlds and how they react to those structures (Grbich, 2013).

The qualitative research was seeking meaning for practitioner's decision-making. That meaning

> lies in the identification of the dominant themes in the encounter between you and your participant through a light form of thematic analysis where the data is kept largely intact.
>
> *(Grbich, 2013, p. 96)*

A thematic approach was used to analyse the transcripts of the qualitative interviews, and open-ended responses to questions in the quantitative instrument to produce participants' descriptions, or meanings, of their professional practice to 'uncover the essence of the phenomena of strategic communication decision-making' (Grbich, 2013). This enabled a better understanding, and interpretation, of the quantitative data that identified factors that influence strategic communication decision-making, and to explain the reasons for possible sectoral differences.

Thematic analysis is a version of content analysis in which a researcher looks for themes in the interview set to enable 'comparisons and contrasts between the different respondents' (Gomm, 2004, p. 189). Bryman's (2008) definition of thematic analysis is that it involves the 'extraction of key themes' (p. 700) in qualitative data, but that it is a diffuse approach with few generally agreed principles to help define such key themes. Bryman (2008) argued that thematic analysis 'lacks a clearly specified series of procedures' (p. 555). Nevertheless, Bryman (2008) noted that key themes are likely to reflect a researcher's awareness of ideas and topics that recur in the data. Gibson and Brown (2009) described this as investigating commonalities, differences, and relationships in the data and they argue that an important aspect of using this approach is for the researcher to work out the context of a given piece of data and why it is distinctive. A thematic approach enables a systematic analysis of the meanings made from the phenomena being investigated (Marks & Yardley, 2004). The prime reason for including semi-structured, face-to-face qualitative interviews in this project was to enable that kind of analysis. However, Marks and Yardley (2004) cautioned that a challenge for researchers using thematic analysis is to 'draw the richness of the themes from the raw information' (p. 68) without reducing the insights to a trivial level.

Thematic analysis involves decisions about what the themes will be and what will count as evidence of them, then coding transcripts to indicate examples of the themes (Gomm, 2004). After these decisions, a thematic analysis involves indicating what respondents said about themes and how these comments may relate to another theme (Gomm, 2004). Grbich (2013) warned that in descriptions resulting from thematic analysis, a researcher should reflect the essence of the experience as closely as possible.

Reflexivity

Researchers engaged in investigations of the kind reported in this book, especially when they have also practised in the field, and written about and taught the subject matter, as I have, need to accept that they are part of the research process (Flick, 2005). That is, a researcher cannot be separated from their 'background, life experiences and memories...which inevitably filter impressions of the actions and behaviour of others' (Grbich, 2013, p. 113). Elliott (2005), too, noted that authors' intellectual biographies shape all research accounts requiring a reflexive approach that makes authors' perspectives clear. Maso (2003) argued that, because research is largely subjective and kept 'reasonably in check by a number of more or less general methodological rules and considerations,' researchers 'are required to come clean' through the use of reflexivity about how their subjectivities affected the research (p. 40). Daymon and Holloway (2002) described this as qualitative researchers being part of phenomena they analyse and argue that researchers should thus reflect on their reactions to their research. This should happen in all stages of data collection, analysis, and report writing and should include reflecting on actions, feelings, and conflicts experienced during the process (Daymon & Holloway, 2002). Wellington and Szczerbinski (2007) suggested reflexivity involves evaluating research for both content and method. That is, researchers should evaluate their own role, position, and 'their effects on what is being researched' (Wellington & Szczerbinski, 2007, p. 49).

Bryman's (2008) definition of reflexivity in research suggests why it was important that I engaged in this practice during the project. That definition encourages social researchers to reflect on the implications for the social world of the knowledge they generate from their methods, values, biases, decisions, and 'mere presence in the very situations they investigate' (p. 698). Daymon and Holloway (2002) made a similar point when they argued that a researcher needs to engage in critical self-reflection because their role is 'inherently tied up with' (p. 242) how findings are derived and interpreted, or how the researcher has 'constructed knowledge' (p. 242) in the field. This means a researcher should examine 'their own assumptions, prior experience and bias' in data collection and analysis (Wellington & Szczerbinski, 2007, p. 223). I engaged in reflexive practice during the development of the research questionnaire and interview protocol to make sure that questions were sufficiently open-ended to 'decentre' my assumptions and replace them with the 'voices of participants' (Grbich, 2013, p. 114). A similar reflexive approach became regular practice post the face-to-face interviews, especially as interviewee responses often challenged my assumptions about professional strategic practice that were grounded in an assumption that senior practitioners always implement communication activities from the perspective of a strategic plan. They don't—which was a personal revelation during the research process, perhaps even what Daymon and Holloway (2002) described as a conflict between my assumptions and the reality of professional practice.

Reactions such as these during the semi-structured, face-to-face interviews caused me to reflect on the assumptions underlying the investigation. This led to a view that the tactical focus revealed by the research was an important dimension in building an understanding of Australian strategic communication practice—a perspective that resonates with Maso's (2003) argument that the limitations researchers impose on themselves should be flexible and that,

> no information should be excluded as long as there is a chance that it could be relevant to their search. As for openness, this means that they must be receptive to everything they encounter.
>
> *(Maso, 2003, p. 48)*

This was reflexivity as self-critique (Grbich, 2013) of all aspects of the research process. Self-critique was especially important in developing the definition that Research Question 3 seeks because I accept that using elements of grounded theory in this inductive way requires reflexivity. A reflexive approach to the research process also generated a deeper appreciation of how integrated research helped to understand and explain both data sets as they related to senior practitioners' personal experiences.

Headline research results and tables

Participant demographics

Of those invited to participate in the online survey, 43% (n = 80) responded. The largest group to respond (n = 20) worked in communication consultancies; the smallest group were professional lobbyists (n = 3). Federal and State Government practitioners were the second largest (n = 16) group in the sample.

The data confirmed the seniority of the sample. The majority (79.7%, n answered this question = 79) had practised professional communication for 11 or more years—32.9% for more than 20 years. More female respondents (n = 15) than male respondents (n = 11) had practised for more than 20 years. Most (90.1%) were at a chief executive of consultancy, or general manager/director public affairs/communication, level in their organisations. Job descriptions of the nine respondents who answered 'Other' for this question were titles such as 'Owner and director of consultancy,' 'Senior Officer,' 'Manager,' 'Director, Marketing,' 'Assistant Director, Strategy and Campaigns,' 'Principal,' and 'Group Manager, Media and Research.'

The gender balance was almost even: 49% male (n = 39), 51% female (n = 40). More females than males worked for not-for-profit organisations, and slightly more females than males were consultants. The total number of practitioners in these two categories represented 43% of the 79 respondents who provided organisational details. Females working for consultancies and not-for-profit organisations comprised almost 49% of the total sample.

The following tables provide data about respondents' answers to Likert-scale questions.

TABLE A1.1 Respondents' organisation

	%
Communication/PR consultancy/agency	27.8
Private sector business	12.7
Federal Government agency	12.7
State/Territory Government agency	7.6
Professional lobbying firm	3.8
Industry association	7.6
University	12.7
Not-for-profit group	12.7
	100%
	(79)

Table A1.1 shows the percentage of respondents who worked for specific organisation types. Respondents were asked: 'Select the option that best describes your organisation.'

TABLE A1.2 Respondents' organisations by gender

	% Male	% Female
Communication/PR consultancy/agency	25.6	30.0
Private sector business	18.0	7.5
Federal Government agency	12.8	12.5
State/Territory Government agency	5.1	10.0
Professional lobbying firm	5.1	2.5
Industry association	10.4	5.0
University	17.9	7.5
Not-for-profit group	5.1	25.0
	100%	100%
	(39)	(40)

Table A1.2 shows respondents' organisation by gender. Thus, 18% of all males and 7.5% of all females worked for private sector business.

TABLE A1.3 Number of years in practice

	% Male	% Female
Less than 5 years	5.1	15.0
Between 6 and 10 years	7.7	12.5
Between 11 and 15 years	25.6	27.5
Between 16 and 20 years	23.1	17.5
For more than 20 years	38.5	27.5
	100%	100%
	(39)	(40)

Table A1.3 shows respondents' years of experience in communication practice, and gender. More than half of the respondents (53.2%) had over 15 years of experience; more male practitioners had between 16 and 20+ years of experience than female practitioners.

TABLE A1.4 How respondents described their jobs

	% Male	% Female
Chief Executive/Executive Chair/Practice Leader	25.6	15.0
Director PR/Affairs/Corporate Communication	53.8	47.5
Senior Consultant	5.1	10.0
General Manager	10.4	7.5
Public sector departmental Branch Head	–	2.5
Other job description	5.1	17.5
	100%	100%
	(39)	(40)

Table A1.4 shows respondents' job titles as an indicator of their seniority, and gender. Respondents were asked to indicate from a pre-set list: 'My job is best described as (select only one).' Responses to 'Other' included: Male: Agency Principal; Group Manager, Media and Research. Female: Assistant Director; Senior Officer Marketing Communication; sole PR person in organisation; Director Marketing; Public Relations Manager; Assistant Director, Strategy and Communication; Owner and Director of Consultancy.

TABLE A1.5 Issues management contexts: total respondents

		Response		
		Yes	No	Don't Know
Context	**%**	**%**	**%**	
A:	How issues impact on current business activities	100.0	–	–
B:	Identifying issues likely to emerge in the mid term (up to 5 years in the future)	86.7	9.3	4.0
C:	Predicting issues that might occur in the long-term business environment (beyond 5 years)	45.9	50	4.1

Note: The questionnaire enabled respondents to answer for more than one context.

Table A1.5 shows responses to the three issues management contexts participants were asked to consider. The three contexts are based on Baghai et al.'s (2000) three horizons for business growth (see Chapter 8).

TABLE A1.6 Priority ranking for issue categories

Rank	Category	Rating average	n respondents
1	Issues about our organisation's reputation, values, and credibility	3.54	65
2	Relationships we have with our stakeholders	4.08	66
2	Current Australian political issues	4.08	61
3	Regulatory issues that affect our industry	5.00	74
4	Economic issues	5.03	58
5	Emerging Australian political issues	5.08	62
6	Our competitive business environment	5.26	62
7	Social and cultural issues that impact on our operating environment	5.62	58
8	Issues about the natural environment that may impact on our organisation	7.06	69

Table A1.6 shows how respondents ranked issues with which they are concerned in their decision-making about strategic communication directions. The ranking set out in the table is based on calculations of rating averages. The table also shows the number of respondents who ranked these issues.

TABLE A1.7 Priority ratings: strategic communication drivers by business planning horizon

Strategic communication driver	Planning Horizon				
	Overall	Current	Mid	Long	SD
Reputation, values, credibility	3.54	3.58	3.56	3.60	0.02
Relationships with stakeholders	4.08	4.09	4.09	4.11	0.01
Current Australian political issues	4.08	4.08	4.12	4.12	0.02
Industry regulatory issues	5.00	4.97	5.06	5.03	0.05
Economic issues	5.03	4.98	5.14	5.09	0.08
Emerging Australian political issues	5.08	5.08	5.12	5.12	0.02
Competitive business environment	5.26	5.31	5.35	5.41	0.05
Impact of socio-cultural issues	5.62	5.61	5.56	5.55	0.03
Impact of natural environment issues	7.06	7.03	7.01	6.98	0.03

Table A1.7 shows the priorities senior practitioners give to specific issues in their strategic planning decisions. The data are reported as overall priorities, and in the context of current, mid- and long-term planning. The data show these priorities are consistent across planning horizons.

TABLE A1.8 Importance of communication strategy by gender

Importance of communication strategy	% Overall	% Gender responded Female	Male
Totally unimportant	1.3	–	2.6
Unimportant	1.3	–	2.6
Neither important nor unimportant	2.6	2.6	2.6
Important	30.8	35.9	25.6
Critically important	64.0	61.5	66.6
	100%	100%	100%
	(78)	(39)	(39)

Table A1.8 shows that, overall, respondents overwhelmingly believe communication strategies are important or critically important to their organisations or clients (total = 95%). Table A1.8 also suggests that female respondents were more likely to believe in the 'importance/critical importance' of communication strategies to their organisations or clients than were male respondents (F = 97%; M = 92%). However, Table A1.8 also illustrates that more male respondents believe communication strategies are 'critically important' (67%) to their organisations or clients than do female respondents (62%).

TABLE A1.9 Contexts in which respondents manage current and emerging issues

Issues management context	Response	% Overall	% Gender responded Female	Male
A: How issues impact on current business activities	Yes	100.0	100.0	100.0
B: Identifying issues likely to emerge in the mid term	Yes	86.7	83.4	89.5
(up to 5 years in the future)	No	9.3	8.3	10.5
	Don't know	4.0	8.3	–
		100%	100%	100%
C: Predicting issues that might occur in the long-term	Yes	45.9	48.6	42.1
business environment (beyond 5 years)	No	50.0	42.9	57.9
	Don't know	4.1	8.5	–
		100%	100%	100%

Table A1.9 shows that respondents all have a tactical focus on dealing with day-to-day issues and fewer plan how they can deal with mid-term issues. A minority of respondents have a long-term strategic focus.

REFERENCES

Ackermann, F., and Eden, C. (2011). Strategic management of stakeholders: theory and practice, *Long Range Planning*, 44(3), pp. 179–196. https://doi.org/10.1016/j.lrp.2010.08.001

Alexander, D. (2006). Reframing leadership communication: consequences for organisational leaders resulting from communication failure: an Australian case study, *Empowerment, Creativity and Innovation: Challenging Media and Communication in the 21ˢᵗ Century* (ANZCA and University of Adelaide).

Al-Aly, Z., Xie, Y., and Bowe, B. (2021). High-dimensional characterization of post-acute sequalae of COVID-19. *Nature*. 594, pp. 259–264 https://doi.org/10.1038/s41586-021-03553-9

An, S.-K., and Gower, K.K. (2009). How do the news media frame crises? A content analysis of crisis news coverage, *Public Relations Review*, 35(2), pp. 107–112. https://doi.org/10.1016/j.pubrev.2009.01.010

Anderson, D.S. (1992). Identifying and responding to activist publics: a case study, *Journal of Public Relations Research*, 4(3), pp. 151–165. https://doi.org/10.1207/s1532754xjprr0403_02

Ansoff, H.I. (1980). Strategic issue management, *Strategic Management Journal*, 1(2), pp. 131–148. https://doi.org/10.1002/smj.4250010204

Argenti, P.A, and Forman, J. (2002). *The Power of Corporate Communication: Crafting the Voice and Image of Your Business*, McGraw-Hill, Boston.

Argenti, P.A., Howell, R. A., and Beck, K.A. (2005). The strategic communication imperative, *MIT Sloan Management Review*, 46(3), pp. 82–89, https://sloanreview.mit.edu/article/the-strategic-communication-imperative/

Australian Charity Guide (2012). http://www.australiancharityguide.com/ September 2012. Accessed 14 September 2012.

Australian Government, Register of Lobbyists (2012). http://lobbyists.pmc.gov.au/ Accessed 16 September, 2012.

Australian Stock Exchange (2012). Browse top companies, www.asx.com.au accessed 14 September 2012.

Bach, D. (2007). David Bach on nonmarket strategy, *Management-Issues*, 3 October 2007, http://www.management-issues.com/2007/10/3/mentors/david-bach-on -nonmarket-strategy.asp accessed 1 April 2013.

Bach, D. (2010). *The Next Frontier in Competitive Advantage*, http://www.youtube.com/ watch?v=DDE5GzuYqUY accessed 3 March 2014.

Bach, D., and Allen, D.B. (2010). What every CEO needs to know about Nonmarket strategy, *MIT Sloan Management Review*, 51(3), pp. 41–48, https://sloanreview.mit.edu /article/what-every-ceo-needs-to-know-about-nonmarket-strategy/

Baghai, M., Coley, S., and White, D. (2000). *The Alchemy of Growth: Practical Insights for Building the Enduring Enterprise*, Basic Books, New York.

Baines, P.R., and Viney, H. (2010). The unloved relationship? Dynamic capabilities and political-market strategy: a research agenda, *Journal of Public Affairs*, 10(4), pp. 258–264. https://doi.org/10.1002/pa.346

Bakir, V. (2006). Policy agenda setting and risk communication: greenpeace, shell, and issues of trust, *International Journal of Press/Politics*, 11(3), pp. 67–68. https://doi.org/10 .1177/1081180X06289213

Baron, D.P. (1999). Integrated market and nonmarket strategies in client and interest group politics, *Business and Politics*, 1(1), pp. 7–34. https://doi.org/10.1515/bap.1999.1.1.7

Barone, E., Ranamagar, N., and Solomon, J.F. (2013). A Habermasian model of stakeholder (non)engagement and corporate (ir)responsibility reporting, *Accounting Forum*, 37(3), pp. 162–181. https://doi.org/10.1016/j.accfor.2012.12.001

Barrett, D.J. (2002). Change communication: using strategic employee communication to facilitate major change, *Corporate Communications: An International Journal*, 7(4), pp. 219–231. https://doi.org/10.1108/13563280210449804

Berman, S.L., Wicks, A.C., Kotha, S., and Jones, T.M. (1999). Does stakeholder orientation matter? The relationship between stakeholder management models and firm financial performance, *Academy of Management Journal*, 42(5), pp. 488–506. https://doi.org/10.5465/256972

Beer, M., and Eisenstat, R.A. (2004). How to have an honest conversation about your business strategy, *Harvard Business Review*, 82(2), pp. 82–89.

Beinhocker, E.D. (1999). On the origin of strategies, *The McKinsey Quarterly*, Number 4, pp. 47–57.

Bentele, G. and Nothhaft, H. (2010). Strategic communication and the public sphere from a european perspective, *International Journal of Strategic Communication*, 4(2), pp. 93–166. https://doi.org/10.1080/15531181003701954

Bentele, G., and Wehmeier, S. (2007). Applying sociology to public relations: A commentary. *Public Relations Review*, 33(3), pp. 294–300. https://doi.org/10.1016/j .pubrev.2007.05.009

Berger, B.K. (2005). Power over, power with, and power to public relations: critical reflections on public relations, the dominant coalition, and activism, *Journal of Public Relations Research*, 17(1), pp. 5–28. https://doi.org/10.1207/s1532754xjprr1701_3

Bernays, E.L. (1952). *Public Relations*, University of Oklahoma Press, Norman.

Bickman, L. and Rog, D.J. (eds.) (2009). *The SAGE Handbook of Applied Social Research Methods*, SAGE Publications, Thousand Oaks.

Bickman, L. and Rog, D.J. (2009). Applied research design: a practical approach, in L. Bickman, and D.J. Rog (eds.) *The SAGE Handbook of Applied Social Research Methods*, SAGE Publications, Thousand Oaks, pp. 3–43.

Biesta, G. (2010). Pragmatism and the philosophical foundations of mixed methods research, in A. Tashakkori and C. Teddlie (eds.) *SAGE Handbook of Mixed Methods in Social & Behavioral Research*, 2nd ed., SAGE Publications, Thousand Oaks, pp. 95–117.

Bigelow, B., Fahey, L., and Mahon, J. (1993). A typology of issue evolution, *Business and Society*, 32 (Spring), pp. 18–29. https://doi.org/10.1177/000765039303200104

Bisel, R.S. (2010). A communicative ontology of organisation? A description, history, and critique of CCO theories for organisation science, *Management Communication Quarterly*, 24(1), pp. 124–131. https://doi.org/10.1177/0893318909351582

Blood, W., and Holland, K. (2004). Risky news, madness and public crisis: a case study of the reporting and portrayal of mental health and illness in the Australian press, *Journalism*, 5(3), pp. 323–342. https://doi.org/10.1177/1464884904044940

Blumler, J.G. (2001). The third age of political communication, *Journal of Public Affairs*, 1(3), pp. 201–209. https://doi.org/10.1002/pa.66

Bower, J.L. and David, D.K. (2007). How managers' everyday decisions create or destroy your company's strategy, *Harvard Business Review*, 85(2), pp. 72–79. PMID:17345681

Bowler, W.M. (2006). Organisational goals versus the dominant coalition: A critical view of the value of organisational citizenship behaviour, *Journal of Behavioural and Applied Management*, 7(3), pp. 258–273. https://doi.org/10.21818/001c.16670

Bradley, C., Dawson, A., and Montard, A. (2013). Mastering the building blocks of strategy, *McKinsey Quarterly*, 2013(4), pp. 36–47, https://www.mckinsey.com/business-functions/strategy-and-corporate-finance/our-insights/mastering-the-building-blocks-of-strategy

Brønn, P.S. (2001). Communication managers as strategists? Can they make the grade? *Journal of Communication Management*, 5(4), pp. 313–326. https://doi.org/10.1108/13632540110806857

Brønn, P.S. and Brønn, C. (2002). Issues management as a basis for strategic direction, *Journal of Public Affairs*, 2(4), pp. 247–258. https://doi.org/10.1002/pa.117

Brown, R.E. (2010). Symmetry and its critics: antecedents, prospects and implications for symmetry in a postsymmetry era, in R.L. Heath (ed.) *The SAGE Handbook of Public Relations*, SAGE, Los Angeles, pp. 277–292.

Bryman, A. (2008). *Social Research Methods*, 3rd ed., Oxford University Press, Oxford.

Bryman, A., and Bell, E. (2003). *Business Research Methods*, Oxford University Press, Oxford.

Bucholtz, R.A. (1988). *Public Policy Issues for Management*, Prentice Hall, New Jersey.

Bull, G. (translator) (1995). *Niccolò Machiavelli, The Prince*, Penguin Books, London.

Burkart, R. (2009). On Habermas: understanding and public relations, in Ø. Ihlen, B. van Ruler, and M. Fredriksson (eds.) *Public Relations and Social Theory: Key figures and Concepts*, Routledge, New York, pp. 141–165.

Burton, D. (2000). *Research Training for Social Scientists*. London: SAGE Publications Ltd

Burton, R.M., Eriksen, B., Håkonsson, D.D., and Snow, C.C. (2006). *Organisational Design: The Evolving State-of-the-art*, Springer, New York.

Bütschi, G., and Steyn, B. (2006). Theory on strategic communication management is the key to unlocking the boardroom, *Journal of Communication Management*, 10(1), pp. 106–109. https://doi.org/10.1108/13632540610646436

Caldas-Coulthard, C.R. and Coulthard, M. (1996). *Texts and Practices: Readings in Critical Discourse Analysis*, Routledge, London.

Calhoun, C. (ed.) (1992). *Habermas and the Public Sphere*, The MIT Press, Cambridge, Massachusetts.

Calhoun, C. (1992). Introduction: Habermas and the public sphere, in C. Calhoun (ed.) *Habermas and the Public Sphere*, The MIT Press, Cambridge, Massachusetts, pp. 1–48.

Callon, M. (1999). Actor-network theory the market test, *The Sociological Review*, 47(S1), pp. 181–195. https://doi.org/10.1111/j.1467-954X.1999.tb03488.x

Callon, M., and Latour, B. (1981). Unscrewing the big Leviatha: how actors macro-structure reality and how sociologists help them to do so, in K. Knorr and A. Cicourel (eds.) *Advances in Social Theory and Methodology*, Routledge and Kegan Paul, London, pp. 277–303.

Cameron, G.T., Cropp, F., and Reber, B.H. (2001). Getting past platitudes: factors limiting accommodation in public relations, *Journal of Communication Management*, 5(3), pp. 242–261. https://doi.org/10.1108/13632540110806802

Cancel, A.E., Cameron, G.T., Sallot, L.M., and Mitrook, M.A. (1997). It depends: A contingency theory of accommodation in public relations, *Journal of Public Relations Research*, 9(1), pp. 31–63. https://doi.org/10.1207/s1532754xjprr0901_02

Choo, G. (2009). Audiences, stakeholders, publics, in R. Tench and L. Yeomans (eds.) *Exploring Public Relations*, Prentice Hall, Harlow, pp. 222–236.

Chong, D., and Druckman, J.N. (2007). A Theory of Framing and Opinion Formation in Competitive Elite Environments, *Journal of Communication*, 57(1) pp. 99–118, https://doi.org/10.1111/j.1460-2466.2006.00331.x

Christen, C.T. (2005). The restructuring and reengineering of AT&T: Analysis of a public relations crisis using organisational theory, *Public Relations Review*, 31(2), pp. 239–251. https://doi.org/10.1016/j.pubrev.2005.02.015

Clement, R.W. (2005). The lessons from stakeholder theory for U.S. business leaders, *Business Horizons*, 48(3), pp. 255–264. https://doi.org/10.1016/j.bushor.2004.11.003

Coombs, W.T., and Holladay, S.J. (2009). Further explorations of post-crisis communication: effects of media and response strategies on perceptions and intentions, *Public Relations Review*, 35(1), pp. 1–6. https://doi.org/10.1016/j.pubrev.2008.09.011

Collins, K.M.T. (2010). Advanced sampling designs in mixed research: current practices and emerging trends in the social and behavioural sciences, in A. Tashakkori, and C. Teddlie (eds.) *SAGE Handbook of Mixed Methods in Social & Behavioral Research*, 2nd ed., SAGE Publications, Thousand Oaks, pp. 353–377.

Cornelissen, J. (2005). *Corporate Communications: Theory and Practice*, Sage, London.

Creswell, J.W. (1994). *Research Design: Qualitative and Quantitative Approaches*, Sage, Thousand Oaks.

Crotty, M. (1998). *The Foundations of Social Research: Meaning and perspective in the research process*, Allen and Unwin, Crows Nest.

Cupchik, G. (2001). Constructivist Realism: An Ontology That Encompasses Positivist and Constructivist Approaches to the Social Sciences, http://www.qualitative-research.net/index.php/fqs/article/view/968 accessed 19 May 2014.

Currivan, D.B. (2004). Sampling frame, in M.S. Lewis-Beck, A. Bryman, and T.F. Liao (eds.) *The SAGE Encyclopedia of Social Science Research Methods*, http://srmo.sagepub.com/view/the-sage-encyclopedia-of-social-science-research-methods/n884.xml accessed 23 July 2012.

Cutlip, S.M., Center, A.H., and Broom, G.M. (2006). *Effective Public Relations*, 9th ed., Pearson, Upper Saddle River.

Cyert, R.M., and March, J.G. (1963). *A Behavioural Theory of the Firm*, Prentice-Hall, Inc., Englewood Cliffs.

Dakin, S. (1989). Research for workforce morale, in S.A. White (ed.) *Values and Communication*, Longman, Melbourne.

Daymon, C. and Holloway, I. (2002). *Qualitative Research Methods in Public Relations and Marketing Communications*, Routledge, London.

De Bussy, N. (2013). Refurnishing the Grunig edifice: strategic public relations management, strategic communication and organisational leadership, in K. Sriramesh,

A. Zerfass, and J-N Kim (eds.) *Public Relations and Communication Management: Current Trends and Emerging Topics*, Routledge, New York, pp. 79–92.

De Bussy, N. M., and Wolf, K. (2009). The state of Australian public relations: Professionalism and paradox, *Public Relations Review*, 35(4), pp. 376–381. https://doi.org/10.1016/j.pubrev.2009.07.005

Deephouse, D.L., and Heugens, P.P.M.A.R. (2009). Linking social issues to organisational impact: the role of infomediaries and the infomediary process, *Journal of Business Ethics*, 86(4), pp. 541–553. https://doi.org/10.1007/s10551-008-9864-3

Deetz, S. (2001). Conceptual foundations, in F.M. Jablin, and L.L. Putnam (eds.) *The New Handbook of Organisational Communication: Advances in Theory, Research and Methods*, SAGE, Thousand Oaks, pp. 3–46.

Deetz, S. (2003). Corporate governance, communication, and getting social values into the decisional chain, *Management Communication Quarterly*, 16(4), pp. 606–611. https://doi.org/10.1177/0893318902250236

Deetz, S. (2008). Engagement as co-generative theorising, *Journal of Applied Communication Research*, 36(3), pp. 289–297. https://doi.org/10.1080/00909880802172301

De Figueiredo, J.M., and de Figueiredo, R.J. (2002). Managerial decision-making in non-market environments: An experiment, *Advances in Strategic Management*, 19(2002), pp. 67–96. https://doi.org/10.1016/s0742-3322(02)19003-6

Deng, X., Zilong, T., and Abrar, M. (2010). The corporate political strategy and its integration with market strategy in Transitional China, *Journal of Public Affairs*, 10(4), pp. 372–382. https://doi.org/10.1002/pa.371

DiFonzio, N., and Bordia, P. (2002). Corporate rumour activity, belief and accuracy, *Public Relations Review*, 28(1), pp. 1–19. https://doi.org/10.1016/s0363-8111(02)00107-8

Donaldson, L. (2006). The contingency theory of organisational design: challenges and opportunities, in R.M. Burton, B. Eriksen, D.D. Håkonsson, and C.C. Snow (eds.) *Organisational Design: The evolving state-of-the-art*, Springer, New York, pp. 20–40.

Dougall, E. (2008). Issues Management, *The Science beneath the Art of Public Relations*, Institute for Public Relations' online topics, http://www.instituteforpr.org/topics/issues-management/ accessed 28 December 2013.

Durham, F. (2005). Public relations as structuration: a prescriptive critique of the starlink global food contamination case, *Journal of Public Relations Research*, 17(1), pp. 29–47. https://doi.org/10.1207/s1532754xjprr1701_4

Economo, H.D., and Zorn, T.E., (1999). Communication during downsizing: how downsizing survivors construct effective corporate communication, *Asia Pacific Public Relations Journal*, 1(2), pp. 19–41. Not digitised.

Edwards, L. (2009). Public relations theories: an overview, in R. Tench, and L. Yeomans (eds.) *Exploring Public Relations*, 2nd ed., Prentice Hall, Harlow, pp. 149–173.

Elliott, J. (2005). *Using Narrative in Social Research: Qualitative and Quantitative Approaches*, Sage Publications, London.

Entman, R.M. (1993). Framing: towards clarification of a fractured paradigm, *Journal of Communication*, 43(4), pp. 51–58. https://doi.org/10.1111/j.1460-2466.1993.tb01304.x

Entman, R.M. (2007). Framing Bias: media in the distribution of power, *Journal of Communication*, 57(1), pp. 163–173. https://doi.org/10.1111/j.1460-2466.2006.00336.x

Falkheimer, J. (2007). Anthony Giddens and public relations: a third way perspective, *Public Relations Review*, 33(3), pp. 287–293. https://doi.org/10.1016/j.pubrev.2007.05.008

Falkheimer, J. (2009). On Giddens: interpreting public relations through Anthony Giddens's structuration and late modernity theory, in Ø. Ihlen, B. van Ruler, and

M. Fredriksson (eds.) *Public Relations and Social Theory: Key figures and Concepts*, Routledge, New York, pp. 103–118.

Falkheimer, J., and Heide, M. (2018). *Strategic Communication: An Introduction*, Routlege, Milton Park.

Fassin, Y. (2009). The stakeholder model refined, *Journal of Business Ethics*, 84(1), pp. 113–135. https://doi.org/10.1007/s10551-008-9677-4

Fassin, Y. (2012). Stakeholder management, reciprocity and stakeholder responsibility, *Journal of Business Ethics*, 109(1), pp. 83–96. https://doi.org/10.1007/s10551-012 -1381-8

Flick, U. (2005). *An Introduction to Qualitative Research*, 2nd ed., Sage Publications, London.

Frandsen, F., and Johansen, W. (2010). Strategy, management, leadership and public relations, in R.L. Heath (ed.) *The SAGE Handbook of Public Relations*, SAGE, Thousand Oaks, pp. 293–306.

Frandsen, F., and Johansen, W. (2014). Corporate image, reputation and identity, in R. Tench and L. Yeomans (eds.) *Exploring Public Relations*, 3rd ed., Pearson, Harlow, England, pp. 181–194.

Fredriksson, M. (2009). On Beck: risk and subpolitics in reflexive modernity, in Ø. Ihlen, B. van Ruler, and M. Fredriksson (eds.) *Public Relations and Social Theory: Key figures and Concepts*, Routledge, New York, pp. 21–42.

Freeman, R.E. (1984). *Strategic Management: A Stakeholder Approach*, Pitman Publishing Inc., Boston.

Freeman, R.E. (2003). Lecture – Stakeholder Management Revisited: What's the State of the Art? Leuven, 20 November, cited in Y. Fassin (2009), The Stakeholder Model Refined, *Journal of Business Ethics*, 84(1), pp. 113–135. https://doi.org/10.1007/s10551 -008-9677-4

Freitag, A.R., and Picherit-Duthler, G. (2004). Employee benefits communication: proposing a PR-HR cooperative approach, *Public Relations Review*, 30(4), pp. 475– 482. https://doi.org/10.1016/j.pubrev.2004.08.006

Gast, A., and Zanini, M. (2012). The social side of strategy, *McKinsey Quarterly*, May, http://www.mckinsey.com/insights/strategy/the_social_side_of_strategy?p=1 accessed 22 November 2013.

Ghemawat, P. (2010). Finding your strategy in the new landscape, *Harvard Business Review*, March, pp. 54–60, https://hbr.org/2010/03/finding-your-strategy-in-the -new-landscape

Gibson, W.J., and Brown, A. (2009). *Working with Qualitative Data*, SAGE Publications Ltd., England.

Giddens, A. (1986). *The Constitution of Society*, University of California Press, Berkeley.

Gillions, P. (2009). Issues management, in R. Tench, and L. Yeomans (eds.) *Exploring Public Relations*, Prentice Hall, Harlow, pp. 175–197.

Gillis, T.L. (2004). In time of change, employee communication is vital to successful organisations, *Communication World*, 21(2), pp. 8–9.

Goffman, E. (1974). *Frame Analysis: An Essay on the Organisation of Experience*, Harper & Row, New York.

Gomm, R. (2004). *Social Research Methodology: A Critical Introduction*, Palgrave Macmillan, Houndmills, Hampshire.

Gower, K.K. (2006). Public relations research at the crossroads, *Journal of Public Relations Research*, 18(2), pp. 177–190. https://doi.org/10.1207/s1532754xjprr1802_6

Grace, D. (2013). The ethics of business communication, in L. Tynan, D. Wolstencroft, B. Edmondson, D. Swanson, A. Martin, D. Grace, and A. Creed (eds.) *Communication for Business*, Oxford University Press, South Melbourne, pp. 185–217.

Grace, D., and Cohen, S. (2013). *Business Ethics*, 5th ed., Oxford University Press, South Melbourne.

Grbich, C. (2004). *New Approaches in Social Research*, SAGE Publications, London.

Grbich, C. (2013). *Qualitative Data Analysis: An Introduction*, 2nd ed., SAGE Publications, London.

Gregory, A. (2000). Systems theories and public relations practice, *Journal of Communication Management*, 4(3), pp. 266–277. https://doi.org/10.1108/eb023525

Gregory, A. (2009a). Management and organisation of public relations, in R. Tench and L. Yeomans (eds.) *Exploring Public Relations*, 2nd ed., Prentice Hall, Harlow, pp. 19–34.

Gregory, A. (2009b). Public relations as planned communication, in R. Tench and L. Yeomans (eds.) *Exploring Public Relations*, 2nd ed., Prentice Hall, Harlow, pp. 175–197.

Gregory, A., and Halff, G. (2013). Divided we stand: Defying hegemony in global public relations theory and practice? *Public Relations Review*, 39(5), pp. 417–425. https://doi.org/10.1016/j.pubrev.2013.04.006

Griffin, J.J., Fleisher, G.S., Brenner, S.N., and Boddewyn, J.J. (2001). Corporate public affairs research: chronological reference list, *Journal of Public Affairs*, 1(1), pp. 9–32. https://doi.org/10.1002/pa.46

Griffith, S.B. (translator) (2011). *Sun Tzu: The Art of War*, Watkins Publishing, London.

Grunig, J.E. (2001). Two-way symmetrical public relations; Past, present, and future, in R.L. Heath (ed.) *Handbook of Public Relations*, Sage Publications Inc., Thousand Oaks, California, pp. 11–30.

Grunig, J.E. (2009). Paradigms of global public relations in an age of digitalisation, *PRism* 6(2), http://praxis.massey.ac.nz/fileadmin/Praxis/Files/globalPR/GRUNIG.pdf accessed 4 September 2013.

Grunig, J.E. (ed.) (1992). *Excellence in Public Relations and Communication Management*, Lawrence Erlbaum Associates, Hillsdale, New Jersey.

Grunig, J.E. (1992). Communication, public relations, and effective organisations: an overview of the book, in J.E. Grunig (ed.) *Excellence in Public Relations and Communication Management*, Lawrence Erlbaum Associates, Hillsdale, New Jersey, pp. 1–28.

Grunig, J.E. (2006). Furnishing the edifice: ongoing research on public relations as a strategic management function, *Journal of Public Relations Research*, 18(2), pp. 151–176. https://doi.org/10.1207/s1532754xjprr1802_5

Grunig, J.E. and Hunt, T.T. (1984). *Managing Public Relations*, Holt, Rinehart and Winston, New York.

Grunig, J.E. and Repper, F.C. (1992). Strategic management, publics, and issues, in J.E. Grunig (ed.) *Excellence in Public Relations and Communication Management*, Lawrence Erlbaum Associates, Hillsdale, New Jersey, pp. 117–157.

Grunig, J.E., and White, J. (1992). The effect of worldviews on public relations theory and practice, in J.E. Grunig (ed.) *Excellence in Public Relations and Communication Management*, Lawrence Erlbaum Associates, Hillsdale, New Jersey, pp. 31–64.

Guth, D.W., and Marsh, C. (2006). *Public Relations: A Values-Driven Approach*, 3rd ed., Pearson Education, Boston.

Habermas, J. (1979). *Communication and the Evolution of Society*. Boston: Beacon Press, cited in K. Hallahan, D. Holtzhausen, B. van Ruler, D. Verčič, and K. Siramesh (2007). Defining strategic communication, *International Journal of Strategic Communication*, 1(1), pp. 3–35.

Habermas, J. (1987). *The Theory of Communicative Action: Volume 2 – Lifeworld and System: A Critique of Functionalist Reason* (T. McCarthy, Trans.), Polity Press, Cambridge.

Habermas, J. (1989). *The Structural Transformation of the Public Sphere* (T. Burger with F. Lawrence, Trans.), MIT Press, Cambridge, MA, cited in K. Hallahan, D.

Holtzhausen, B. van Ruler, D. Verčič, and K. Siramesh (2007). Defining strategic communication, *International Journal of Strategic Communication*, 1(1), pp. 3–35. https://doi.org/10.1080/15531180701285244

Habermas, J. (1990). *Moral Consciousness and Communicative Action* (C. Lenhardt and S.W. Nicholsen, Trans.), Polity Press, Cambridge, MA.

Habermas, J. (1992). Further reflections on the public sphere, in C. Calhoun (ed.) *Habermas and the Public Sphere*, The MIT Press, Cambridge, MA, pp. 421–461.

Hackley, C. (2000). Silent running: Tacit, discursive and psychological aspects of management in a top UK advertising agency, *British Journal of Management*, 11(3), pp. 239–254. https://doi.org/10.1111/1467-8551.00164

Hallahan, K. (1999). Seven models of framing: implications for public relations, *Journal of Public Relations Research*, 11(3), pp. 205–242. https://doi.org/10.1207/s1532754xjprr1103_02

Hallahan, K. (2001). The dynamics of issues activation and response: an issues process model, *Journal of Public Relations Research*, 13(1), pp. 27–59. https://doi.org/10.1207/s1532754xjprr1301_3

Hallahan, K. (2010). Public relations media, in R.L. Heath (ed.) *The SAGE Handbook of Public Relations*, SAGE, Los Angeles, pp. 623–641.

Hallahan, K., Holtzhausen, D., Van Ruler, B., Verčič, D., and Siramesh, K. (2007). Defining strategic communication, *International Journal of Strategic Communication*, 1(1), pp. 3–35. https://doi.org/10.1080/15531180701285244

Hamel, G. (1996). Strategy as revolution, *Harvard Business Review*, 74(4), pp. 69–82, https://hbr.org/1996/07/strategy-as-revolution

Hammersley, M. (ed.) (2004). *Social Research: Philosophy, Politics and Practice*, Sage Publications, London.

Harrington, L.K. (1996). Ethics and public policy analysis: stakeholders' interests and regulatory policy, *Journal of Business Ethics*, 15(4), pp. 373–382. https://doi.org/10.1007/bf00380358

Harris, P., and Moss, D. (2001). Editorial: understanding public affairs, *Journal of Public Affairs*, 1(1), pp. 6–8. https://doi.org/10.1002/pa.45

Harrison, K. (2011). *Strategic Public Relations: A Practical Guide to Success*, Palgrave Macmillan, South Yarra.

Hartcher, P. (2021). Too-great expectations: Morrison's masterstroke of political mismanagement, *The Sydney Morning Herald*, 17–18 April 2021, https://www.smh.com.au/politics/federal/too-great-expectations-morrison-s-masterstroke-of-political-mismanagement-20210416-p57jy8.html

Hatch, M.J., and Cunliffe, A.L. (2006). *Organisation Theory: Modern, Symbolic and Postmodern Perspectives*, 2nd ed., Oxford University Press, New York.

Hay, C. (2002). *Political Analysis: A Critical Introduction*, Palgrave, Houndmills, Basingstoke.

Hays, B.A., and Swanson, D. J. (2012). Public relations practitioners' use of reverse mentoring in the development of powerful professional relationships, *Prism*, 9(2), http://www.prismjournal.org/homepage.html accessed 10 July 2013.

Heath, R.L. (1993). A rhetorical approach to zones of meaning and organisational prerogatives, *Public Relations Review*, 19(2), pp. 141–155. https://doi.org/10.1016/0363-8111(93)90004-v

Heath, R.L. (2000). A rhetorical perspective on the values of public relations: cross roads and pathways toward concurrence, *Journal of Public Relations Research*, 12(1), pp. 69–91. https://doi.org/10.1207/s1532754xjprr1201_5

Heath, R.L. (ed.) (2001). *Handbook of Public Relations*, Sage Publications Inc., Thousand Oaks, California.

Heath, R.L. (2001). Rhetorical enactment rationale for public relations: the good organisation communicating well, in R.L. Heath (ed.) *Handbook of Public Relations*, Sage, Thousand Oaks, pp. 31–50.

Heath, R.L. (2006). Onward into more fog: thoughts on public relations' research directions, *Journal of Public Relations Research*, 18(2), pp. 93–144. https://doi.org/10.1207/s1532754xjprr1802_2

Heath, R.L. (ed.) (2010). *The SAGE Handbook of Public Relations*, SAGE, Los Angeles.

Heath, R.L., and Ni, L. (2010). Community relations and corporate social responsibility, in R. L. Heath (ed.) *The SAGE Handbook of Public Relations*, SAGE, Los Angeles, pp. 557–568.

Heath, R.L., and Palenchar, M. (2000). Community relations and risk communication: a longitudinal study of the impact of emergency response messages, *Journal of Public Relations Research*, 12(2), pp. 131–161. https://doi.org/10.1207/S1532754XJPRR1202_1

Heath, R.L., and Palenchar, M.J. (2009). *Strategic Issues Management: Organisations and Public Policy Challenges*, 2nd ed., Sage, Los Angeles.

Helin, S., Jensen, T., and Sandström, J. (2013). 'Like a battalion of tanks': a critical analysis of stakeholder management, *Scandinavian Journal of Management*, 29(3), pp. 209–218. https://doi.org/10.1016/j.scaman.2012.11.010

Henderson, A. (2005). Activism in 'Paradise': identity management in a public relations campaign against genetic engineering, *Journal of Public Relations Research*, 17(2), pp. 117–137. https://doi.org/10.1207/s1532754xjprr1702_4

Hendry, J. (2002). Strategic decision making, discourse, and strategy as social practice, *Journal of Management Studies*, 37(7), pp. 955–977. https://doi.org/10.1111/1467-6486.00212

Henry, G.T. (1990). *Practical Sampling*, SAGE Publications, Inc., Thousand Oaks, http://srmo.sagepub.com/view/practical-sampling/SAGE.xml accessed 23 July 2012.

Heugens, P.P., van Riel, C.B., and Bosch, F.A. (2004). Reputation management capabilities as decision rules, *Journal of Management Studies*, 41(8), pp. 1349–1377. https://doi.org/10.1111/j.1467-6486.2004.00478.x

Hill, C.W.L, and Jones, G.R. (2008). *Strategic Management: An Integrated Approach*, 8th ed., Houghton Mifflin Company, Boston.

Hodge, B.J., Anthony, W.P., and Gales, L.M. (2003). *Organisation Theory: A strategic approach*, 6th ed., Prentice Hall, Upper Saddle River, New Jersey.

Holmström, S. (2009). On Luhmann: contingecy, risk, trust, and reflection, in Ø. Ihlen, B. van Ruler, and M. Fredriksson (eds.) *Public Relations and Social Theory: Key Figures and Concepts*, Routledge, New York, pp. 186–211.

Holtzhausen, D. (2010). Communication in the public sphere: the political context of strategic communication, *International Journal of Strategic Communication*, 4(2), pp. 75–77. https://doi.org/10.1080/15531181003730037

Huebner, H., Varey, R., and Wood, L. (2008). The significance of communicating in enacting decisions, *Journal of Communication Management*, 12(3), pp. 204–223. https://doi.org/10.1108/13632540810899407

Ihlen, Ø., van Ruler, B., and Fredriksson, M. (2009). *Public Relations and Social Theory: Key figures and Concepts*, Routledge, New York.

Ihlen, Ø., and Verhoeven, P. (2009). Conclusions on the domain, context, concepts, issues and empirical avenues of public relations, in Ø. Ihlen, B. van Ruler, and M. Fredriksson (eds.) *Public Relations and Social Theory: Key figures and Concepts*, Routledge, New York, pp. 323–340.

Ihlen, V., and van Ruler, B. (2009). Introduction: applying social theory to public relations, in Ø. Ihlen, B. van Ruler, and M. Fredriksson (eds.) *Public Relations and Social Theory: Key figures and Concepts*, Routledge, New York, pp. 1–20.

Ingley, C., Mueller, J., and Cocks, G. (2011). The financial crisis, investor activists and corporate strategy: will this mean shareholders in the boardroom? *Journal of Management and Governance*, 15(4), pp. 557–587. https://doi.org/10.1007/s10997-010 -9130-9

Illia, L., Lurati, F., and Casalaz, R. (2013). Situational theory of publics: exploring a cultural ethnocentric bias, *Journal of Public Relations Research*, 25(2) pp. 93–122, https://doi.org/10.1080/1062726X.2013.758581

Issue Management Council (n.d.). Origins of Issue Management, http://issuemanagement .org/learningmore/origins-of-issue-management/ accessed 28 December 2013.

Jablin, F.M. and Putnam, L.L. (eds.) (2001). *The New Handbook of Organisational Communication: Advances in Theory, Research and Methods*, SAGE, Thousand Oaks.

Jacob, S.A., and Furgerson, S.P. (2012). Writing interview protocols and conducting interviews: tips for students new to the field of qualitative research, *The Qualitative Report*, 17(T&L Art, 6), pp. 1–10.

Jaques, T. (2007). Issue management and crisis management: an integrated, non-linear, relational construct, *Public Relations Review*, 33(2), pp. 147–157. https://doi.org/10 .1016/j.pubrev.2007.02.001

Jaques, T. (2009a). Integrating issue management and strategic planning: unfulfilled promise or future opportunity? *International Journal of Strategic Communication*, 3(1), pp.19–33. https://doi.org/10.1080/15531180802606539

Jaques, T. (2009b). Issue and crisis management: quicksand in the definitional landscape, *Public Relations Review*, 35(3), pp. 280–286. https://doi.org/10.1016/j.pubrev.2009.03 .003

Jaques, T. (2010). Embedding issue management: from process to policy, in R.L. Heath (ed.) *The SAGE Handbook of Public Relations*, Sage Publications Inc., Thousand Oaks, CA, pp. 435–446.

Jaques, T. (2012). Is issue management evolving or progressing towards extinction? *Public Communication Review*, 2(1), pp. 35–44. https://doi.org/10.5130/pcr.v2i1.2183

Jarzabkowski, P. (2008). Shaping strategy as a structuration process, *Academy of Management Journal*, 51(4), pp. 621–650. https://doi.org/10.5465/amj.2008.33664922

Johnston, J., and Zawawi, C. (eds.) (2009). *Public Relations Theory and Practice*, 3rd ed., Allen & Unwin, Crows Nest.

Jones, K., and Bartlett, J.L. (2009). The strategic value of corporate social responsibility: A relationship management framework for public relations practice, *Prism*, 6(1), http://praxis.massey.ac.nz/prism_on-line_journ.html accessed 6 November 2013.

Jordan, P.J. (2004). Dealing with organisational change: can emotional intelligence enhance organisational learning? *International Journal of Organisational Behaviour*, 8(1), pp. 456–471, http://hdl.handle.net/10072/5388

Jupp, V. (ed.) (2006). *The SAGE Dictionary of Social Research Methods*, SAGE Publications, London.

Kalton, G. (1983). *Sampling Frames. Introduction to Survey Sampling*, SAGE Publications, Inc., Thousand Oaks.

Kang, J., and Cheng, I.-H. (2008). Application of Contingency Theory Frameworks to Issue Management: A Case Study of the Restaurant Industry's Obesity Issues management. Paper presented at the annual meeting of the NCA 94th Annual Convention, TBA, San Diego, Nov 20, 2008, http://www.allacademic.com/meta/ p260518_index.html accessed 13 January 2011.

Kanihan, S.F., Hansen, K.A., Blair, S., Shore, M., and Myers, J. (2013). Communication managers in the dominant coalition: power attributes and communication practices,

Journal of Communication Management, 17(2), pp. 140–156. https://doi.org/10.1108/13632541311318747

Kegan, R., and Lahey, L. (2001). The real reason people won't change, *Harvard Business Review*, 79(10), pp. 84–92, https://hbr.org/2001/11/the-real-reason-people-wont-change

Kim, S., and Rader, S. (2010). What they can do versus how much they care: assessing corporate communication strategies on Fortune 500 web sites, *Journal of Communication Management*, 14(1), pp. 59–80. https://doi.org/10.1108/13632541011017816

King, C.L. (2010). Emergent communication strategies, *International Journal of Strategic Communication*, 4(1), pp. 19–38. https://doi.org/10.1080/15531180903415814

King, W.R. (1982). Using strategic issues analysis, *Long Range Planning*, 15(4), pp. 45–49. https://doi.org/10.1016/0024-6301(82)90090-5

Knorr, K., and Cicourel, A.C. (eds.) (1981). *Advances in Social Theory and Methodology*, Routledge and Kegan Paul, London.

Kotter, J.P. (1995). Leading change: why transformation efforts fail, *Harvard Business Review*, 73(2), pp. 59–67, https://hbr.org/1995/05/leading-change-why-transformation-efforts-fail-2

Kotter, J.P. (1999). Change leadership, *Executive Excellence*, 16(4), pp. 16–17.

Kuhn, T. (2008). A communicative theory of the firm: developing an alternative perspective on intra-organisational power and stakeholder relationships, *Organisation Studies*, 29(8–9), pp. 1227–1254. https://doi.org/10.1177/0170840608094778

L'Etang, J. (2005). Critical public relations: some reflections, *Public Relations Review*, 31(4), pp. 521–526. https://doi.org/10.1016/j.pubrev.2005.08.011

Lane, A. (2007). Empowering publics: the potential and challenge for public relations practitioners in creative approaches to two-way symmetric public relations. *Australian Journal of Communication*, 34(1), pp. 71–86, https://search-informit-org.ezproxy.canberra.edu.au/doi/10.3316/ielapa.200708021

Laroche, H. (2004). The power of moderation, *MIT Sloan Management Review*, 46(1), pp. 19–21, https://sloanreview.mit.edu/article/the-power-of-moderation/

Lauer, L.D. (2001). All together now: a strategic institutional approach to integrated marketing, in F. Albrighton, and J. Thomas (eds.) *Managing External Relations*, Open University Press, Buckingham, pp. 129–142.

Lauzen, M.M. (1997). Understanding the relation between public relations and issues management, *Journal of Public Relations Research*, 9(1), pp. 65–82. https://doi.org/10.1207/s1532754xjprr0901_03

Lawrence, P.R., and Lorsch, J.W. (1967). *Organisation and Environment: Managing Differentiation and Integration*, Harvard University, Boston.

Ledingham, J. A. (2003). Explicating relationship management as a general theory of public relations, *Journal of Public Relations Research*, 15(2), pp. 181–198. https://doi.org/10.1207/s1532754xjprr1502_4

Leitch, S. and Motion, J. (2010). Publics and public relations, in R.L. Heath (ed.) *The SAGE Handbook of Public Relations*, SAGE, Thousand Oaks, pp. 99–110.

Lewis, L.K. (2000). Communicating change: four cases of quality programs, *Journal of Business Communication*, 37(2), pp. 128–155. https://doi.org/10.1177/002194360003700201

Lewis-Beck, M.S., Bryman, A., and Liao, T.F. (eds.) (2004). *The SAGE Encyclopedia of Social Science Research Methods*, http://srmo.sagepub.com/view/the-sage-encyclopedia-of-social-science-research-methods/n884.xml accessed 23 July 2012.

Luoma-aho, V., and Vos, M. (2010). Towards a more dynamic stakeholder model: acknowledgning multiple issue arenas, *Corporate Communications: An International Journal*, 15(3), pp. 315–331. https://doi.org/10.1108/13563281011068159.

Mackey, S. (2003). Changing vistas in public relations theory. *PRism*, 1(1), http://www.prismjournal.org/vista.html accessed 4 June 2013.

Mackey, S. (2009). Public relations theory, in J. Johnston, and C. Zawawi (eds.) *Public Relations Theory and Practice*, 3rd ed., Allen & Unwin, Crows Nest, pp. 47–77.

Macnamara, J., Lwin, M.O., Hung-Baesecke, F., and Zerfass, A. (2021). *Asia-Pacific Communication Monitor 2020/21. Strategic Issues, Competency Development, Ethical Challenges and Gender Equality in the Communication Profession. Results of a Survey in 15 Countries and Territories*, APACD, EUPRERA, Hong Kong, Brussels.

Macnamara, J. (2012). *Public Relations: Theories, Practices, Critiques*, Pearson, Frenchs Forest.

Macnamara, J., and Zerfass, A. (2012). Social media communication in organisations: the challenges of balancing openness, strategy, and management, *International Journal of Strategic Communication*, 6(4), pp. 287–308. https://doi.org/10.1080/1553118x.2012.711402

Mahon, J.F., and Bigelow, B. (1992). Green collaboration: dealing with the enemy to solve environmental issues and problems, in S.A. Waddock (ed.) *Proceedings of the Third Annual International Association of Business and Society Conference*, https://www.pdcnet.org/iabsproc/content/iabsproc_1992_0003_0125_0138

Mahoney, J. (2006). Towards a new construct for communication during organisational change, *Empowerment, Creativity and Innovation: Challenging Media and Communication in the 21st Century* (ANZCA and University of Adelaide), https://www.researchgate.net/profile/James-Mahoney-3/publication/237218720_Towards_a_New_Construct_for_Communication_During_Organizational_Change/links/550b5d6c0cf2855640970a3a/Towards-a-New-Construct-for-Communication-During-Organizational-Change.pdf

Mahoney, J. (2019). *Defining a Profession, PRIA Members' Views about Continuing Professional Development and Technical Skills Training, Survey Report*, Public Relations Institute of Australia, Sydney.

Mahoney, J. (2010). Strategic communication: making sense of issues management, *Proceedings, Communication Policy and Research Forum*, Sydney, pp. 174–185. apo-nid69313.pdf

Mahoney, J. (2011a). Horizons in strategic communication: theorising a paradigm shift, *International Journal of Strategic Communication*, 5(3), pp. 143–153. http://dx.doi.org/10.1080/1553118X.2011.53760

Mahoney, J. (2011b). *The Butterflies from Brazil: Issues, Contingency, and Strategic Communication*, Australian and New Zealand Communication Association conference: Communication on the edge 2011, http://www.anzca.net/past-conferences/anzca11-proceedings.html accessed 11 February 2013.

Mahoney, J. (2012). Gillard, Carr and the strategy trap - reshuffling the new-look government's message, *The Conversation*, 2 March, https://theconversation.edu.au/profiles/james-mahoney-3326 accessed 2 March 2012.

Mahoney, J. (2013). *Strategic Communication: Principles and Practice*, Oxford University Press, South Melbourne.

Marchiori, M., and Bulgacov, S. (2012). Strategy as communicational practice in organisations, *International Journal of Strategic Communication*, 6(3), pp. 199–211. https://doi.org/10.1080/1553118x.2012.654550

Marks, D.F., and Yardley, L. (2004). *Research Methods for Clinical and Health Psychology*, SAGE Publications Ltd., London.

Martin, R.L., and Osberg, S. (2007). Social entrepreneurship: the case for definition, *Stanford Social Innovation Review*, Spring, pp. 29–39. https://ssir.org/articles/entry/social_entrepreneurship_the_case_for_definition#

Maso, I. (2003). Necessary subjectivity: exploiting researchers' motives, passions and prejudices in pursuit of answering 'true' questions, in L. Finlay, and B. Gough (eds.) *Reflexivity: A Practical Guide for Researchers in Health and Social Sciences*, Blackwell Science, Oxford, pp. 39–51.

Maxwell, J. A., and Mittapalli, K. (2010). Realism as a stance for mixed methods research, in A. Tashakkori, and C. Teddlie (eds.) *SAGE Handbook of Mixed Methods in Social & Behavioral Research*, 2nd ed., SAGE Publications, Thousand Oaks, pp. 145–167.

McCallum, K. (2011). Journalism and Indigenous health policy, *Australian Aboriginal Studies*, 2011/2, pp. 21–31, https://search.informit.org/doi/10.3316/ielapa.822752773835304

McCarthy, P., and Hatcher, C. (2004). Reputation building: the public communication styles of Carly Fiorina and Rupert Murdoch, *Australian Journal of Communication*, 31(1), pp. 1–18, https://search-informit-org.ezproxy.canberra.edu.au/doi/abs/10.3316/ielapa.200407156

McCombs, M. (2004). *Setting the Agenda: The Mass Media and Public Opinion*, Polity Press, Cambridge, UK.

McCombs, M. (2005). A look at agenda-setting: past, present and future, *Journalism Studies*, 6(4), pp. 543–557. https://doi.org/10.1080/14616700500250438

McDonald, L.M., and Hebbani, A.G. (2011). Back to the future: Is strategic management (re)emerging as public relations' dominant paradigm? *Prism*, 8(1), http://www.prismjournal.org/fileadmin/8_1/mcdonald_hebbani.pdf accessed 19 March 2012.

McGrath, C., Moss, D., and Harris, P. (2010). The evolving discipline of public affairs, *Journal of Public Affairs*, 10(4), pp. 335–352. https://doi.org/10.1002/pa.369

McPhee, R.D. and Zaug, P. (2000). The communicative constitution of organisations: a framework for explanation, *The Electronic Journal of Communication*, 10(1 and 2), http://www.cios.org/EJCPUBLIC/010/1/01017.html (no page numbers), accessed 25 January 2015.

Meznar, M.B., and Nigh, D. (1993). Managing corporate legitimacy: public affairs activities. strategies and effectiveness, *Business and Society*, 32(1), pp. 30–43. https://doi.org/10.1177/000765039303200105

Merrill, C. (2021). Opinion: As a CEO, I want my employees to understand the risks of not returning to work in the office, *The Washington Post*, 7 May 2021, https://www.washingtonpost.com/opinions/2021/05/06/ceo-i-want-my-employees-understand-risks-not-returning-work-office/ accessed 7 May 2021.

Mintzberg, H. (1994). *The Rise and Fall of Strategic Planning*, Prentice Hall, New York.

Mintzberg, H. (2003). Five Ps for strategy, in H. Mintzberg, J. Lampel, J.B. Quinn, and S. Ghoshal (eds.) *The Strategy Process: Concepts, Contexts, Cases*, 4th ed. Prentice Hall, Upper Saddle River, pp. 3–9.

Mintzberg, H., Lampel, J., Quinn, J.B., and Ghoshal, S. (2003). *The Strategy Process: Concepts, Contexts, Cases*, 4th ed. Prentice Hall, Upper Saddle River.

Mintzberg, H., Raisinghani, D., and Theoret, A. (1976). The structure of 'unstructured' decision processes, *Administrative Science Quarterly*, 21(2), pp. 1–30. https://doi.org/10.2307/2392045

Mitrook, M.A., Parish, N.B., and Seltzer, T. (2008). From advocacy to accommodation: a case study of the Orlando Magic's public relations efforts to secure a new arena, *Public Relations Review*, 35(2), pp. 161–168. https://doi.org/10.1016/j.pubrev.2008.03.017

Moloney, K. (2006). *Rethinking Public Relations: PR Propaganda and Democracy*, 2nd ed., Palgrave, Milton Park, Oxon.

Moloney, K. (2009). Public affairs, in R. Tench, and L. Yeomans (eds.) *Exploring Public Relations*, Prentice Hall, Harlow, pp. 441–461.

Montgomery, C.A. (2012). How strategists lead, *McKinsey Quarterly*, July 2012, https://www.mckinseyquarterly.com/article_print.aspx?L2=21&L3=37&ar=2993 accessed 26 July 2012.

Motion J., and Leitch, S. (2007). A toolbox for public relations: the *oeuvre* of Michel Foucault, *Public Relations Review*, 33(3), pp. 263–268. https://doi.org/10.1016/j.pubrev.2007.05.004

Motion, J. and Leitch, S. (2009). On Foucault: a toolbox for public relations, in Ø. Ihlen, B. van Ruler, and M. Fredriksson (eds.) *Public Relations and Social Theory: Key figures and Concepts*, Routledge, New York, pp. 83–101.

Murphy, P. (2000). Symmetry, contingency, complexity: accommodating uncertainty in public relations theory, *Public Relations Review*, 26(4), pp. 447–462. https://doi.org/10.1016/s0363-8111(00)00058-8

Nash, L. (1995). The real truth about corporate 'values', *The Public Relations Strategist*, 1(2), pp. 7–16, https://apps.prsa.org/Intelligence/TheStrategist/

Olufowote, J. (2003). Structuration Theory and Communication Research: Developing and Applying an Organisational-Evaluative Framework, paper presented at the annual meeting of the International Communication Association, San Diego, May 27, 2003, http://citation.allacademic.com/meta/p_mla_apa_research_citation/1/1/1/4/8/p111480_index.html accessed 21 March 2011.

Pang, A., Jin, Y., and Cameron, G.T. (2010). Strategic management of communication: insights from the contingency theory of strategic conflict management, in R.L. Heath (ed.) *The SAGE Handbook of Public Relations*, SAGE, Los Angeles, pp. 17–34.

Pascale, R.T., and Sternin, J. (2005). Your company's secret change agents, *Harvard Business Review*, 83(5), pp. 72–81. https://hbr.org/2005/05/your-companys-secret-change-agents

Peters,T.J. and Waterman, R.H. (1984). *In Search of Excellence: Lessons from America's Best-Run Companies*, Harper & Row, Sydney.

Plowman, K.D. (2013). Creating a model to measure relationships: U.S. Army strategic communication, *Public Relations Review*, 39(5), pp. 549–557. https://doi.org/10.1016/j.pubrev.2013.07.001

Phillips, R. (2003). Stakeholder legitimacy, *Business Ethics Quarterly*, 13(1), pp. 25–41. https://doi.org/10.5840/beq20031312

Phillips, R., Freeman, R.E., and Wicks, A. (2003). What stakeholder theory is not, *Business Ethics Quarterly*, 13(4), pp. 479–502. https://doi.org/10.5840/beq200313434

Porter, M.E. (2008). The five competitive forces that shape strategy, *Harvard Business Review*, 86(1), pp. 78–93.

Public Affairs Council (2014). What is public affairs? http://pac.org/faq#WhatPA accessed 2 February 2014.

Public Relations Institute of Australia (2012). Registered Consultancies, http://www.pria.com.au/resources/choosing-a-consultancy accessed 14 September 2012.

Putnam, L.L., and Nicotera, A.M. (2010). Communicative constitution of organisation is a question: critical issues for addressing it, *Management Communication Quarterly*, 24(1), pp. 158–165. https://doi.org/10.1177/0893318909351581

Quinn, J.B. (2003). Strategies for change, in H. Mintzberg, J. Lampel, J.B. Quinn, and S. Ghoshal (eds.) *The Strategy Process: Concepts, Contexts, Cases*, 4th ed., Prentice Hall, Upper Saddle River, pp. 10–16.

Ragan Communication Leadership Council (2021). *Communications Benchmark Report, 2021 Edition, Executive Summary*, Ragan Communications, https://www.ragan.com /white-papers/communications-benchmark-report-2021/thank-you accessed 3 July 2021.

Raupp, J., and Hoffjann, O. (2012). Understanding strategy in communication management, *Journal of Communication Management*, 16(2), pp. 146–161. https://doi .org/10.1108/13632541211217579

Reber, B.H., and Cameron, G.T. (2003). Measuring contingencies: using scales to measure public relations practitioner limits to accommodation, *Journalism and Mass Communication Quarterly*, 80(2), pp. 431–446. https://doi.org/10.1177/107769900308000212

Recardo, R.J. (1995). Overcoming resistance to change, *National Productivity Review*, 14(2), http://80-global.factiva.com accessed on 19 September, 2005.

Reed, M. (2010). Is communication *Constitutive* of organisation?, *Management Communication Quarterly*, 24(1), pp. 151–157. https://doi.org/10.1177/0893318909351583

Reese, S.D. (2007). The framing project: a bridging model for media research revisited, *Journal of Communication*, 57(1), pp. 148–154. https://doi.org/10.1111/j.1460-2466 .2006.00334.x

Regester, M., and Larkin, J. (2005). *Risk Issues and Crisis Management: A Casebook of Best Practice*, 3rd ed., Chartered Institute of Public Relations, Kogan Page, London.

Rensburg, R., and de Beer, E. (2011). Stakeholder engagement: A critical element in the governance of corporate reputation, *Communitas*, 16, pp. 151–169, https://www .semanticscholar.org/paper/Stakeholder-engagement-%3A-a-crucial-element-in -the-Rensburg-Beer/12f7d8b6e48e342de1881a104c10a4d973878b78

Roberts, L. (2021). COVID-19 patients from Australian ICUs still reporting symptoms six months after infection. *ABC News Online*, https://www.abc.net.au/news/health /2021-05-10/covid-19-what-we-know-about-the-long-term-impacts-on-body -mind/100113934 accessed 10 May 2021.

Roper, J. (2005). Organisational identities, identification and positioning: learning from political fields, *Public Relations Review*, 31(1), pp. 139–148. https://doi.org/10.1016/j .pubrev.2004.11.012

Roper, J., and Toledano, M. (2005). Taking in the view from the edge: issues management recontextualised, *Public Relations Review*, 31(4), pp. 479–485. https://doi.org/10.1016 /j.pubrev.2005.08.005

Rumelt, R. (2011). The perils of bad strategy, *McKinsey Quarterly*, June 2011, https:// www.mckinseyquarterly.com/Strategy/Strategic_Thinking/The_perils_of_bad _strategy_2826 accessed 28 June 2011.

Sandhu, S. (2009). Strategic communication: an institutional perspective, *International Journal of Strategic Communication*, 3(2), pp. 72–92. https://doi.org/10.1080 /15531180902805429

Scheufele, D. (1999). Framing as a theory of media effects, *Journal of Communication*, 49(1), pp. 103–122. https://doi.org/10.1111/j.1460-2466.1999.tb02784.x

Scheufele, D., and Tewksbury, D. (2007). Framing, agenda setting, and priming: the evolution of three media effects models, *Journal of Communication*, 57(1), pp. 9–20. https://doi.org/10.1111/j.0021-9916.2007.00326.x

Schofield, J.W. (2004). Increasing the generalisability of qualitative research, in M. Hammersley (ed.) *Social Research: Philosophy, Politics and Practice*, Sage Publications, London, pp. 200–225.

Schwarzkopf, D.L. (2006). Stakeholder perspectives and business risk perception, *Journal of Business Ethics*, 64(4), pp. 327–342. https://doi.org/10.1007/s10551-006-0002-9

Seitel, F.P. (2011). *The Practice of Public Relations*, 11th ed., Pearson, Boston.

Sheehan, K. (2001). E-mail survey response rates: a review. *Journal of Computer-Mediated Communication*, 6 (2). https://doi.org/10.1111/j.1083-6101.2001.tb00117.x

Shih, T., & Fan, X. (2009). Comparing response rates in e-mail and paper surveys: A meta-analysis. *Educational Research Review*, 4(1), pp. 26–40. https://doi.org/10.1016/j.edurev.2008.01.003

Shin, J.-H., Cameron, G.T., and Cropp, F. (2006). Occam's Razor in the contingency theory: A national survey on 86 contingent variables, *Public Relations Review*, 32(3), pp. 282–286. https://doi.org/10.1016/j.pubrev.2006.05.005

Silber, T. (2021). Planning and carrying out communications strategies, *Ragan's PR Daily*, 9 July, https://www.prdaily.com/planning-and-carrying-out-communications-strategies/?utm_source=RDH&utm_medium=email&utm_campaign=RDH+(2021-07-12)&utm_content=article+title&utm_term=5&oly_enc_id=7465J3023134E0R accessed 14 July 2021

Sriramesh, K., Zerfass, A., and Kim, J.-N. (eds.) (2013). *Public Relations and Communication Management: Current Trends and Emerging Topics*, Routledge, New York.

Sison, M.D. (2010). Recasting public relations roles: agents of compliance, control or conscience, *Journal of Communication Management*, 14(4) pp. 319–336. https://doi.org/10.1108/13632541011090437

Smith, B.G. (2012). Public relations identity and the stakeholder-organisation relationship: a revised theoretical position for public relations scholarship, *Public Relations Review*, 38(5), pp. 838–845. https://doi.org/10.1016/j.pubrev.2012.06.011

Smith, B.G. (2013). The internal forces on communication integration: co-created meaning, interaction, and postmodernism in strategic integrated communication, *International Journal of Strategic Communication*, 7(1), pp. 65–79. https://doi.org/10.1080/1553118x.2012.734883

Smith, J.M. (2013). The stakeholder imperative, *American Journal of Preventative Medicine*, 44(1, Supplement), pp. S1–S4. https://doi.org/10.1016/j.amepre.2012.09.011

Smudde, P.M., and Courtright, J.L. (2011). A holistic approach to stakeholder management: A rhetorical foundation, *Public Relations Review*, 37(2), pp. 137–144. https://doi.org/10.1016/j.pubrev.2011.01.008

Sommerfeldt, E.J. (2012). The dynamics of activist power relationships: a structurationist exploration of the segmentation of activist publics, *International Journal of Strategic Communication*, 6(4), pp. 269–286. https://doi.org/10.1080/1553118x.2012.686256

Spitzeck, H., and Hansen, E.G. (2010). Stakeholder governance: how stakeholders influence corporate decision making, *Corporate Governance*, 10(4), pp. 378–391. https://doi.org/10.1108/14720701011069623

Stengel, R. (2009). The responsibility revolution, *Time*, September 21, pp. 24–27.

Steyn, B., and de Beer, E. (2012). Conceptualising strategic communication management (SCM) in the context of governance and stakeholder inclusiveness, *Communicare*, 31(2), pp. 29–55, https://www.semanticscholar.org/paper/Conceptualising-strategic-communication-management-Steyn-Beer/26f137dd5fd00e579dc53b2dcb70c6d0e05239f8

Steyn, B., and Niemann, L. (2010). Enterprise strategy: a concept that explains corporate communication's strategic contribution to the macro-organisational level, *Journal of Communication Management*, 14(2), pp. 106–126. https://doi.org/10.1108/13632541011034574

Stones, R. (2005). *Structuration Theory*, Palgrave Macmillan, Houndmills, Basinstoke.

Strong, F. (2021). Survey: Communicators more valued than ever before, *Ragan's PR Daily*, July 15, 2021, https://www.prdaily.com/survey-communicators-more-valued-than-ever-before/?utm_source=RDH&utm_medium=email&utm_campaign =RDH+(2021-07-15)&utm_content=article+title&utm_term=4&oly_enc_ id=7465J3023134E0R accessed 16 July 2021.

Ströh, U. (2006). The impact of organisational change communication approaches on employee relationships: an experimental study, *Asia Pacific Public Relations Journal*, 7, pp. 247–276. Not digitised.

Ströh, U. (2007). Relationships and participation: a complexity science approach to change communication, *International Journal of Strategic Communication*, 1(2), pp. 123–137. https://doi.org/10.1080/15531180701298916

Tashakkori, A., and Teddlie, C. (2009). Integrating qualitative and quantitative approaches to research, in L. Bickman and D.J. Rog (eds.) *The SAGE Handbook of Applied Social Research Methods*, SAGE Publications, Thousand Oaks, pp. 283–317.

Tashakkori, A., and Teddlie, C. (eds.) (2010). *SAGE Handbook of Mixed Methods in Social & Behavioral Research*, 2nd ed., SAGE Publications, Thousand Oaks.

Taylor, P. (1999). Loss and grief: issues for organisational change and development, *HERDSA Annual International Conference*, Sydney.

Teddlie, C., and Tashakkori, A. (2009). *Foundations of Mixed Methods Research: Integrating Quantitative and Qualitative Approaches in the Social and Behavioral Sciences*, SAGE Publications, Thousand Oaks.

Tench, R., and Yeomans, L. (eds.) (2009). *Exploring Public Relations*, 2nd ed., Prentice Hall, Harlow.

Tench, R., and Yeomans, L. (eds.) (2014). *Exploring Public Relations*, 3rd ed., Pearson, Harlow, England.

Tench, R., Verhoeven, P., and Zerfass, A. (2009). Institutionalising strategic communication in Europe – An ideal home or mad house? Evidence from a survey in 37 countries, *International Journal of Strategic Communication*, 3(2), pp. 147–164. https://doi.org/10.1080/15531180902806237

Theunissen, P., and Wan Nordin, W.N. (2012). Revisiting the concept of 'dialogue' in public relations, *Public Relations Review*, 38(1), pp. 5–13. https://doi.org/10.1016/j.pubrev.2011.09.006

Thomson, S., and John, S. (2007). *Public Affairs in Practice: A Practical Guide to Lobbying*, Chartered Institute of Public Relations, Kogan Page, London.

Tsetsura, K. (2010). Social construction and public relations, in R.L. Heath (ed.) *The SAGE Handbook of Public Relations*, SAGE, Los Angeles, pp. 163–175.

Tullberg, J. (2013). Stakeholder theory: some revisionist suggestions, *The Journal of Socio-Economics*, 42, pp. 127–135. https://doi.org/10.1016/j.socec.2012.11.014

Turnbull, N. (2001). Issues and crisis management in a convergent environment, *Journal of Public Affairs*, 1(1), pp. 85–92. https://doi.org/10.1002/pa.53

Tynan, L., Wolstencroft, D., Edmondson, B., Swanson, D., Martin, A., Grace, D., and Creed, A. (2013). *Communication for Business*, Oxford University Press, South Melbourne.

Universities Australia (2012). Key contacts within universities, Directors of Public Relations/Communications at Australia's Universities, http://www.universitie saustralia.edu.au/page/461/about-us/committees---contacts/key-contacts/pr---comms/ accessed 14 September 2012.

Van Gorp, B. (2007). The constructionist approach to framing: bringing culture back in, *Journal of Communication*, 57(1), pp. 60–78. https://doi.org/10.1111/j.1460-2466.2006.00329_3.x

Van Leuven, J.K., and Slater, M.D. (1991). How publics, public relations, and the media shape the public opinion process, *Public Relations Research Annual*, 3(1–3), pp. 165–178. https://doi.org/10.1207/s1532754xjprr0301-4_8

Van Leuven, T., (1996). The representation of social actors, in C. R. Caldas-Coulthard and M. Coulthard (1996), *Texts and Practices: Readings in Critical Discourse Analysis*, Routledge, London.

Van Riel, C.B.M., and Frombrun, C.J. (2008). *Essentials of Corporate Communication: Implementing Practices for Effective Reputation Management*, Routledge, London.

Varey, R.J. (2002). *Marketing Communication Principles and Practice*, Routledge, London.

Vasquez, G.M. (1996). Public relations as negotiation: an issue development perspective, *Journal of Public Relations Research*, 8(1), pp. 57–77. https://doi.org/10.1207/s1532754xjprr0801_03

Wartick, S.L., and Rude, R.E. (Fall, 1985). Issues management: corporate fad or corporate function? *California Management Review*, 29(1), pp. 124–140. https://doi.org/10.2307/41165231

Waters, R.D. (2013). The role of stewardship in leadership: applying then contingency theory of leadership to relationship cultivation practices of public relations practitioners, *Journal of Communication Management*, 17(4), pp. 324–340. https://doi.org/10.1108/jcom-05-2012-0041

Waters, R.D., Burnett, E., Lamm, A., and Lucas, J. (2009). Engaging stakeholders through social networking: how non-profit organisations are using Facebook, *Public Relations Review*, 35(2), pp. 102–106. https://doi.org/10.1016/j.pubrev.2009.01.006

Weaver, D.H. (2007). Thoughts on agenda setting, framing and priming, *Journal of Communication*, 52(1), pp. 142–147. https://doi.org/10.1111/j.1460-2466.2006.00333.x

Wellington, J., and Szczerbinski, M. (2007). *Research Methods for the Social Sciences*, Continuum, London.

White, J., and Dozier, D. (1992). Public Relations and Management Decision Making, in J. E. Grunig (ed.) *Excellence in Public Relations and Communication Management*, Lawrence Erlbaum Associates, Hillsdale, New Jersey, pp. 91–108.

Whittle, A., and Spicer, A. (2008). Is actor network theory critique? *Organisation Studies*, 29(4), pp. 611–629. https://doi.org/10.1177/0170840607082223

Wilcox, D.L., and Cameron, G.T. (2012). *Public Relations Strategies and Tactics*, 10th ed., Pearson, Boston.

Wilson, L.J. (2001). Extending strategic planning to communication tactics, in R.L. Heath (ed.) (2001), *Handbook of Public Relations*, Sage, Thousand Oaks, pp. 215–222.

Wilson, L.J., and Ogden, J.D. (2008). *Strategic Communications Planning*, 5th ed., Kendall-Hunt, Dubuque.

Wilson, L.J. (1994). Excellent companies and coalition-building among the Fortune 500: a value-and relationship-based theory, *Public Relations Review*, 20(4), pp. 333–343. https://doi.org/10.1016/0363-8111(94)90094-9

Wolfe, M., Jones, B.D., and Baumgartner, F.R. (2013). A failure to communicate: agenda setting in media and policy studies, *Political Communication*, 30(2), pp. 175–192. https://doi.org/10.1080/10584609.2012.737419

Wood, J., Wallace, J., Zeffane, R.M., Chapman, J., Fromholtz, M., and Morrison, V. (2004). *Organisational Behaviour – A Global Perspective*, 3rd ed., Wiley, Milton, QLD.

Wood, E. (2014). Corporate communication, in R. Tench, and L. Yeomans (eds.) *Exploring Public Relations*, 3rd ed., Pearson, Harlow, England, pp. 448–463.

Yim, M.C. (2021). Fake, faulty, and authentic stand-taking: what determines the legitimacy of corporate social advocacy? *International Journal of Strategic Communication*, 15(1), pp. 60–76, https://doi.org/10.1080/1553118X.2020.1856853

Yin, R.K. (2009). How to do better case studies, in L. Bickman, and D.J. Rog (eds.) *The SAGE Handbook of Applied Social Research Methods*, SAGE Publications, Thousand Oaks, pp. 254–282.

Zerfass, A., Buhmann, A., Tench, R., Verčič, D., and Moreno, A. (2021). *European Communication Monitor 2021. CommTech and Digital Infrastructure, Video-conferencing,and Future Roles for Communication Professionals. Results of a Survey in 46 Countries*, EUPRERA/EACD, Brussels.

Zerfass, A. (2009). Institutionalising strategic communication: theoretical analysis and empirical evidence, *International Journal of Strategic Communication*, 3(2), pp. 69–71. https://doi.org/10.1080/15531180902810205

Zerfass, A., and Huck, S. (2007). Innovations, communication, and leadership: new developments in strategic communication, *International Journal of Strategic Communication*, 1(2), pp. 107–122. https://doi.org/10.1080/15531180701298908

INDEX

Printed in the United States
by Baker & Taylor Publisher Services